THE SOURCES OF HISTORY:
STUDIES IN THE USES OF HISTORICAL EVIDENCE

GENERAL EDITOR: G. R. ELTON

THE SOURCES OF HISTORY

STUDIES IN THE USES OF HISTORICAL EVIDENCE

GENERAL EDITOR: G. R. ELTON

The purpose of this series of books is, broadly, to present to students and readers of history some understanding of the materials from which history must be written and of the problems which these raise. The books will endeavour to bring out the inescapable links between historical sources and historical reconstruction, will help to define promising lines of fruitful research, and will illumine the realities of historical knowledge. Each volume will be concerned with a logical span in the history of a given nation, civilisation or area, or with a meaningful historical theme, and it will confine itself to all the primary material extant for that sector. These materials it will consider from the point of view of two crucial questions: what can we know, and what have we no right to expect to learn, from what the past has left behind?

The Sources of History
Studies in the Uses of Historical Evidence

Early Christian Ireland
Introduction to the Sources

KATHLEEN HUGHES

CAMBRIDGE UNIVERSITY PRESS

CAMBRIDGE

LONDON · NEW YORK · MELBOURNE

CAMBRIDGE UNIVERSITY PRESS
Cambridge, New York, Melbourne, Madrid, Cape Town, Singapore, São Paulo

Cambridge University Press
The Edinburgh Building, Cambridge CB2 8RU, UK

Published in the United States of America by Cambridge University Press, New York

www.cambridge.org
Information on this title: www.cambridge.org/9780521214513

First published by The Sources of History Ltd in association with
Hodder and Stoughton Ltd 1972
First published by the Cambridge University Press 1977
Reprinted 1979
This digitally printed version 2008

A catalogue record for this publication is available from the British Library

ISBN 978-0-521-21451-3 hardback
ISBN 978-0-521-07389-9 paperback

*To my undergraduates
who have been
my pupils and teachers*

Contents

General Editor's Introduction

By what right do historians claim that their reconstructions of the past are true, or at least on the road to truth? How much of the past can they hope to recover: are there areas that will remain for ever dark, questions that will never receive an answer? These are problems which should and do engage not only the scholar and student but every serious reader of history. In the debates on the nature of history, however, attention commonly concentrates on philosophic doubts about the nature of historical knowledge and explanation, or on the progress that might be made by adopting supposedly new methods of analysis. The disputants hardly ever turn to consider the materials with which historians work and which must always lie at the foundation of their structures. Yet, whatever theories or methods the scholar may embrace, unless he knows his sources and rests upon them he will not deserve the name of historian. The bulk of historical evidence is much larger and more complex than most laymen and some professionals seem to know, and a proper acquaintance with it tends to prove both exhilarating and sobering—exhilarating because it opens the road to unending enquiry, and sobering because it reduces the inspiring theory and the new method to their proper subordinate place in the scheme of things. It is the purpose of this series to bring this fact to notice by showing what we have and how it may be used.

G. R. ELTON

Preface

I have written this book because it is needed. One should not write history in compartments, as this book is arranged; but it seemed the clearest way of introducing the various kinds of source material, the problems which each presents and the sort of questions it will answer. The fourth chapter, on the annals, is much more detailed than the rest of the book; but here so little work has been done that it seemed of no use to produce conclusions without setting out the evidence by which I reached them. The rest of the book is description and discussion of material which is well known to certain people. All the same, I have learned a lot in writing it, and I hope that something may be learned from reading it.

The trouble in writing a book like this is that the range of source material to be included is very wide. I am a specialist in only some of it. This book had to be as reliable a guide as possible, so I have consulted a wide range of experts. I should like to record my warmest gratitude to them for the generosity with which they have made available their learning. I am responsible for any final errors in my own book, but their criticism has made it a much better book than it would otherwise have been.

I am most heavily indebted to Professor Dan Binchy who, with his combination of linguistic and historical disciplines, criticised Chapters 2, 3 and 4 at an early stage, and Chapters 7 and 9 in a late draft. My debt to Professor Kenneth Jackson is also heavy; he made very helpful criticisms of Chapters 5 and 6, and checked and corrected my translations. Miss Ann Hamlin generously provided preliminary ideas and detailed criticism for Chapters 1 and 8.

In addition to these three, many people have allowed me to

consult them on more specific points: Professor Ó Cuív on Chapter 9, Mr Michael Dolley on coins, Dr Charles-Edwards on the legal evidence for farming, Professor Byrne on genealogies, Mrs Flanagan on place-names, Dr Bernard Wailes on the plough. Professor Bieler very kindly checked the photostat of a manuscript for me, Miss Roe gave me her views on the dating of the scripture crosses, Dr Raftery showed me the Tara brooch, explaining its craftsmanship. I also had valuable discussions with a number of people, too many to mention all of them; but I must especially name Professor O'Kelly. Professor Dorothy Whitelock has been the friend at hand who, though she is not a specialist on Irish history, has asked stimulating questions on many occasions.

There is one aspect of the subject which I have completely omitted in this book—the linguistic one. I have tried here to introduce early Irish history to people with little or no Irish. Anyone who wants to do research into the subject will have to learn Irish, and is strongly advised to go to some university where he can take a formal course. Old and Middle Irish are too difficult for most people to pick up satisfactorily by themselves.

Any university teacher will recognise how much a book like this owes to one's own undergraduates. This year I am especially grateful to Susan Evans, Siân Victory, Michael Hunter and David Dumville, all of whom have commented on various sections. I should also like to thank the staffs of the Royal Irish Academy and of the Cambridge University Library, especially Mr Nigel Hancock; and to acknowledge the admirable policy of my own university and college in granting sabbatical leave.

Newnham College   KATHLEEN HUGHES
Cambridge
August 1971

Abbreviations

AFM	*Annals of the Kingdom of Ireland by the Four Masters.*
AI	*Annals of Inisfallen.*
ALI	*Ancient Laws of Ireland,* Rolls Series, 6 vols (Dublin 1865–1901).
AU	*Annals of Ulster.*
BGSIHS	*Bulletin of the Group for the Study of Irish Historic Settlement.*
CCC	*Caithréim Cellacháin Caisil.*
CG	*Crith Gablach,* ed. D. A. Binchy, Mediaeval and Modern Irish Series 11 (Dublin 1941).
CGG	*Cogadh Gaedhel re Gallaibh.*
CGH	M. A. O'Brien, *Corpus Genealogiarum Hiberniae I* (Dublin 1962).
CS	*Chronicon Scottorum.*
Councils	A. W. Haddan and W. Stubbs, *Councils and Ecclesiastical Documents relating to Great Britain and Ireland,* 3 vols (Oxford 1869–73).
EHR	*English Historical Review.*
HBS	*Henry Bradshaw Society.*
Hughes, CEIS	K. Hughes, *The Church in Early Irish Society* (London 1966).
IER	*Irish Ecclesiastical Record.*
IHS	*Irish Historical Studies.*
ITS	*Irish Texts Society.*
JCHAS	*Journal of the Cork Historical and Archaeological Society.*

JEH	*Journal of Ecclesiastical History.*
JRSAI	*Journal of the Royal Society of Antiquaries of Ireland.*
Kenney, *Sources*	J. F. Kenney, *Sources for the Early History of Ireland. Vol I. Ecclesiastical* (New York 1929. Reprint 1968).
LC	*Lebor na Cert.*
LG	*Lebor Gabála Érenn.*
LL	*The Book of Leinster,* ed. R. I. Best, O. Bergin and M. A. O'Brien, 5 fascs (Dublin 1954–67).
Lowe, *CLA*	E. A. Lowe, *Codices Latini Antiquiores. A palaeographical guide to Latin manuscripts prior to the ninth century,* 10 parts (Oxford 1934–63).
LU	*Lebor na hUidre,* ed. R. I. Best and O. Bergin (Dublin 1929).
MD	E. Gwynn, *The Metrical Dinnshenchas,* Todd Lecture Series 8–12, 5 vols (Dublin 1900–35).
Migne, *PL*	J. P. Migne, *Patrologia Latina,* 221 vols (Paris 1844–64).
PBA	*Proceedings of the British Academy.*
Plummer, *BNE*	C. Plummer, *Bethada Náem nÉrenn,* 2 vols (Oxford 1922).
Plummer, *HE*	*Venerabilis Baedae Opera Historica.*
Plummer, *VSH*	C. Plummer, *Vitae Sanctorum Hiberniae,* 2 vols (Oxford 1910).
PRIA	*Proceedings of the Royal Irish Academy.*
SLH	*Scriptores Latini Hiberniae.*
Stokes, *Lismore*	W. Stokes, *Lives of the Saints from the Book of Lismore* (Oxford 1890).
St. Ir. Law	*Studies in Early Irish Law* (Dublin 1936).
Tig.	*Annals of Tigernach.*
UJA	*Ulster Journal of Archaeology.*
ZCP	*Zeitschrift für celtische Philologie.*

CHAPTER 1

Archaeology

Historians would often like archaeology to be a kind of computer which would give definite answers to fundamental general questions about the material culture of a people. But this is just what archaeology does least well, for such answers would imply a synthesis of a large body of material. Modern archaeology is a comparatively new study. Not only is the archaeologist's interpretation of his material, just like the historian's, sometimes in dispute, but also his evidence is often scattered and scanty. He is therefore reluctant to offer a general analysis and usually confines himself to descriptions of a particular dig, and only occasionally, as in the articles by Dr Proudfoot[1] or Professor Duignan[2] or in the chapter by Dr and Mrs de Paor[3] and in various papers by Professor O'Kelly, does the archaeologist face the questions which the historian finds most urgent.

I

The historian first wants an aerial view of the country; then he wants to come nearer and see where the residential sites were located, how many people lived in them and how communications were maintained between them. If all this information could be fed into an archaeological computer it should be possible to form an estimate of the total size of the population.

No definite answer is yet possible, but some of the most thought-provoking suggestions as to what the country looked like have been made by the work on pollen analysis. This enables the scientist to discover what kind of vegetation covered a particular

[1] 'The economy of the Irish rath', *Medieval Archaeology V* (1961), 94–122.
[2] 'Irish agriculture in early historic times', *JRSAI* (1944), 124–45.
[3] Chapter 3 on 'The Life of the People' in *Early Christian Ireland*.

area. Its disadvantages are that it provides a method of only relative dating, so that the sequence has to be placed in the historian's time scale by a process such as carbon 14 being applied to particular points in the series. Moreover, a considerable number of samples are necessary in order to reach a reliable conclusion. Whereas students of early English history may see at a glance from the Ordnance Survey map of Britain in the Dark Ages what pattern was created by pagan Anglo-Saxon cemeteries and which areas were empty of burials and early place names, students of Irish history at a comparable period have no such tools: there is no Ordnance Survey map of Ireland for the Early Christian period, there were no fifth-century barbarian invaders, while place-name studies are far less advanced than in England. Recent work on pollen analysis is therefore extraordinarily important.

In 1956 Professor Mitchell published a paper in which he examined samples of pollen taken from fourteen different bogs situated in different places over Ireland.[1] His *zone viii* covers about 3,000 years, from 2,500 BC to AD c. 500, his *zone ix* stretches from AD c. 500 to c. 1700. Probably the tree from which most may be inferred concerning agricultural practice is the elm, for this tree needs fresh, fertile soils in fairly open conditions, the sort of soil which men need for ploughing and pasture. Professor Mitchell's tentative conclusion (he calls it only 'speculation') is that agriculture reached Ireland not later than 2,500 BC, that forest, especially elm forest on dry ground, was cleared and that subsequently plantain invaded the cleared patch, that the cleared patch was abandoned, to be taken over by hazel and birch. The country thus became a mosaic of virgin forest, patches of tillage, areas of rough pasture and secondary forest, as well as bog, lake and mountain. Round about AD 500 (the dating is by radiocarbon process) there was a dramatic fall in the growth of the elm, which almost certainly means an advance in agriculture. The production of cereals and vegetables may have increased in the early Christian period, while in the Viking period the emphasis seems to be

[1] 'Post-boreal pollen diagrams from Irish raised bogs', *PRIA*, LVII B (1956), 185–251.

on pastoral farming. The evidence shows that from Neolithic times on there were successive phases of agriculture.

Since Professor Mitchell's pioneer study on samples from widely-scattered Irish sites in 1956, pollen analysis has been intensively applied to other sites. For example at Littleton Bog, ten miles north-west of Cashel, cereal pollen was continuously present after about AD 300, while elm, ash and hazel were being cleared.[1] At Beaghmore, in Co. Tyrone, there was large-scale clearance of forest and scrub between c. 100 BC and AD c. 350, followed by regeneration of woodland; subsequently there was further clearance, together with an increase in plaintains which suggests pastoral agriculture.[2] So far, most of the work on pollen analysis concerns the pre-Christian period,[3] but the technique opens up new possibilities in environmental studies.

Our next question concerns population, and here archaeology has shown the dimensions of the problem rather than provided the answers. The typical Irish habitation site has various names: ring-fort, *rath*, *dún*, *cathair*, *cashel* and a few more.[4] 'Ring-fort' is the collective term now used to describe them all. The other words are ancient, they seem to have different connotations and, except for the *dún* which is found all over Ireland, their distribution is different.[5] The *rath* was always dug, so that the bank was formed from the soil thrown up out of the ditch. But though *rath* normally indicates an earthwork, it may have a stone facing or a wooden facing or palisade of close-set posts. The *cashel* and *cathair* are both made of stone, the *cashel* being especially heavily distributed in the north and the *cathair* in the south-west.

[1] G. F. Mitchell, *JRSAI*, XCV (1965), 121–32.

[2] J. R. Pilcher, *UJA*, XXXII (1969), 73–90, especially p. 89.

[3] See A. G. Smith, 'Late-glacial and post-glacial vegetational and climatic history of Ireland: a review', *Irish Geographical Studies*, ed. N. Stephens and R. E. Glasscock (Belfast 1970), 65–88.

[4] M. J. O'Kelly, 'Problems of Irish ring-forts,' *The Irish Sea Province in Archaeology and History*, ed. D. Moore (Cardiff 1970), 50–4.

[5] The information on the distribution of place-names is from an unpublished lecture by Mrs Deirdre Flanagan, delivered in 1971 to the Council for Name Studies in Great Britain and Ireland.

There have been various estimates of the number of ring-forts in Ireland: thirty to forty thousand gives some indication. They were not all in occupation at the same time, for some of the excavated sites date from the Neolithic or Early Bronze Age, while others, which look like normal structures of the Early Christian period, were built AD c. 1600. Since less than a hundred sites have been adequately examined it is impossible to make any estimate of Irish population between c. 500 and c. 1200.[1] In addition to the ring-forts there were unenclosed sites, such as that at Craig Hill, Co. Antrim.[2]

Many of the ring-forts are in naturally defensible positions, on raised (though not very high) ground, commanding good views. A recent survey of ring-forts in West Cork shows that they were mainly built on good agricultural land, between the 200- and 400-foot contour.[3] This must mean that the area was not over-populated, that there was plenty of good land for everyone.

The enormous ramparts surrounding some sites were marks of status. An Irish Law Tract, *Crith Gablach*, speaks of the measurements of a king's *dún* and of the ramparts erected by the king's unfree clients.[4] The community at Cahercommaun with its formidable fortifications was one of peaceful cattle-ranchers. The size of the population here has been estimated at forty or fifty. Garranes and Ballycatteen may have been chieftains' residences and we know that the crannog of Lagore was a royal site.[5] A hill-fort like Downpatrick may have been a tribal centre, while other ring-forts were small single-family enclosures containing a

---

[1] There is no map of the distribution of ring-forts all over Ireland, but the map for Co. Down in *The Archaeological Survey of Northern Ireland: County Down* (Belfast 1966) 110 gives an indication of their frequency. Proudfoot, *op. cit.*, 98 gives a map of the forty-seven sites excavated between 1925 and 1955.

[2] D. M. Waterman, *UJA*, XIX (1956), 87–91.

[3] E. M. Fahy, *BGSIHS*, I (1970), 5–6.

[4] *Crith Gablach*, ed. D. A. Binchy, lines 566–72. Mac Neill, *PRIA*, XXXVI (1923), C 305.

[5] H. Hencken, *PRIA*, LIII (1950), C 1–247. A crannog is an artificial island constructed on a lake out of timbers, brushwood, peat, etc.

dwelling house and farm buildings. Thus the population would vary very considerably from site to site. Nor are burial places of much use in estimating population, for they were often used over long periods and may have served areas varying in size. They do, however, enable us to say that, like people elsewhere at the same period, men were not long-lived: at Castleknock between about 850 and 1050 only 2·5 per cent of the skeletons were of people over the age of fifty.[1] Many died in infancy and childhood (23 per cent under fifteen);[2] young people under twenty were in the best health (6·25 per cent deaths) and most people died between twenty and fifty (68·1 per cent).

It is clear from the documents that communications were fairly good. Abbots frequently went on circuit, monks travelled, provincial kings must have covered quite a lot of ground in most years. We know that there were certain main roads,[3] and there must have been local track-ways. The Geological Survey of Ireland's map of bogs and the Ordnance Survey's map of river ways both show at a glance where routes would be likely. Major settlements are often at a confluence of natural routes; Clonmacnoise, where the land highway meets the Shannon, or Glendalough, which now seems so remote in the midst of its mountains, but which is actually near a junction of valleys. The written sources sometimes refer to bridges, and Professor O'Kelly's examination of the timbers uncovered in dredging operations in the Cashen River has allowed him to reconstruct a large wooden bridge which must be earlier than the mid-sixteenth century, but which it is impossible to date precisely.[4] The open passes in the northern midlands between water or forest, which probably served as roads, are quite often straddled by a ditch and bank about three to six miles long, presumably to prevent cattle

[1] J. H. Scott, *UJA*, XX (1957), 4–7. These figures compare fairly closely with prehistoric finds.

[2] Probably too low an estimate, since infants' bones decay more quickly than adults.

[3] See Colm O Lochlainn, 'Roadways in Ancient Ireland', in *Féil-sgríbhinn Eóin mhic Néill*, ed. J. Ryan (Dublin 1940), 465–74 with map.

[4] *JRSAI*, XCI (1961), 135–52.

raiding.[1] But though archaeology sometimes offers corroborative evidence about trackways, our main information about early Irish routes and communications is at present from the written records.

In spite of all the difficulties, archaeology does give us a bird's eye view of man in his environment which adds substantially to our written sources. For instance, historical sources tell us very little indeed about the limestone plateau of the Burren in northern Co. Clare. It is today empty and silent, yet if you go here alone the awareness of man's past presses upon you with an almost frightening urgency, for wherever you turn your head there are signs of the human past, from dolmens to forts, ancient fields and churches. It is a crowded landscape, with forts and fields once occupied, which must then have been abandoned for new pastures. The historian who is unwilling to look at man in relation to the land can have no such experience.

II

After settlement and population, the historian wants to know about agriculture[2] and technology. Each Irish ring-fort produced its own basic food supplies. These were sometimes supplemented by hunting and to a lesser degree by fishing and fowling, as deers' antlers, fish and bird bones, limpet and periwinkle shells demonstrate. It is difficult to compare the relative importance of pastoral and agrarian farming, though it is usually assumed that the main wealth of the farm lay in the animal husbandry. First in importance here were the cows, which provided summer food of milk products and winter food of meat. 50,000 lb. of animal bones, mostly cattle, were dug up at Lagore. Long-legged pigs foraged for themselves in the woodland and were only second in importance to the cows. Comparatively few sheep's bones have been found, but this is almost certainly because sheep were kept partly, or perhaps mainly, for wool and were not as popular on the

---

[1] O. Davies, 'The Black Pig's Dyke', *UJA*, XVIII (1955), 29–36.
[2] For the evidence on farming provided by the law tracts, see *infra*, 51–3, 61–4.

menu as beef and pork. There were some hens. Much of the farmer's time must have been spent on herding and milking the cows, while cattle raiding was a very useful sport for the aristocracy. Cattle murrain always hit the community very hard and was recorded in the annals much more readily than a poor harvest. The importance of cattle is further emphasised because they were a unit of exchange; nevertheless tillage was widely practised, for querns have been found on very many sites and mills are mentioned in the laws, where even the lowest grade of freeman of full age and status who is recognisable at law (*ócaire*) has a share in a kiln, a mill and a barn and a fourth share in a plough.[1] Pollen analysis shows that wheat, rye, barley and oats were all grown, but not the proportion of each. Very little work has been done on Irish ploughs and field systems: the two may be associated, for the type of the plough may be one factor determining the shape of the field.[2] As early as 1934 and 1935 the late Professor Ó Ríordáin, in his excavations at Cush, Co. Limerick, examined the field systems which are related to the dwellings there.[3] He did the same for the site called 'The Spectacles' at Lough Gur,[4] and Professor O'Kelly has discussed the fields at Beginish,[5] but with these and one or two other notable exceptions[6] Irish archaeologists have either not had the opportunity or the inclination to conduct such surveys.

New evidence has now been made available by the recent publication of some of Dr St Joseph's aerial photographs,[7] which show a number of ring-forts with adjacent fields. Unfortunately the sites have not been dated by excavation, though it seems very likely that the photographs reveal fields which were

---

[1] *CG*, lines 95–7, p. 101.
[2] Nightingale, 'Ploughing and field shape', *Antiquity*, XXVII (1953), 20–6.
[3] *PRIA*, XLV (1940), C 83–181.
[4] *Ibid.*, LII (1949), C 39–111.
[5] *Ibid.*, LVII (1956), C 159–94.
[6] See V. B. Proudfoot, 'Ancient Irish field systems', *Advancement of Science*, XIV (1958), 369–71. For some legal evidence, see *infra*, 61–4.
[7] E. R. Norman and J. K. S. St Joseph, *The Early Development of Irish Society* (Cambridge 1969). See *infra*, 34–6.

in use during the period with which we are here concerned. The fields for which we have archaeological evidence are mostly small—the average size of those at 'The Spectacles' was one-seventh of an acre.[1] Many are roughly square or rectangular, but some are irregular in shape. This suggests a small, easily manœuvred plough drawn by a small ox-team. We have a few iron coulters and plough-shares,[2] varying in weight and size; for example the share from Leacanabuaile weighs 3lb. 14 oz., that from Lagore weighs 6 lb. 6 oz. An iron coulter with a long shank was found at Cor in Co. Donegal.[3] There is no archaeological evidence for a mouldboard, the part of the plough which turns the sod. But in any case the more vital improvement in technology may have come with the iron share and coulter, which could bite into the ground, cutting matted grass roots and lifting the sod to air and drain the soil. In the hands of a skilful ploughman such a plough may have been able to turn the sod on its side.[4]

The Irish word for plough is *arathar*, cognate with the Latin *aratrum*, and this is usually recognised as a light plough. There must, however, have been considerable variation of efficiency between the good-sized iron share and coulter and the wooden ploughshares which also existed.[5] Wooden ploughshares do not suggest a very productive tillage; but we should remember that

[1] Cf. the early field system in Goodland townland, Co. Antrim, where there were rectilinear enclosures about 100 yards square or two acres in extent. These may have been used for tillage or grazing. *JRSAI*, XCIX (1969), 39–54.

[2] The coulter makes a vertical cut into the ground, the share cuts a horizontal furrow slice.

[3] *JRSAI*, XCII (1962), 153.

[4] The literary and archaeological evidence for a mouldboard in Europe at a comparable period is disputable. There were certainly different plough types, but exactly what were the components of each is far from clear. I now understand that Dr Lucas is working on Irish ploughs.

[5] e.g. *JRSAI*, XCVII (1967), 12. One of the problems is why so few plough parts have survived. Is this because they were often made of wood, or of wood tipped with metal? A plough past service would be abandoned in a ditch or field, not brought back to the ring-fort: thus it might not come in the way of the excavator.

the Irish had plenty of manure from their cattle, and their fields would have been more fertile in consequence. Some fields must have been left fallow, perhaps for several years, so that stock could be grazed on them before they were again ploughed up.

In addition to the plough the farmer's main implements were knives, spades (perhaps used with the plough), shears, and sickles for reaping the crop. Occasionally a corn-drying kiln has been identified.[1] There is literary evidence for mills, but most of the raths must have had their corn ground by hand in the querns. How to use the quern was a part of the education of the *ócaire*'s daughter, for which the foster-parent was responsible.[2]

Some of the farmer's equipment was of iron. There were specialists in iron smelting. At St Gobnet's House, Ballyvourney, excavation revealed fifty-seven small 'furnace bottoms' with fragments of eighty more, formed from the hot debris of smelting which falls into the bottom of the furnace. Here the blast furnaces were worked on a charcoal fuel.[3] There are also traces of slag and iron smelting on many small Irish ring-forts. This means either that each farmer made his own iron tools, or that black-smiths travelled round, possibly within the *tuath* (petty kingdom), doing any necessary work.[4] Much of the farm equipment was of wood, and the timbers used in the construction of the crannogs show the high standard of carpentry. At Lagore axes, a hammer, a chisel and various other carpenter's tools were recovered during the excavation. One main domestic industry pursued in many homes was spinning and weaving. In many forts there are spindle-whorls and loom-weights, though it is only occasionally, on a crannog site like Lagore, that pieces of cloth showing the actual weave have survived.

[1] At Garranes, Letterkeen, Ballymacash. See Proudfoot, *Medieval Archaeology*, V (1961), 108.

[2] This is in a gloss on the tract on Fosterage, *ALI*, II, 152. For the *ócaire*, see *supra*, 23.

[3] M. J. O'Kelly, *JCHAS*, LVII (1952), 18-40.

[4] The suggestion of A. E. P. Collins, *UJA*, XXXI (1968), 57. In a recent lecture to the Society for Medieval Archaeology, Professor O'Kelly pointed out that iron slag has been found even on a site as remote as the Skellig rock.

Thus on the Irish farm the basic tools were manufactured; herds were kept; corn was grown, harvested, dried, stored and ground; from the sheep's wool thread was spun, cloth woven and clothes made. Archaeology tells us very little about the organisation of agriculture, but it shows us the farmstead as the microcosm of physical life.

III

So we come to house and home, the subject on which the excavations inform us amply and which has been so well written up that I shall treat it very briefly here.[1] In most of Ireland the houses were of wood or perhaps even less durable material such as turf sods, so that unless conditions were exceptionally favourable, only post-holes survive; in the west the remains of stone houses are still standing. Some have sleeping places partitioned off, or areas by the wall which may have been used as beds;[2] some have benches along the walls.[3] The hearth was usually away from the wall towards the centre of the house. Some houses have post-holes, the posts in which must have been used to hang cooking vessels over the fire or to support a loom. Drainage was sometimes provided: at Leacanabuaile a covered drain ran from inside the largest house down the slope through the entrance. In the rectangular stone house on Church Island, near Valencia, there is a water pit with an overflow drain to maintain a convenient level.[4] Under the house is sometimes found a souterrain, a stone passage and small chamber probably used for storing butter and meat.

Very little pottery has been found on Irish sites, with the exception of the 'souterrain ware' in the north. The literary sources speak of cauldrons, but probably the most common

---

[1] See M. and L. de Paor, *Early Christian Ireland*, 79 ff.
[2] F. Henry, 'Remains of the Early Christian period on Inishkea North, Co. Mayo', *JRSAI*, LXXV (1945), 127-55.
[3] At White Fort, Drumaroad, see D. Waterman, *UJA*, XIX (1956), 73-86.
[4] M. J. O'Kelly, *PRIA*, LIX (1958), C 74-5.

vessels were of wood or skin. At Lagore there were tubs and
buckets made with staves, lathe-turned bowls, mugs, scoops,
boxes and plates.[1]

Outside the house the ground within the enclosure was sometimes paved. But though the ring-fort is the most common
homestead of this period now known, there were other houses,
without enclosures, possibly occupied by the lower classes of
society, such as the eight houses set in small fields at Beginish,[2]
or the four houses at 'The Spectacles', with paths, cobbled areas
and farm-buildings.[3] It looks as if the house and souterrain of
Viking Age date at Craig Hill, Co. Antrim, formed an open
settlement.[4] The unenclosed sites are, of course, much more difficult to identify, and may have been much more frequent than
excavation suggests.

Only occasionally, as in the exceptionally well-preserved royal
residence at Lagore, are luxury objects found. Many sites have
produced glass beads, bracelets, bone combs, simple pins of
bronze or iron, occasionally more elaborate brooches used to
fasten the cloak. Gaming pieces and dice have also been found,
and a fine carved gaming board turned up in one of the Ballinderry crannogs.[5] Weapons, other than knives, are rather scarce.
Spearheads, the most common weapons, were used in hunting,
and archaeology suggests that for the majority of the population
society was fairly peaceful. This serves to emphasise the aristocratic character of the literary sources.

IV

The volume of overseas trade must have been small, for early
Ireland had no coinage and did not even use foreign coins.[6] The

[1] H. Hencken, 'Lagore Crannog', *PRIA*, LIII (1950), C 152–60.
[2] M. J. O'Kelly, *PRIA*, LVII (1956), C 159–94.
[3] S. P. Ó Ríordáin, *PRIA*, LII (1949), C 57–62.
[4] D. Waterman, *UJA*, XIX (1956), 87–91.
[5] H. Hencken, 'Ballinderry Crannog No. 1', *PRIA*, XLIII (1936), C 103–239.
[6] For coins see *infra*, 37–40.

Irish unit of value was a *cumal* or female slave, estimated at six *sets* (or chattels), where a *set* was worth half a milch cow. This shows the importance of cows, precious objects and slaves in the economy, but it is a very clumsy predecessor of a coinage, and trade must have been by exchange and barter. In the late-fifth, sixth and early-seventh centuries some pottery was being imported, but it was not until the Viking settlements that trade on any considerable scale was maintained. From the end of the ninth century the Dublin Vikings were using foreign coins and at the end of the tenth century they began to strike their own. Some of their goods reached the Irish, especially their jewellery and their swords. Until the recent series of excavations in Viking Dublin there has been very little archaeological evidence (other than coins) for Viking trading settlements in Ireland. Now the spectacular discoveries are providing solid material evidence for the claims of the written sources.

The situation of Dublin corresponded to the mercantile needs of Viking settlers. It was built on the boulder clay which rose in a low hill to the south of the Liffey estuary. The main street of the town ran from east to west along the top of the ridge, parallel to the river where the ships could be drawn up. A quantity of eleventh-century French pottery has been found on the Winetavern Street site, while on the High Street site there is French pottery and there are sherds of Gam Green, Bristol, type.[1] It is likely that other Viking sites such as Limerick would tell the same story.

In spite of the absence of a native coinage, a certain amount of internal trade among the Irish themselves must have gone on. The most important members of the aristocracy may have kept their own craftsmen; at Lagore there is evidence for bronze working and for the manufacture of millefiori and glass studs, though amber had to be imported for the jewellery. But there were also settlements pursuing crafts. At Garranes, in Co. Cork, about the year 500, there is little evidence for domestic activity but plenty for specialised craftsmanship in metal working, with

[1] B. Ó Ríordáin, *BGSIHS*, I (Dec. 1970), 31.

the allied pursuits of glass manufacture and enamelling.[1] Sixty bronze objects were found here, as well as pieces of millefiori glass and champlevé enamel. It is perhaps significant that this site provided an unusual amount of pottery, for its inhabitants had something to trade in exchange for oil and wine. The beads and bracelets of glass and jet found on many Irish ring-forts, probably the bronze pins and certainly the occasional silver brooch like that at Cahercommaun, were not made at home but purchased. There is evidence for granite from the Mourne Mountains found some distance away:[2] it is possible to identify the stone from which querns were made and to see that they were traded. A site like Church Island, Valencia, must have imported some necessities; here it was timber and slate for building and charcoal and ore for iron smelting.[3] How did craftsmen like those at Garranes dispose of their wares? How important were Irish fairs in the small luxury trade? Archaeology poses such questions for the historian.

v

What I have written so far will have given some idea of the limitations of archaeology as a source for the historian. It is difficult to make safe generalisations when so few of the sites have been excavated. Moreover, many of the digs have been inevitably on a very small scale or under rescue conditions and the questions most vital to the historian, concerning land and population, agriculture and technology, can be satisfactorily answered only where there is a large and expensive excavation with ancillary aids such as aerial photography, pollen analysis, soil study. In such circumstances it is possible to survey the land surrounding a site for the field systems which throw light on economic institutions. We should also bear in mind that the work so far undertaken has been unevenly distributed over Ireland. Much has been completed,

[1] S. P. Ó Ríordáin, 'The excavation of a large earthern ring-fort at Garranes, Co. Cork', *PRIA*, XLVII (1942), C 77–150.

[2] See, for example, St John's Point, *Down Survey*, 295–6. I owe this reference to Miss Hamlin.

[3] M. J. O'Kelly, *PRIA*, LIX (1958), C 116–18.

both field survey and excavation, in Co. Down, and is readily available in the *Survey*; a considerable amount of work in Co. Armagh is now awaiting publication; there has been a good deal of excavation in Co. Cork and Co. Limerick; but elsewhere work has been much less concentrated. So it is impossible to tell as yet whether there was much local variation in economic conditions.

Accurate dating is also often very difficult. Sometimes the date of a site may rest on one piece of metalwork, which has to be placed in a typological sequence which can take no account of conservative or progressive tastes. Moreover, radiocarbon determination of 'known age' samples indicates that some adjustment in quoted dates may be necessary, though this affects earlier periods more than those with which we are dealing. There is always a considerable margin of uncertainty in radiocarbon dating and where dating needs to be more specific, as it does in the historic period, this becomes a serious drawback. Tree-ring dating (dendrochronology) may eventually provide absolute dating for oakwood. At present sequences of rings are available for the Early Christian period, but there is not yet any continuous series up to the present day, so that early samples cannot yet be placed in any absolute chronological context. More samples are needed, and waterlogged sites such as crannogs provide particularly good material.

In spite of the difficulties, archaeology gives the historian information and enlarges his understanding beyond the boundaries of his written sources. First of all, the sheer number of habitation sites (which can easily be seen in a country not much industrialised and sparsely inhabited) prises open the spectator's imagination. By about 1100 the land (other than bog) below about 800 feet must have been fairly thoroughly cleared. Of course all these sites were not inhabited at once. Presumably families shifted their residences, so that even if a lot of heavy virgin forest had been cut down there must have been plenty of secondary woodland. But Ireland was probably a fairly prosperous and well-inhabited country by early medieval standards.

Archaeology gives plentiful information about some stony areas in the west, of which historical documents tell almost nothing. I have already mentioned the Burren; the Aran Islands, Donegal, the Waterville and Dingle peninsulae should be added. The annals, on the other hand, deal with the eastern and central districts of Ireland,[1] and even ecclesiastical written sources are scanty for the far west. For instance, we know absolutely nothing about Killabuonia on the Waterville peninsula; the patron (as far as we know) is not mentioned in the Martyrologies of Oengus or Tallaght, there is no Life and the place never occurs in the annals. Yet there is here a large and important ecclesiastical site with several remaining buildings and a spring which still contains votive offerings. If one climbs the steps to the inner enclosure, the tent-shaped founder's tomb is on the right and there is an incised cross-slab; the dry-stone church behind it is now in ruins.[2] Who was this saint, and what part did the church play in the life of the community? Similar problems are presented by the four huge cashels and one promontory fort on Inishmore, the biggest of the Aran islands. Dun Aonghusa has three enormous semi-circular walls and a chevaux-de-frise. When and by whom were these forts built, where did the labour come from, and who lived in them? Tradition says that they were the home of the Fir Bolg, who were expelled from the mainland of Ireland by the People of the Goddess Danu, but this explanation is not likely to satisfy either the historian or the archaeologist.

The archaeological and historical evidence is sometimes complementary. The written sources may mention a place without describing it. For instance, Skellig Michael has an occasional reference in annals and ecclesiastical sources, but here the material remains give us an extraordinarily complete picture of the physical life of a small, ascetic community. Built on a terrace just beneath the peak of the rock island are six dry-stone houses with a well,

---

[1] *Infra*, 99 ff.

[2] This, and many other sites on the Waterville peninsula, are surveyed by F. Henry, 'Early Irish monasteries, beehive huts and dry-stone houses in the neighbourhood of Caherciveen and Waterville', *PRIA*, LVIII (1957), C 45–166.

and beyond them lies a small, isolated oratory, just beneath them are a boat-shaped oratory and graveyard and a rectangular church; below this lies a little garden, then steps lead down steeply to three landing places.[1] Many of the saints named in the Martyrologies cannot be located: Miss Ann Hamlin has found ecclesiastical material on a number of sites in north-east Ireland which are not mentioned in the documents. The texts invite us to think that many ecclesiastical foundations lasted a comparatively short time, and the archaeology gives life to this picture.

Occasionally the archaeological evidence may suggest an exciting hypothesis to the historian. Professor Bernard Wailes has recently been digging at Knockaulin, in Co. Kildare, where there was a ritual or ceremonial site in the pre-Christian period.[2] Here, in the third and fourth phases of the site, there was a small timber structure with a heavily burned floor, outside it a circle of huge post-holes for some wooden 'henge' monument, the whole surrounded by two concentric wooden palisades. A fibula dates from the first centuries AD, and other finds are consistent with the Iron Age. The whole structure was deliberately dismantled, the posts taken up. Five miles away is Kildare, an early and important church site, with its patron Brigit (which means 'the exalted one').[3] The historian immediately thinks of the pagan goddess Bríg and of Giraldus' story of the never-dying fire.[4] Have the two sites any connection?

Sometimes the archaeological material seems to be at variance with the literary evidence. There is, for instance, considerable discrepancy between the poverty of finds on most Irish sites and the solid body of equipment attributed to the free and noble grades of Irish society in the law tracts. The *mruigfer*, one of the free but non-noble grades, has all the apparatus of his house in its proper place, including two cauldrons, a vat for ale, iron cups

---

[1] L. De Paor, *JRSAI*, LXXXV (1955), 174–87.

[2] 'Excavations at Dún Ailinne, Co Kildare, 1968–69 Interim Report', *JRSAI*, C (1970), 79–90. For 1970, *J. Kildare Arch. Soc.*, XIV (1970), 507–17.

[3] Binchy, *Celtic and Anglo-Saxon Kingship* (Oxford 1970), 12.

[4] J. O'Meara, *PRIA*, LII (1949), C 150.

and kneading troughs and mugs, a washing trough, tubs, candle-sticks, knives; also an adze, auger, saw, shears, axe, whetstone, billhook, hatchet, spears for cattle-killing, a plough and its accessories.[1] Mr and Mrs de Paor say that 'archaeological research has added a good deal to, and subtracted something from, this picture'. I would definitely attach more weight here to the literary evidence than to the absence of archaeological evidence. It might be argued that the tract provides a schematized account of status, saying rather what each grade should have had than what it had in fact. English medieval village sites offer an instructive analogy, for the finds on them are often quite minor and trivial, whereas manorial sources such as court rolls prove that peasants had quite elaborate equipment.[2] The Irish farmer's wooden tools would have rotted away under normal temperate conditions, while his iron ones would have been handed on, so that finds today are not representative of the amount of equipment then current.

This observation brings us back to the written sources as the core of the historian's evidence. Archaeologists have informed us well about house and home and artefacts, but the historian needs the results from more studies of the whole environment.[3] Excavation of individual sites in the traditional manner will build up more knowledge. This is in itself valuable, and on some specially well-chosen site it may transform all the historian's accepted ideas, but it is generally likely to produce evidence of the same character as that which we already possess. What the historian now most needs is research on a large scale in order to build up knowledge of population and the use of the land.

[1] *CG*, lines 171–82. Translated E. Mac Neill, *PRIA*, XXXVI (1923), C 291 and L. and M. de Paor, *Early Christian Ireland*, 78–9.

[2] R. K. Field, 'Worcestershire peasant buildings, household goods and farming equipment in the later Middle Ages', *Medieval Archaeology*, IX (1965), 105–45. I owe this reference to Miss Hamlin.

[3] The recently formed Group for the Study of Irish Historic Settlement is for this purpose.

Appendix I: Aerial Photography

Until recently aerial photography has been applied to Irish sites in a haphazard way, but the publication of E. R. Norman and J. K. St Joseph, *The Early Development of Irish Society: the evidence of aerial photography* (Cambridge 1969), has now provided a magnificent series of photographs.

Photographs taken from the air under the right conditions will show up certain features which cannot be seen, or will emphasise features which can only be seen with difficulty, from ground level. Any features in relief, such as banks and ditches, are sharply distinguished in oblique light. Aerial photographs show differences in vegetation which are brought about by differences in the soil, so that a filled-in ditch is likely to produce denser and taller crops than the surrounding area, while stone-work below the surface will cause poor and stunted growth. After fresh ploughing the soil covering ground which has been anciently disturbed may be slightly different in colour from the surrounding soil. Long-rooted cereal crops like wheat, oats and þarley show the most marked contrasts in growth, especially in the second half of the growing season, and conditions of drought betray buried structures particularly well.[1]

Ireland is a wet country and much of the land is pasture, but air photography has nonetheless produced very interesting results. It has brought to light some unknown ring-forts, though so far these form a very small proportion of the total number.[2] The photographs perform certain unique functions. There are superb views showing forts in relation to their natural environments—crannogs in lakes

[1] For the application of air photography to archaeology in general, see *The Uses of Air Photography*, ed. J. K. St Joseph (London 1966).

[2] One hundred and sixty or so is a small percentage of thirty or forty thousand.

34

or cashels on cliff edges—so that the geographical factors which have determined the choice of site make a most vivid impact on the imagination. Moreover, we may see sites in relation to each other; clusters of ring-forts, sometimes within a short distance of each other, sometimes actually overlapping.

Most important of all, the photographs show the ring-forts in relation to adjacent earth-works and field systems. This is vital new evidence. Archaeologists have nearly always confined themselves to what has happened inside the fort, but the historian wants to know the physical background of farming and economy. Consequently the enclosures adjacent to the ring-fort or near by, perhaps for keeping cattle, and the scores of small, irregularly-shaped fields which have been revealed are the most exciting additions to our knowledge. It is also worth noting that in the collection of unpublished air photographs there are examples of strip-farming. None of these was clearly identified as an early site, and it was assumed that they belonged to a post-Norman period.[1] Possible literary evidence for strip-farming[2] is not, in fact, contradicted by the evidence of aerial photography.

Of course aerial photography will not date things, and the historian needs a chronology. These fields and cattle-enclosures may have been in use much later. But it seems likely that most of them were laid out when the ring-forts were first occupied. The adjacent forts were probably not all inhabited at the same time. To this day in parts of western Ireland you can see a modern house beside a cabin (now used as a shed but once the main dwelling), beside a ruin. It may have been easier to build a new ring-fort than to clean up and repair an old one.

It might be possible from aerial photographs to plot earthworks and trackways. For instance, the road which ran across the centre of Ireland was called an *escir*, a word which means a ridge separating two areas of lower ground. One would expect the line of this to be visible from the air. Irish roads were used by wheeled vehicles, so they must have been fairly well drained. No doubt

---

[1] I owe this information to Dr Norman.
[2] *Infra*, 52.

modern roads overlie many of them, but aerial photographs might show natural lines of communication more clearly than any other means.

Aerial photography does not replace archaeology, but it adds enormously to our knowledge of the surroundings of excavated sites, it can guide the archaeologist in future excavation and might help the cartologist of early Ireland.

Appendix II: Coins

Well over two thousand Roman coins have been found in Ireland. These seem to represent three different types of activity. A few were probably brought by early travellers and tourists. For instance, around New Grange a number of gold, silver and copper coins have come to light, mostly of the fourth century, including uniface pendants, the kind of gold coins with blank backs and suspension loops which were given to Roman veterans. These may have been left as votive offerings. Other coins, from the end of the fourth and early fifth centuries, seem to be loot brought by Irish raiders from Britain. The Ballinrees hoard (also sometimes called the Coleraine hoard), which dates from c. 420 and includes over 1,500 silver coins as well as silver plate and ingots, is a clear example of loot. The boy Patrick was captured as a slave on such a raid from Britain.[1] But the great majority of coins which occur as single finds can be shown to have been brought into the country in the last century or so as souvenirs, and later abandoned.

The Irish themselves did not use coins, and there are few coin hoards before the tenth century, when the Norse of Dublin started to import coins on a considerable scale. Finds of the ninth century present evidence of Viking activity. The Mullaghboden hoard is the only find from the whole of Great Britain and Ireland which is composed exclusively of Carolingian coins.[2] The circumstances of its deposit may therefore be exceptional. All the coins are from Aquitaine and date from c. 830–45, so we may infer that they were assembled in 845 or soon after. The Vikings were

[1] See Ó Ríordáin, 'Roman material in Ireland', *PRIA*, LI (1947), C 35–82. A critical re-appraisal, by Mr J. D. Bateson, incorporating much new material, is appearing in *PRIA*.

[2] R. H. M. Dolley in *Oslo Universitetets Oldsaksamlings Årbok* (1960–61), 49–62.

ravaging in Aquitaine in 845, and in 846 destroyed Noir-moutier, before many of them returned to Ireland. So this hoard looks like part of Viking pillage from Aquitaine. The Hiberno-Norse were also in contact with England. In one of the cabinets of the National Museum of Ireland Mr Dolley has recently found six coins of Burgred of Mercia and Æthelred and Alfred of Wessex, which were probably concealed c. 875.[1]

During the first half of the tenth century the Scandinavians in England were minting their own imitations of English coins, and there were close contacts between Dublin and the Viking colonies in northern England.[2] So we may expect English pennies and Viking imitations from York and Chester in central east Ireland. There are also Kufic coins, mostly falling within the first half of the century, showing that the Hiberno-Norse had contact with people trading and raiding in Arab territories. The hoards tend to 'bunch' around the decade c. 970–80, and so emphasise the importance of the battle of Tara (980), when Máel-Sechnaill, the Uí Néill overlord, defeated the Foreigners of Dublin and the Isles and, according to the annals, banished their power from Ireland. The coin evidence suggests that in this decade life for the Hiberno-Norse was insecure, so that they buried their treasure and in a number of cases were unable to recover it. The hoards also show that after this time the Viking hold on Meath and Louth was broken.[3] The dramatic success of Brian should not blind us to the achievements of the Uí Néill.

About 995 the Hiberno-Norse of Dublin began to mint their own coins on English models. At first they were of good weight, later debased. For thirty years after 999 (the Irish victory at Glen Mama) only three coin-hoards in Ireland have come to light, though we know from Irish coins in Scandinavia that the Dublin mint had a considerable output during this period. Mr Dolley

---

[1] *British Numismatic Journal*, XXXIV (1965), 32–5.

[2] For what follows see R. H. M. Dolley, *The Hiberno-Norse Coins in the British Museum* (London 1966).

[3] Compare Dolley's distribution maps of tenth- and eleventh-century hoards, *op. cit.*, 35 and 45.

suggests that the Dubliners were not especially disturbed by the battle of Clontarf, where the brunt of the fighting must have fallen on the Irish and the Vikings from the Isles. Still, the battle was fought just outside Viking Dublin, and it seems extraordinary that the Hiberno-Norse did not hide their property in case of loot. The lack of coin hoards around 1014 (the date of Clontarf) does, however, suggest that the after-effects of the battle were not great, and that the Dubliners survived to recover their valuables. Our views of Clontarf are almost inevitably coloured by saga.

For a generation or so the Dublin penny found its way to Scandinavia, though in dwindling quantity. Then it seems that regular trading contact between Scandinavia and Ireland virtually ceased. By this time the Irish penny was inferior to the English penny in weight, so that it must have been a less good competitor for trade. Dublin was the only mint in Ireland to issue coins. During the period c. 995 to c. 1105 most of the hoards are from the south-eastern quarter of Ireland, witnessing to Hiberno-Norse influence in Leinster. But it is clear that most of Ireland was still a coinless economy. The very different picture which numismatics present of the Norwegian and Danish spheres of influence should provide strong warning against generalisations about the effects of Viking settlement in different parts of the British Isles.[1]

Towards the end of our period a new type of coin appears. These are bracteates. A thin flan of silver was laid on some material such as leather or wood, with a hard substance below. The die was put on top and struck. This does not give the normal obverse and reverse. Some seeming bracteates were found at Scrabo, in Co. Down (a hoard which Mr Dolley maintains was the product of a single mint, presumably Dublin, and struck c. 1135),[2] but these are in fact the last of the coins struck by traditional methods.[3] A number of authentic bracteates have now come to light in the 1962–70 excavations at Dublin, nearly all of

---

[1] See *infra*, 149 ff.
[2] *Op. cit.*, 142.
[3] It is the thinness of the metal that gives the impression of a bracteate.

them in base silver and struck (as Mr Dolley thinks) at the Dublin mint between c. 1150 and c. 1170,[1] The hoard of bracteates found at Castlelyons near Fermoy, in Co. Cork, differs not only in technique, but in style, from most Hiberno-Norse coins. 'They drew their ultimate inspiration from English pennies, but the engraver is infinitely freer in his treatment, and in particular is not afraid boldly to improvise.'[2] Moreover the weight-standard is different, for these bracteates are in good silver. In 1966 Mr Dolley suggested that these coins might have been struck by Toirdelbach Ua Conchobair (1119–56) about the middle of the century. Since then another bracteate in fairly pure silver has been excavated at Dublin, though it was probably not struck there but in some Irish mint. The last phase of coinage in pre-Norman Ireland therefore shows the very close inter-relationship of the Irish and Hiberno-Norse in the twelfth century. It now looks as if the Hiberno-Norse practice of striking coins may actually have begun to spread to the Irish before the Anglo-Normans arrived.

[1] I am most grateful to Mr Dolley for letting me see the typescript of his report on the coins from Dublin up to June 1971.

[2] Dolley, *Sylloge*, 142.

CHAPTER 2

The Secular Laws

I

Irish secular law is recorded in a series of tracts compiled in the seventh and eighth centuries. They are accompanied by later commentary and gloss, and the whole corpus forms a very considerable body of material. They were transmitted, orally at first, in the secular law schools by professional jurists, who were the successors of a pre-Christian learned class. They are in no sense the king's law, but statements of customary practices.

The law tracts would answer a mass of questions on almost every subject connected with the institutions of the country. Where does power reside, and what constitutes a right to it? How is law enforced, what are the sanctions and who applies them? In what does wealth consist, how do you inherit it and can you get rich? Is farming private or co-operative? What are the relations between landlord and tenant? What is the character of royal authority? Is there any conception of public as distinct from personal authority? One could formulate many more questions of this kind to which the law tracts provide the key. They would allow you not only to construct a political theory for early Ireland but to have some idea of how the society actually worked.

If the law tracts are so early and so informative, why have so few scholars chosen to work on them? By no means all the tracts are in a reliable edition, and the work of editing them is one of extreme difficulty. The texts have survived only in much later manuscripts, accompanied by gloss and commentary which in the nineteenth-century edition are sometimes not correctly distinguished from the text. The bulk of the material may be estimated from the fact that the five volumes of text in the Rolls

Series represent a little more than half of the extant manuscript material. This is an unsatisfactory edition and often a misleading translation. The language of the law tracts is archaic, and even the good Irish scholar has great difficulty in understanding it. However, there are now excellent editions, usually with translations, of a number of tracts, and Professor Binchy's corpus of Irish law is soon to go to press. This diplomatic edition will make the study of Irish law a possibility for the next generation, but it will remain the field of the philologist and legal specialist before it can be used by the historian.

Largely owing to the work of Professor Mac Neill and, more particularly, Professor Thurneysen in the last generation[1] and Professor Binchy in this, the historian with some Old-Irish can now make a beginning in trying to understand the law tracts. But he must expect hard work, for their language is not only archaic, it is also technical. Take for instance this passage from the law of status which says that it is about to define the qualifications of each grade of society:

> What is the measure of the compurgatory oath (*imthach*) and the enforcing-suretyship (*naidm*) and the paying-suretyship (*ráth*) and the evidence (*fiadnaise*) and the honour-price (*lóg n-enech*) and the hospitality (*biathad*) and the sick-maintenance (*othrus*) and the protection (*snádud*) and the client-price (*taurchrec*) and the house-custom (*bés tige*) of each of them?[2]

In these few lines of Old-Irish every single term needs to be properly defined before the passage can be understood. This is why Professor Binchy's glossary to *Crith Gablach* is such an important contribution to the subject. All the texts which he has edited have been explained, and his lectures in *Early Irish Society* (1954) and *Celtic and Anglo-Saxon Kingship* (1970) together with

---

[1] See Binchy, *The Irish Jurist*, I (1966), 84–7; II (1967), 106–15.

[2] *CG*, lines 19–22. Mac Neill, *PRIA*, XXXVI (1923), C 282. I will give the references to Mac Neill's translation in footnotes, but the notes to Professor Binchy's edition should be consulted for corrections even by readers who cannot understand the text.

the glossary to *Críth Gablach* have made it possible for the historian, even for one who knows no Irish, to gain some idea of Irish institutions.

There is another difficulty still for the historian. How far do the statements of the law tracts represent real life? Schematisation was the lawyer's leading characteristic. This is easily recognisable and not very serious when we have to deal, for instance, with the day-to-day occupations of a king: Sunday for drinking, Monday for judgment, for adjusting the kingdom, Tuesday for playing chess, Wednesday for watching deer-hounds at the chase, Thursday for the society of his wife, Friday for horse-racing, Saturday for adjusting disputes between territories.[1] This gives us some idea of what were thought to be the proper interests of a king, and it matters very little whether or not kings stuck to so rigid a time-table. But when we come to distinctions in status, with the exact property-qualification of each sub-division, it is important to know how far these distinctions were really apparent in early Irish society. What happens if a man gains or loses a cow or two? What happens if all his cows die off through disease?[2] The historian also wants to know to what extent the sanctions described in the laws were actually applied. Moreover, when the laws were written down they were already ancient: were institutions already beginning to change? Only a beginning has been made in the work of setting the law tracts alongside other sources like the annals in order to arrive at the historical reality.

The tracts will not, of course, answer questions about society after 800. The glosses and commentaries vary considerably in date. Sometimes the commentators have misunderstood a passage, and the glossators sometimes indulge in fantastic explanations. The late Professor Bergin provided an English parody of a not uncommon kind of pseudo-etymological gloss.[3] He took the

---

[1] *CG*, lines 542–7. Mac Neill, *op. cit.*, 304.

[2] Binchy, *PBA*, XXIX (1943), 224–5, thinks that the detailed classification of grades was on paper only, and that in practice the classification was king, nobles and free commoners.

[3] Quoted Binchy, *ibid.*, 212.

Shakespearian phrase 'Darraign your battle', where 'darraign' comes from Old French *deraigner* and means 'dispose your troops in battle array'. Had the Irish glossators got to work on this, we might have:

> *Darraign*, that is *do ruin*, from its destructiveness; or *die ere you run*, that is, they must not retreat; or *dare in*, because they are brave; or *tear around*, from their activity; or *dear rain*, from the showers of blood.

Such glosses show the lawyers at work. They seem to add little to our understanding of the text, though they sometimes help a modern editor to restore a text which has been corrupted by later scribes. It might, however, be possible for a scholar with sufficient expertise to put the text alongside gloss and commentary to see how institutions changed.

The law tracts provide one of the least explored and most potentially productive sources of Irish history. Every time a tract is properly edited new material is made available. This mine of information is as yet only partially accessible to the historian.

II

First of all let us consider kin and status. The law tracts underline the fundamental importance of the family; important socially, essential for purposes of inheritance and for applying sanctions to keep order. The old legal unit of kin was the *derbfine*, the four-generations family group, though during the period covered by the law tracts this was narrowing to the *gelfine*, the three-generations group. Within the family group there was a recognised 'senior', who inherited a special portion of the family property and discharged certain obligations as head of the family.[1] Irish society concentrated its power in the male line. When a man died his male heirs inherited his estates, though his daughters received a share of the chattels. In the earlier period daughters could not inherit land, though a man without sons could 'appoint'

[1] C. Plummer, *Ériu*, X (1928), 113–14; Binchy, *St. Ir. Law*, 141–2.

a daughter who originally had to marry her nearest agnatic kinsman (uncle or cousin). Later the laws were modified so that if a man had no sons, and if male heirs failed within the *gelfine*, his daughters inherited his land.

This is all made more complicated by the fact that a woman might have children by more than one husband, while a man very probably had children by more than one wife. For Irish society was polygamous. This does not mean that society was permissive. On the contrary, marriages must have been carefully arranged and illegal unions carried severe deterrents.[1] But a man might have a chief wife and a subordinate wife or wives (the usual word—a borrowing—is *adaltrach*), who are all described as 'lawful women'. Probably the *adaltrach* was taken to provide sons when the chief wife had failed to produce any. Then there are various classes of concubine, living in at least a semi-permanent relation, all recognised by law, for there are complicated rules regulating liability and inheritance. This usage must have gone back to pre-Christian times, and some of the lawyers were uneasy at the discrepancy between common practice and Church teaching. In the following passage a lawyer tries to justify native practice by appealing to Biblical history:

> There is a dispute in Irish law as to which is more proper, whether many sexual unions or a single one: for the chosen [people] of God lived in plurality of unions (a gloss refers to David, Solomon and Jacob) so that it is not easier to condemn it than to praise it.[2]

Most men did not have several wives all the time, or there would not have been enough women to go round, even allowing for the fact that more men than women were killed in war, more followed a life of ascetic religion or died in infancy. The desire for children, which comes out clearly in the law tracts, was

---

[1] In a case of abduction the abductor bears all the woman's liabilities, while her family gain all her assets (Binchy, *St. Ir. Law*, 182). The wanton can obtain no sick-maintenance and no fines for injury (*Bretha Crólige, Ériu*, XII [1938], 34).

[2] *Bretha Crólige, op. cit.*, 44. The ecclesiastical legislation provides much stricter marriage rulings. See *infra*, 79.

probably dictated largely by economic pressures. Conception, not merely cohabitation, was the aim,[1] and the *adaltrach* with sons enjoyed a higher status than the one without.

The children of nearly all legally recognised marriages belonged to the father's kin,[2] yet the connection between the woman and her own family was not severed. The more informal the marriage tie, the closer was the link between the woman and her own family. The law tracts work out degrees of responsibility, a subject of great importance in a society where law is privately enforced. For example, the liability for a mother's misdeeds falls partly on her sons,[3] partly on her own family, in proportions varying according to the type of wife she is; for the chief wife was a heavier liability on her own sons (or husband) than the woman of a less formal union, where her own kin bore a greater responsibility.

The extent of a man's legal liability and the amount which he received in compensation for injuries depended on his honour-price. Thus status was a concept of Irish law as fundamental as kin, since it decided rights and obligations. Status was determined in the first place by birth, but birth did not give inviolable rights. For instance, a man might lose status by giving false evidence or by failing to fulfil his obligations as a surety,[4] while a king must behave suitably to maintain his position—he must not be wounded in the back while fleeing from an enemy, he has to have constant attendance and so on.[5]

But status also implied a certain economic standing, which a man had to have in order to fulfil his obligations. The *ócaire*, a man of the free and honourable grades of society,[6] had seven

[1] See *Bretha Crólige, op cit.*, 31, 67.

[2] There are a few exceptions, e.g. if a woman married a foreigner. See *St. Ir. Law*, 183.

[3] Or, if these are not legally responsible, on her husband. *Ibid.*, 181.

[4] *CG*, lines 303-7, Mac Neill, *op. cit.*, 295. See also *Uraicecht Becc* for changes in status, *ALI*, V, 14-20, translated Mac Neill, *op. cit.*, 273.

[5] *CG.*, 530-41; Mac Neill, *op. cit.*, 303-4.

[6] The tracts distinguish various grades of freeman and various grades of noble.

cows with a bull, seven pigs with a brood sow, seven sheep, a horse for working and riding, enough land to graze seven cows for a year, a fourth share of a plough, an ox, a plough-share, goad and halter, a share in a kiln, a mill and a barn. He gave protection to a man of equal status, and his own honour-price was paid to him for various injuries against him. The validity of a man's legal action depended on his status,[1] and one of superior status might 'overswear' an inferior. The principle behind these complicated arrangements is that, in a system of law based on payments and privately enforced, a man had to be able to provide economic support for his undertakings. The Viking Age, when nobles might be beggared overnight, must have produced legal chaos.

The law was for the protection of the privileged classes of society. *Críth Gablach* deals only with the independent farmers and nobility. (The unfree are rarely discussed in the laws.) It defines the property qualification, the rights and the honour-price of each grade. An effort of imagination is needed to understand that a freeman was glad to have his property minutely catalogued—the size of his house, the precise amount of stock his farm supported, his kitchen equipment, how many suits of clothes he had to his back—for with it went his rights, such as the price he could command from a lord, what hospitality he could claim, how far his legal capacity extended. All this was part of his privilege. Beneath him the unfree classes were increasingly dependent on another's will. The ideas of freedom and law were closely bound together in Ireland, as in other medieval societies.

III

So far I have mentioned two of the fundamental principles of Irish law, kin and status. But these men lived not in a legal system but in a real world of closely-interlocking personal relationships: the tenant needed a lord, the lord wanted clients, the land had to be farmed. The status of a lord was measured by the number of his

[1] CG, lines 89–97, 114; Mac Neill, *op. cit.*, 286–7, 288. Cf. Thurneysen, *Cáin Aicillne*, §19, ZCP, XIV (1923), 361–2.

clients. The lowest of the noble grades of society (the *aire désso*) had ten clients, the noble at the other end of the scale, immediately below the heir to the kingship (*aire forgill*), had forty clients. These clients were of two kinds, free and base.

Free clientship was an honourable state. The free client gave his lord personal service, accompanied him and formed part of his retinue. He held stock of his lord on a kind of hire-purchase system, for, after a heavy rent for seven years, the stock became the free client's own property. The noble grades of society took rent from their clients in food-render, but the man immediately below the noble grade (the *fer fothlai*) had rent from his clients in corn: he had to do his brewing himself.[1] The *fer fothlai* is the only non-noble freeman whom the tract on status sees as rich enough to have clients. If a man of this grade had surplus stock he either sold it to buy himself more land or used it as the capital to acquire clients. Below this grade the law tract is interested in the price which the client commanded from a lord.

Free clientship was the means by which the lord invested capital and commanded personal service. Base clientship was the means by which the lord invested capital in return for food, rent and for manual labour, such as reaping his harvest or building his fort. In addition to the fief of stock, or more occasionally land, the lord gave the base client a preliminary payment determined by the client's status, and in return gained the right to a share in compensation payable to the client for certain injuries done to him. But the base client was not entirely unfree, and his relationship with the lord could be terminated. Both free and base clients owned land of their own,[2] on to which they put the cattle which formed the lord's investment. Land could also be rented if a man had more stock than his pasture would carry.

Beneath the base clients in the social scale was the *fuidir*, who

---

[1] *CG*, lines 253–5. Mac Neill, *op. cit.*, 293.

[2] This is generally speaking true, though in *CG*, which belongs to an old stratum in the law tracts, one of the lowest grades of freemen (*fer midboth*) may be 'without the taking of inheritance until old age', and, for most of his life at any rate, was not cultivating his own land (*CG*, 69–71).

was legally and economically dependent on his lord. His lord, not his kindred, provided support for him in legal and economic matters. These were the people who did much of the agricultural work on the lord's own land. Even the *fuidir* was not bound to the soil, though if he left his lord he abandoned his holding, which was his means of livelihood, and his freedom to leave his lord was so hedged about with restrictions[1] that it must have been very difficult for him to take such a step. The hereditary serf (*senchléithe*) was part of the property of the lord.

It is difficult to find out anything from reliable secondary authorities about Irish economic history, yet the law tracts give a lot of information about farming. Only the expert, however, can understand and interpret it. Here I am heavily indebted to Dr Charles-Edwards, who very generously sent me a long statement about farming in common. I shall summarise its main conclusions here; but so valuable a commentary on obscure material should not go unpublished, so I am printing it, with his permission, in a note at the end of this chapter.

The law tracts provide evidence for farming in common. In the older stratum of the texts, probably dating from c. 600, the members of the four-generations family group who were old enough to acquire their share of the family land joined together for co-operative farming. In the later tracts (perhaps by about 700) the family unit had broken down into the three-generations group, and joint pasturage was not necessarily between kinsmen. In fact there can rarely have been more than three generations living at one time, but a group of people descended from a common great-grandfather will be larger than a group descended from a common grandfather. The family group was thus getting smaller, and legal partnerships between non-kinsmen were becoming more common.

The men ploughed their units of land jointly and had a series of arrangements for common pasturing. The common land—mountain, bog or waste[2]—was used during the summer, from

---

[1] *Cáin Aicillne* §51, ed. Thurneysen, *ZCP*, XIV (1923), 386.
[2] On land, see now G. Mac Niocaill, *Ériu*, XXII (1971), 81–6.

1 May to 1 November, and presumably the stubble was grazed after harvest. It is possible that the arable sometimes consisted of scattered strips in open fields[1] so that joint pasturing on the stubble would be necessary. Some of the land was fenced pasture, and this could also be grazed by a common arrangement whereby each partner put animals into the joint herd, his number depending on the amount of pasture he was able to contribute to the total available.[2] We can also see what happened when a man with land at the boundary of the family property let his fences go to ruin, to the damage of his neighbours' land. His kindred, when challenged by the neighbours, could alienate the pasture to the neighbours for a year as a means of compensating them.[3] The tracts are concerned with the legal arrangements for maintaining fair play and protecting the individual against the neglect of his fellows.

Another tract shows us that water-mills could be either privately or co-operatively owned. There was plenty of water in Ireland. No one could refuse the right to the passage of water across his land, but the mill-owner normally had to pay a fee to the man whose land had been breached or to give him free grinding at the mill. A less wealthy man might find it more convenient to own the mill jointly with the neighbours through whose land the water passed (and possibly others as well), who contributed to its construction and servicing.[4]

It is usually said that Irish farms were small and independent; but the estate of an Irish lord as we see it in the law tracts fits the definition of a 'typical manor', for it had demesne, villein land

---

[1] Dr Charles-Edwards supplies the following references to the *immaire*: *De Maccaib Conaire*, ed. L. Gwynn, *Ériu*, VI (1912), 149; the Middle-Irish introd. to Colman's Hymn, Stokes and Strachan, *Thesaurus Palaeohibernicus*, II, 298; *Cóic Conara Fugill*, ed. Thurneysen, 42 §65; *Vita Tripartita*, ed. Stokes, I, 192, or Mulchrone, lines 2255–6; Cormac's Glossary on *etarche*, ed. W. Stokes, *Three Irish Glossaries* (London 1862), 18. There is no tract on this subject, and the references are incidental. For the evidence of aerial photography see *supra*, 35.

[2] *Comingaire, ALI*, IV, 100.   [3] *Bretha Comaithchesa, ALI*, IV, 128.

[4] Binchy, *Ériu*, XVII (1955), 58–9.

and free holdings.[1] The demesne was worked by the *fuidri* and hereditary serfs[2] (we do not know how large this class was), with help from the base clients at harvest time. The *fuidri* had their own villein holdings, and the lord also let out land and stock to free clients in return for rents and personal services.[3] Units of landholding were thus of varying sizes, from the lord's, down to that of the small freeman who inherited and farmed his share of the family land.

IV

You may be wondering why I have not discussed kingship at the beginning of the chapter. It is because kingship in the law tracts had quite a limited importance for maintaining society in working order. Every man owed duties to his kin, to his lord, to his church, but no duties on a national level were owed to the king. There was no royal law or administration, there was only the most rudimentary public revenue (for lands were attached to the kingship which were inherited by the king's successor and not his natural heirs),[4] there was no central government for day-to-day affairs. The law of status affected the grade of kingship much as it did that of the aristocracy, for there were three grades of king; the petty king, or king of one *tuath* (an area about the size of a modern Irish barony), the king of three or four *tuatha* (pl.) and the king over kings who is the highest grade of king known to the tracts.

There were scores of petty kings in Ireland. Such a king was the representative of his people in any negotiations with another king[5] and he led his troops (drawn from the free tribesmen) into battle; but the tract on status shows how modest was his entourage.

---

[1] Here again I am indebted to Dr Charles-Edwards for correcting and clarifying my ideas.

[2] *Supra,* 51.

[3] *Supra,* 50.

[4] Binchy, *Celtic and Anglo-Saxon Kingship,* 20.

[5] *CG,* lines 494-9, Mac Neill, *op. cit.,* 302. Binchy, *Celtic and Anglo-Saxon Kingship,* 20.

He normally had a suite of twelve for public and nine for private business, though during 'the month of sowing' he had only three, made up of his judge and two of his free clients. In his hall he was attended by his free clients, those 'folk who are company to a king', his wife (presumably the chief wife), a man who was the legal representative of his clients, his judge (who said what the law was but did not execute it), envoys, guests, entertainers of various kinds, hostages (representing each of the aristocratic kin groups), and a guard for the door. The Testament of Catháir, possibly dating from the eighth century, gives a poet's picture of a royal court and a king's possessions:

> Hounds, ale, horses and teams,
> Women, well-bred fosterlings,
> A harvest of honey, wheat of the first reaping,
> Mast for feeding goodly swine
> Shall be in thy populous household,
> Many women and pet animals,
> Musicians for ale-feasts.[1]

The king's court was a social unit. It was also a unit of jurisdiction where all were subject to the same law; its king was the chief of the noble grades and could be sued for private claims by a special process of law.[2]

The powers of the king of three or four *tuatha* were greater. Such a king stood in a personal relationship to his subordinate kings, who contributed their own armies, under their own leadership, to his hostings.[3] Normally the over-king could not interfere in the internal affairs of the petty kingdoms beneath him, but he could convene an assembly of his *tuatha*, and he had administrative powers in certain crises, when there had been defeat in battle or after a pestilence or in time of invasion.[4] The king over kings had similar powers, but over a wider area.

---

[1] M. Dillon, *Lebor na Cert*, *ITS*, 46 (Dublin 1962), 158.
[2] See Binchy, *Celtic and Anglo-Saxon Kingship*, 17.
[3] *Ibid.*, 31-2.
[4] *CG*, lines 514-24, Mac Neill, *op. cit.*, 303.

Who was this 'king over kings'? He has frequently been called the 'high-king', and people have sometimes assumed that he had authority over all Ireland. There is no basis for this in the law tracts;[1] nevertheless, by the eighth century, certain kings were already becoming very powerful overlords over a large area. For example, one tract, compiled about 700, itself mentions the king of Munster as 'supreme over kings', while the Uí Néill kings of the midlands and north formed a kind of dynastic federation[2] under the king of Tara. We shall see later from the evidence of the annals how this tendency towards the growing power of overlords continued after the period when the law tracts were written down. But until the late-tenth century, 'supreme overlord', *imperator*, 'high-king' means a claim to be the greatest king *in* Ireland (whether of Munster or Tara). The 'kingship *of* Ireland' is a term without any political meaning.

We can see from the annals that, as time went on, the chief overlords achieved their ascendancy by a measure of agreement. The kingship of Tara (i.e., of the northern half of Ireland) alternated between the northern and southern branches of the Uí Néill, and normally between the Cenél Éogain in the north and the Clann Colmáin Móir in the south (though this pattern was temporarily broken in the mid-tenth century). The Eoganacht kings of Cashel seem to have been the most powerful overlords in the sourthern half of Ireland until the rise of the Dál Cais in the late-tenth century heralded the reign of Brian Bóruma, the first true king of Ireland. Mac Neill claimed that in the *tuath* the petty kingship was in theory open to all the members of the *derbfine*: anyone whose great-grandfather had held the throne was eligible for the kingship. But in practice a successor was selected (how we do not know) from those eligible in the lifetime of the reigning king. He is given separate status in *Críth Gablach* as the 'second to a king (*tánaise ríg*), because the whole of the *tuath* looks forward to his kingship without opposition to him'.

[1] Binchy, *Ériu*, XVIII (1958), 48 ff.
[2] The phrase is Professor Binchy's: *Celtic and Anglo-Saxon Kingship*, 37.

Without such an arrangement the succession would have been much more troubled than it was in fact.

I have been stressing the limitations on royal power. Yet there was one sense in which the king stood apart from ordinary men. In the pagan period the kingship had been regarded as divine, and some of the attributes of a divine king still clung to kings in the Christian period. We hear of the 'marriage feast' of Tara, by which that king in the fifth and sixth centuries was wedded to his land. There had been similar fertility rites of inauguration for Emain Macha (the old capital of Ulster) and Cruachu (the capital of Connacht).[1] Kings of the historic period had to be willingly accepted by their land. The reign of a true king brought abundance: the seven candles which prove the falsehood of a king include famine, dryness of cows, blight of mast, scarcity of corn. It would be interesting to work out from the annals just how often a run of bad luck had fatal consequences for a king.

v

One of the main purposes of any political organisation is to keep order, yet, as we have seen, the king exercised no general control over the day-to-day business of keeping the peace. Who then applied the sanctions in this society, and why was the law kept at all?

First of all, we are among people who see misdeeds not as a crime against society but as injuries by individuals against individuals. And these injuries have to be paid for. The cost of a deliberate injury would be a considerable deterrent, especially if it injured the honour of one of high status. And there was no escaping the debt. If a man could not pay, then his kin had to pay for him. The pressure of opinion among the kin must have been heavy enough to keep most men in line.

The system of compensation for injuries and kin responsibility is, of course, also found in Germanic societies of the same period,

[1] Cashel was probably Christian from its beginnings or at least early in its history. See Binchy, *Celtic and Anglo-Saxon Kingship*, 40.

and, indeed, in all early legal systems. But the Irish evolved another method of enforcing the law and developed it to an unusual degree. When a contract was made each side took sureties who swore to its fulfilment.[1] The earliest kind of surety to evolve in Irish law was the *naidm*, the enforcing surety, who, with the *aitire* or hostage surety, figures in archaic passages in the law tracts. The enforcing surety pledged himself to compel the debtor to perform his obligations, the hostage surety pledged his person in case of default. In private contracts the *ráth*, the paying surety, replaced these as the normal type of surety. If the enforcing surety failed to make the debtor pay, the *ráth* became liable. In the end the *ráth* could get back the value of his property plus substantial compensation by distraint. A man could never go surety for a person of higher rank than himself (for the obvious reason that he would have been unable to meet his obligations), and the enforcing surety had to be of a higher rank than the principal.

There was yet another sanction which might be applied, the law of distress. It was the normal means used to force an opponent to agree to submit to arbitration. There is a long tract about distress. It deals with such questions as the notice which precedes distress, the circumstances under which it may be levied, how it is to be levied (for example, the animals taken are to be put in safe custody pending a legal enquiry), the persons and classes debarred from taking distress, the alternatives to distress from those too low in the social scale to supply it, how much distress may be levied for various offences. This tract has a long commentary and is heavily glossed. It was obviously important.

Even the freeman can hardly have understood all the intricacies of the law. The Irishman must often have needed a lawyer to press his claims and manage his business. There were various classes of lawyer, up to the jurist who actually pronounced the judgment when the case was tried. But the judge did not put the law into effect. This was the responsibility of kindred and sureties.

[1] On suretyship see Thurneysen, *Die Burgschaft im irischen Recht*; Binchy in *Early Irish Society*, 63–4, and in *Indo-European and Indo-Europeans: Papers presented at the Third Indo-European Conference, 1963* (Philadelphia 1970), 355–67.

In effect, since one could not go surety for a superior and since the value of a man's oath depended on his status, each class of society helped to keep the classes below itself in order. Society was indeed hierarchical and familiar.[1]

Would these sanctions work? Until the Viking Age they would work fairly well, save in the exceptional case where a man was rich and powerful enough to pay for the injuries he did. In one story we see Cú Chulainn going to the smith and demanding a shield with a silver engraving, which had to be different from that on any other shield. The smith answers:

'I cannot do that, for I have spent my skill on the shields (of the other Ulster heroes).'
'I swear by my weapon', said Cú Chulainn, 'that I will kill you if you do not make my shield so.'
'I am under the protection of Conchobar from you.'
'You shall claim the protection of Conchobar and I will kill you all the same.'[2]

If Cú Chulainn could pay the heavy fine for the murder of the smith and compensate Conchobar for the insult done to him he would be cleared without loss of status. But for most people, crime did not pay.

The old social sanctions must have been modified in the Viking Age, for the complex customary law then ceased to be recorded. Why did this breakdown occur? The sanctity of the law must have received severe shocks, for the Vikings had no respect for it. Moreover, the economic backing which a man required to support the rights and obligations of his status might disappear overnight in a Viking raid. Thus some of the foundations on which the law rested were very badly shaken. We do not know what happened in the lower ranks of society, but the annals show us that, at the top, force became increasingly important and that some of the old laws, for instance the law of sanctuary, were no

[1] Binchy, *Early Irish Society*, 54.
[2] See M. Dillon, 'Stories from the law tracts', *Ériu*, XI (1932), 55; R. I. Best, *Ériu*, V (1911), 72, for text.

longer regarded. The secular law tracts, with their extreme complexity, presuppose a stable society. There must have been considerable simplification in the Viking Age.

VI

Irish law provided certain social amenities. A man's status determined the amount of hospitality he should receive, the extent of sick-maintenance to which he had a right, the cost of fostering his son or daughter. The *ócaire*, for instance (the free small farmer), if he were moving about the petty kingdom, might claim hospitality for himself and one other person. The kind and quantity of the food is laid down—milk and curds and corn baked into bread, but no butter. A man could not legally claim hospitality from anyone of lower class than himself. Failure to provide hospitality when it was legally demanded meant loss of honour. The higher a man's status, the better the hospitality he provided.[1]

The *ócaire* was to be accompanied by one attendant when he received sick maintenance. Irish law has detailed provisions for this. Originally, if you injured a man you not only had to pay the relevant fines, you also had to remove him to the house of a third party and arrange for his nursing under a doctor's direction. You might also have to compensate him for his temporary loss of activity and, if the injury proved permanent, make a further payment. The maintenance of the sick man, according to his status, is carefully laid down. But by the eighth century this system had already been replaced by fines and compensation:

Sick maintenance does not exist at the present day, but rather a fee for his proper nursing [is paid] to each according to his rank, to include the doctor's fee and [the expense of] supplying drink and food, and an [eventual] payment for blemish, hurt [or] loss of limb.[2]

[1] There is a delightful poem ascribed to Brigit, beginning: 'I would like a great ale feast for the king of kings,' in which the poet sees himself as a tributary of God. See D. Greene, *Celtica*, II (1952), 151-2.
[2] *CG*, lines 47-9, Mac Neill, *op. cit.*, 284.

By this time the injured man was nursed at home, while the man who did the injury paid a nursing fee. One tract deals in detail with the tariffs of compensation for different types of injury, and with the doctor's fee. The whole subject of sick-maintenance is of great interest because it takes us back to an extremely archaic period of Irish law. The last part of the tract *Bretha Déin Chécht* is written in a rhetorical style without any of the loan-words which came into Irish through the influence of Christianity.[1] This means that this part of the tract must have been composed before the native schools came under Christian influence. As we shall see, the conversion was a gradual affair: it was not until the seventh century that jurists and canonists got together on a large scale.

Fosterage was another of the amenities of society. The education of a girl was more expensive than that of a boy because she needed more attention and was likely to be of less use to the fosterer, and the higher a man's status the greater the fosterage fee he paid. The tract on fosterage mentions the maintenance of the children, and its commentary enlarges on how they are to be equipped and what they are to be taught. The tract is also concerned with liability for their misdeeds. Fosterage was a common practice in the upper ranks of Irish society, probably the more desirable if a man had children by several different women.

These amenities, unlike modern social services, were for the privileged classes. They are one more example of the aristocratic character of Irish society.

VII

In this chapter I have tried to show the kind of information which the law tracts provide. It is essential for the historian to understand how a society functions, and the law tracts tell at least how it *claimed* to function. They are fundamental to our understanding of early Irish history: they add substance and detail to the archaeological evidence; they explain some of the early ecclesiastical legislation; they are illustrated by some of the literature. But they

[1] Binchy, *Ériu*, XX (1966), 3-4.

are undoubtedly highly schematised, and the historian also wants to know how far this ideal society coincided with the facts. For this he must turn to other sources.

NOTE FROM DR CHARLES-EDWARDS ON COMMON FARMING

It is essential to distinguish between two periods, both of which are covered by the law tracts. The older strata of the laws belong to a period when the unit for purposes of inheritance, and also for purposes of co-operation in farming, was the *derbfine*, the kindred consisting of the agnatic descendants of a man's agnatic great-grandfather (I think that Mac Neill was right about the structure of the kindred, and that O Buachalla's criticisms of Mac Neill[1] and O Buachalla's own theory are wrong). The more recent strata of the laws, on the other hand, belong to a period when a man's inner kindred was no longer the *derbfine*, but the *gelfine*, an agnatic kindred consisting of the descendants of a man's grandfather.[2] *Bretha Comaithchesa*[3] belongs to the *gelfine* period, but contains many rules and ideas belonging to the older *derbfine* period. The legal poem now edited by Binchy[4] belongs to the *derbfine* period. Among tracts which deal with specific topics, *Bechbretha*[5] and *Coibnes Uisci Thairidne*[6] belong to the *derbfine* period (though in one place *Bechbretha* has been superficially brought up to date), whereas the tract on *Comingaire*[7] probably belongs to the *gelfine* period.

In the older period there was a group of neighbours, called a *comaithches*, which was composed of those members of the *derbfine* who had reached the age at which they acquired their portion of the *fintiu*.[8] The *comaithches* was the unit for farming co-operation. This is shown in two ways. First, there was a sharp distinction between trespasses committed by the animals of the kinsman on the land of another kinsman, and trespasses committed by animals on land belonging to a man who was not a member of the kindred

---

[1] *JCHAS*, LII (1947), 43–54.
[2] Binchy, *PBA*, XXIX (1943), 223.
[3] *ALI*, IV, 68–159.
[4] 'An archaic legal poem', *Celtica*, IX (1971), 152–68.
[5] *ALI*, IV, 162–203.
[6] Ed. Binchy, *Ériu*, XVII (1955), 52–85.
[7] *ALI*, IV, 100–2.
[8] *Celtica*, IX (1971), 156–7, lines 12–25.

of which the owner of the animals was a member. In other words, trespasses within the bounds of the *fintiu* were on a different footing from trespasses across the bounds of the *fintiu*. In both cases the payments were compensatory rather than punitive, but, within the *comaithches*, compensation was guaranteed by forepledges given by the participants, whereas outside the *comaithches* there was no such guarantee, and it might be necessary to distrain against the offender or his kindred.[1] Secondly, joint pasturing seems, in the earlier period, to have been arranged between close kinsmen, and joint ploughing was undoubtedly a matter for kinsmen.[2] Joint ploughing may perhaps have continued to be the province of kinsmen in the *gelfine* period; but the short tract on *comingaire* shows that this was not true of joint pasturing. The participants are partners (*céili*), not kinsmen, and rules are given which presuppose that the participants will not have holdings of the same size, which they would have had under the older law if they were kinsmen.

The organisation of joint pasturing also varied according to what sort of land was being pastured. Three categories of pasture may be distinguished: arable after harvest, fenced pasture and common land. Common land might be mountain land, bogland or just waste land.[3] It was used during the summer months (1st May until 1st November). Such land appears to have been common to a whole *tuath*. Fenced pasture was of two types, pasture preserved for the winter (*etham díguin*), and pasture also used during the summer (*athlumpaire, athbronnad*). The stubble was, no doubt, grazed after harvest. Some arable, at least, consisted of strips, each man having a number of scattered strips rather than a block.[4] In such circumstances, joint pasturing would be necessary if the stubble was grazed after harvest. The tract on *comingaire* is not primarily concerned with the grazing of common land. The organisation implied is one whereby each man who participates in a *comingaire* partnership contributes a certain amount of pasture which belongs to him alone, and is allowed to put a corresponding number of cattle or other animals into the joint herd. Since the tract assumes that at any one time the joint herd will be on the land of one of the participants, it is fair to conclude that the land involved is fenced pasture, and not unfenced pasture in private ownership like, for example, an open field strip after harvest. On the other hand the tract is not merely dealing with

---

[1] *ALI*, IV, 128.   [2] *St. Ir. Law*, 19.   [3] *ALI*, IV, 124.
[4] *Supra*, 52, note 1.

winter pasture (*etham díguin*), because it contains the proviso that piglets and lambs do not come under the provisions of joint pasturing until 1st August. This suggests that the pasture implied is *athlumpaire* (*athbronnad*).

A different set of assumptions appears to lie behind the opening sections of *Bretha Comaithchesa*.[1] The third paragraph refers to two possible ways in which penalties for trespass can be arranged. The first way requires fences round each man's pasture and the penalties are called *smachta*. The second way requires a forepledge from each man and the penalties are called *caithgi* (MS *caiche*). The evidence of the rest of the tract suggests that *caithgi* are penalties due when human fault is involved in the offence. The natural inference is, then, that the forepledge/*caithgi* arrangement is for joint herding. *Caithgi* are due rather than *smachta*, because a herdsman has failed to prevent trespasses. The pasture involved appears not to have been fenced (the contrast is fencing/*smachta* versus forepledge/*caithgi*) and this implies that the joint herding is not of the same type as that covered by the *comingaire* tract. It is, however, of the type implied in a later section of *Bretha Comaithchesa*[2] which gives rules for the situation when a man with a holding at the boundary of the *fintiu* abandons his holding (probably only temporarily), allowing the fences to go to ruin. His kindred, when challenged by the non-kinsmen neighbours, can alienate the pasture belonging to the *eisert*[3] to the two neighbours for a term of a year. These two neighbours (who are themselves members of one kindred) fence the pasture, put in an equal number of livestock and give forepledges to each other. They have repaired the fences round the *eisert*'s pasture, and they exploit it jointly for a year.

The compiler of *Bretha Comaithchesa* did not succeed in keeping to the scheme announced in his third paragraph. Later he mentions a forepledge in connection with *smachta*.[4] In my view, one of his main sources may well have been the poem on the law of neighbourhood edited by Binchy (first half of seventh century?), and this poem has only one arrangement. A *comaithches* partnership is set up by means of pledges, and the pledges guarantee the payment of *smachta* ('slán cach comaithches/cuirthar gellaib/gelltar smachtaib'). At this period a *comaithches* partnership was simply one role performed by the *derbfine*, so that there was a sharp distinction between

[1] *ALI*, IV, 68–70.   [2] *Ibid.*, 128.
[3] i.e., the man who neglects his holding.   [4] *ALI*, IV, 78, 86.

the partner and non-partner. The idea that the *comaithig* are *derbráithir* lies behind the second paragraph of *Bretha Comaithchesa*[1] ('Cait. Can for-beir co(i)maithches? A ilcomarbus. Cía cruthsaide? Con-rannat comarbai cétamus a ranna ocus a se(a)lba ocus im-fen cách díb fri araile ocus do-beir cách díb díguin diarailiu'; text normalised from Rawl. MS B.487). In the rest of the tract, however, there is only one place where any concern is shown for the role of the kindred, and this, the passage on the *eisert*, is, I think, taken bodily from some older source (I think it belongs to the *derbfine* period). Moreover, in the first paragraph of *Bretha Comaithchesa* the relationships (as neighbours) of *aire* and *aithech*, *airchinnech* and *bachlach* are said to belong to *comaithches*. Such men would not be kinsmen, and *comaithches* in the early period was a partnership of kinsmen.

There is another series of difficulties in *Bretha Comaithchesa* which can be solved in the same way. In the section on the *eisert*[2] one possible answer to the problem his neglect has posed is for the *eisert's* kindred to alienate pasture to the injured parties for a year. Their pasture has been damaged, and the temporarily alienated pasture is adequate compensation. Earlier in the tract the same method of compensation is mentioned, and also another equivalent compensation consisting of one-third, two-thirds or even the whole of a year's rent for the damaged pasture.[3] Whereas in the *eisert* section the compensation payment settles the matter, in the earlier sections of *Bretha Comaithchesa* there is a further penalty paid in sacks of corn (or barley malt).[4] In the legal poem the penalties within the *comaithches* partnership are in sacks.[5] The *eisert* section is dealing with offences across the boundary of the *fintiu* and the penalty is a temporary handing over of pasture; the legal poem is dealing with offences within the *fintiu* and the penalty consists of sacks; *Bretha Comaithchesa* is not quite sure whether it is dealing with offences between kinsmen or not and the penalty consists both of temporary alienation of pasture (or rent) and of sacks. The correct explanation of these differences is perhaps that, with the collapse of the old *comaithches* system based on the *derbfine*, compensatory payments were replaced by a punitive penalty which consisted of both the old payment in sacks appropriate within a *comaithches* partnership and the temporary alienation (or rent) appropriate outside the partnership.

[1] *ALI*, IV, 68.   [2] *Ibid.*, 128   [3] *Ibid.*, 88, 92, 94–6.
[4] *Ibid.*, 78, 90, 94.   [5] *Op. cit.*, line 25.

CHAPTER 3

Ecclesiastical Legislation

The secular laws must be mainly the philologists' field for some
time to come. The ecclesiastical legislation is much easier material
for the historian. It is nearly all in Latin, and though there are
technicalities the language is not archaic. It is unlike the secular laws
in that it is not a fairly homogeneous body of material. It needs to
be considered in separate groups, so I shall start with the canons.

We have a good modern edition of some of the canons with
a reliable translation, the work of Professor Bieler.[1] The great
collection of canons known as the *Collectio Canonum Hibernensis*
was edited by Wasserschleben in 1885,[2] and Dr Sheehy is now
working on a diplomatic edition. There are a considerable number
of manuscripts of the *Collectio*, one transcribed from an Irish
original between 763 and 790 for Albericus bishop of Cambrai and
Arras, and several others of the ninth century.

The canons were promulgated by synods of the sixth and
seventh centuries. We do not really know who attended these
synods. The group of canons known as 'The First Synod of St.
Patrick' has as a sub-title: 'Here begins the synod of the bishops,
namely Patrick, Auxilius, Iserninus.' The contents of these canons
are of mainly ecclesiastical interest, so one would infer that the
synods were composed mainly of clerics. But in the seventh-
century canons there are rulings which must have had the
support of secular society (for example theft from a king, bishop
or scribe which merits a fine or seven *ancillae*[3] or seven years'

---

[1] L. Bieler, *The Irish Penitentials* (Dublin 1963).

[2] H. Wasserschleben, *Die irische Kanonensammlung* (Leipzig 1885).

[3] The major unit of value. *Ancilla* means a female slave. This canon, Bieler,
op. cit., 170, is attributed to Patrick but belongs to a much later period.

penance); and there are passages which do not seem to be specifically ecclesiastical at all, like the rulings concerning damage done by dogs and laying down fines for killing valuable working dogs. The great conferences of Druim Cett (575) and Birr (697) were attended by kings, nobles and churchmen, and it is by no means impossible that laymen were present at the synods.

We know that two distinct parties were represented in seventh-century Irish synods, for their meetings are entitled 'Roman synod' and 'Irish synod'. As we shall see, their interests were different.

The *Collectio* is a compilation drawn up in the early eighth century by two Irish scholars, Cú-Chuimne of Iona and Ruben of Dairinis, possibly the Dairinis on the Blackwater, to the south of Lismore. They quote no authors later than Theodore and Adamnán (who died in 704). They were certainly using written sources —they refer to 'a great forest of writings'—and they were writing within living memory of at least some of the synods whose canons they report.

It is agreed that most of the canons are from seventh-century synods, but there has been disagreement about those attributed to 'The First Synod of Patrick'. Professor Binchy in 1962 revived an old dispute and argued for a seventh-century date.[1] Professor Bieler maintained the fifth-century attribution.[2] I discussed the dating in *The Church in Early Irish Society*,[3] putting the case for the mid-sixth century, and Professor Binchy has subsequently accepted the possibility of a date in the second half of the sixth century.[4]

Once the canons have been put into a context they provide a mass of information about the organisation of the Church. This is enormously important to the historian, because it gives a very different picture from that of the saints' Lives, which is still the

---

[1] *Studia Hibernica*, II (1962), 45–9.
[2] *Mélanges offerts a Mlle Christine Mohrmann* (Utrecht Anvers 1963), 96 ff. *Irish Eccles. Record*, CVII (1967), 9–10.
[3] pp. 44–9.
[4] *Studia Hibernica*, VIII (1968), 53.

generally accepted version of the sixth- and seventh-century Irish Church. The canons are matter-of-fact, contemporary evidence, which is obviously much to be preferred to the saints' Lives, most of which are much later. Moreover the canons tell us about a vital period when revolutionary changes were in motion. An Irishman living about 500 would have found it very hard to predict accurately what the Church would be like in 750. The historian is fortunate in that he can see the change actually happening in the canons.

The canons may be used to elucidate some fundamental facts of Irish ecclesiastical history during this period of rapid development. First, they throw light on the progress of the conversion. But before we can assess this, we need to know the date of the early canons, known as 'The First Synod of St Patrick'. They seem to me to show a Church far too well organised to be a first-generation missionary society (Professor Bieler's view). The Church is divided into territorial dioceses with well-defined boundaries, each under its own bishop. Bishops are not to trespass in each other's sees. Each bishop has jurisdiction within his own diocese, which seems to be coterminous with the petty kingdom. It is the bishop who gives permission to baptise, say mass, build and consecrate a church. Within the dioceses are subordinate churches with priests in charge. There are seven orders of clergy and monasteries under abbots. The clergy are being encouraged to follow civilised Roman customs of dress, both for themselves and their wives. All this would seem to me to put the canons considerably later than the time of Patrick.

One canon, which Professor Binchy discusses in detail, deals with the native law of surety.[1] It provides that if a cleric acts as surety for a pagan (*gentilis*) and the latter defaults, the cleric must pay the debt himself rather than resort to violence to compel the other to discharge his obligations; should he use violence he is *ipso facto* excommunicated. Now in secular law only the highest (and the earliest) type of surety is called the 'enforcing surety'

[1] Canon 8. Binchy, *Studia Hibernica*, VIII (1968), 53.

(*naidm*). He is entitled to use violent means, including bloodshed, against the defaulting principal to enforce his guarantee: he must always be of higher status than the principal, and in the Laws he is classed *grád flatha*, 'one of the noble grades'. Hence the canon implies that some, at least, of the clergy were of sufficiently exalted status in secular law to be recognised as valid 'enforcing sureties'. But since the canon law forbids them to use violence they are ordered to satisfy the debt of the defaulting principal rather than compel him by force; in other words to act like the 'paying surety' (the *ráth*), who is a commoner.[1] This canon suggests a fairly well-organised Church with some clergy of the native nobility,[2] not a missionary Church.

But although the developed organisation of the Church and the legal recognition of at least some of the clergy seem to me to be incompatible with the earliest stages of christianity in Ireland, the society which the canons depict is still quite definitely pagan. Christians are believers in the midst of pagan practices. Pagans swear before their own diviners (*ad aruspicem*: Professor Bieler translates 'before a druid'); pagan beliefs are current; the Church is not allowed to accept alms from pagans, whereas later synods are eager to legislate on payments from the laity. But paganism may linger on in a predominantly christian society. What is much more significant for dating these canons is the contrast which they present to the main body of seventh-century ecclesiastical legislation. Some of the later canons impose fines (for example for injuring important clerics) which must have been sanctioned by

---

[1] Professor Binchy writes: 'It is even just barely possible that this type of surety, who appears later in time than the *naidm*, and whose functions are those of the *fideiussor* of Roman law, was first introduced in the wake of christianity. But the native name for him is an argument against this, as one would expect a borrowing of a Latin term.' The whole question has been discussed by Professor Binchy in 'Celtic suretyship, a fossilised Indo-European institution?' *Indo-European and Indo-Europeans: Papers presented to the Third Indo-European Conference, 1963* (Philadelphia 1970), 355–67.

[2] In isolation, it could imply a Church where the clergy have been incorporated into the noble grades of society, as they later were; but see *infra*, 71 for Canon 7.

society. Yet these early canons carry no penalties other than penance and excommunication. Whereas seventh-century ecclesiastical lawyers were trying to adjust the Church to the secular law, christians are here expressly told to avoid the secular courts and to bring their cases to the Church for trial. And a priest may be prevented from attending matins and vespers because he is 'under the yoke of servitude' (*iugo servitutis*). Whatever this difficult phrase actually means[1] it seems inconsistent with priests automatically belonging to the noble grades of society as they do in the seventh century, once the clergy had been incorporated into the native law of status.

I think that these canons must therefore be considerably later than the Church of Patrick (to which Professor Bieler assigns them) and before the main bulk of seventh-century legislation. If a sixth-century dating for the canons is accepted, their testimony must be preferred to that of the literary sources. They reveal a Church separating itself off from a pagan society, with clerics who are not yet completely incorporated into the aristocracy, with a system of jurisdiction not yet supported by secular law. They thus invalidate the old view of a conversion completed by 500.

The Church established in fifth-century Ireland was the Church as it existed elsewhere in the western world, organised in territorial dioceses, each under the jurisdiction of a bishop. But by the seventh century Ireland had a Church where powers of jurisdiction were held mainly by abbots, with bishops exercising only sacramental functions. The abbot might be a bishop himself, but usually was not. The Church was now organised no longer in territorial dioceses but in monastic *paruchiae*, groups of widely scattered houses acknowledging a particular head. Thus Iona, founded by the priest and abbot Columcille, was the chief church of the *paruchia* of Columcille, and other houses in Scotland and Ireland, including Derry, in the north, and Durrow, in Co. Offaly in the south-west midlands, belonged to this confederation. When and

[1] Binchy, *Studia Hibernica*, VIII (1968), 53–4.

why did this unique change from episcopal to monastic organisation occur?

It is generally accepted that it happened in the sixth century. This is what the annals imply and what ninth- and tenth-century historians understood. But the legislation shows that it did not happen as quickly and neatly as is usually supposed. Some synods of the seventh century were still legislating for a Church governed by bishops, though monasteries were flourishing.[1] The episcopal organisation of the earlier period cannot have been entirely superseded by the seventh century. As late as the early eighth century, when the *Collectio* was drawn up, its compilers thought it worth while to include canons emphasising the administrative authority of bishops. Some seventh-century canons even suggest an episcopal hierarchy, for they speak not only of the 'bishop' but of the 'bishop of bishops', who presumably held some position analogous to the 'king over kings'. Armagh in the late-seventh or eighth century[2] claims to take precedence over 'all the churches and all the monasteries of all the Irish'. In the Book of the Angel we see her trying to establish a hierarchy of jurisdiction with cases referred to herself and ultimately to Rome, even while, at the same time, she was trying to build up a *paruchia* of monastic type.[3] The canons show that a monastic and an episcopal Church existed side by side for perhaps most of the seventh century, though the episcopal organisation in the end was so thoroughly submerged that only the legislation reveals its existence.

No satisfactory explanation has ever been put forward as to why that change occurred.[4] Monasticism became very popular during the sixth century, but this does not account for the change in constitution. We should expect monasteries to be founded, bishops to take monastic vows and surround themselves with monastic clergy, but why was the territorial diocese not retained?

[1] *Infra*, 76.
[2] Book of the Angel, Hughes, *CEIS*, 278.
[3] The evidence is from the Book of the Angel, translated Hughes, *CEIS*, 276-9, and discussed 111-20.
[4] See Professor Binchy in *Studia Hibernica*, VII (1967), 219.

Why does Ireland not have monastic bishops like Martin of Tours? The *tuath* or petty kingdom was the political and legal unit of early Ireland, and the diocese seems to have been co-terminous with the *tuath*. So why was a Church under diocesan organisation superseded?

I cannot provide a satisfactory answer, but I think that there are certain considerations which must have some bearing on this problem. First, we must remember that Ireland had never known Roman organisation at all and had none of the central administration which formed the background to the Roman-style bishopric. Gaul might have its eccentrics like St Martin, but the concept of diocesan territorial boundaries and diocesan jurisdiction was firmly rooted. When the monasticism of the desert, which had already sloughed off much of Roman administration, was transplanted to Ireland it might well develop along other channels.

You would expect that native ideas of kin and kingship would influence the Irish monastic constitution. They do. An Irish word for abbot is *comarba*, 'heir'. The abbot was the heir of the founder, sometimes of the same dynastic family. A glance at the genealogical table of the early abbots of Iona drawn up by Bishop Reeves[1] shows that up to 724 all the twelve abbots of Iona except the sixth and the tenth belonged to the same kindred. Hereditary succession can be shown for several churches in the eighth century.[2] Professor Ryan has proved early Clonmacnoise abbots to be of diverse kin groups.[3] Nevertheless, the secular laws show that, though the founder's physical kinsmen were not always his spiritual heirs, the idea of kin was dominant. If a successor could not be found among the founder's kin he must be sought from the donor's kin; failing this from the tribe of the monks (*manaig*).[4] The commentary on the law sets out the proper precedence for seeking the founder's heir.[5] Thus we can see the native ideas of

---

[1] *Adamnán's Life of Columba* (Dublin 1857), facing p. 342.

[2] Hughes, *CEIS*, 162–4. Cf. 210–11. See also T. Ó. Fiaich, 'The Church of Armagh under lay control', *Seanchas Ardmhacha*, V (1969), 76–8.

[3] *Féil-sgríbhinn Eóin MhicNéill*, ed. J. Ryan (Dublin 1940), 590–7.

[4] *Infra*, 94–5.   [5] *ALI*, III, 72–4.

kin affecting monasticism. But why should they not have been applied to the territorial bishop? After all, at Iona the abbots were celibate; it was not their sons who were their heirs. Irish bishops might have been succeeded by their nephews or more distant kinsmen. So the native institution of kin does not completely account for the Irish system.

The other native institution which affected Irish monasticism was kingship. The bishop stood in a similar relationship to his diocese as did the petty king to his *tuath*; but the head of a great monastic *paruchia* was like a 'king over kings'. In the sixth and seventh centuries the influence of certain kings was already extending outside their own kingdoms. The Uí Néill had already established a confederation of *tuatha*. At the same time the great saints and their 'heirs' were establishing even more widespread confederations. The link was a personal one between the patron (or his successor) and the subordinate church represented by its abbot. Once the monastic *paruchiae* had started to grow, the analogy of overlordship must have been apparent.

But why did monastic *paruchiae* start at all? I think that the changeover of constitution must have some connection with endowments. Armagh, named after the pagan goddess Macha, was founded two miles from Emain Macha, which seems to have been her chief seat.[1] Kildare was founded five miles from Knockaulin where there was a pagan sanctuary, and its patron saint, Brigit, bears the name of an Irish goddess. Kilcullen, connected with Iserninus, one of Patrick's fellow-workers, was near to Knockaulin; Killashee, dedicated to Auxilius, was between Knockaulin and Naas. Ardbraccan was built beside 'the tree of Tortan'. There was a sacred fire at Seir, founded by Ciarán, 'first-born of the saints of Ireland'. Emly, another early church, seems to have been a holy place in pagan times. All these were episcopal churches. How were they supported? Is it not likely that lands originally used for the upkeep of pagan sanctuaries

---

[1] Although the sanctuary recently excavated at Emain seems to belong to a period long before Christianity.

were turned over to the Church?[1] If so, there would be a definite limit to the funds available.

The monastic *paruchiae*, on the other hand, had almost unlimited powers of expansion. If enthusiasm for the ascetic life seized a whole family they could agree to turn their property over to monasticism.[2] Such monasteries might spring up in many places. Sometimes churches were founded directly under the patronage of a great saint. Other churches subsequently sought to enter such a *paruchia*, as when Aed of Sletty, towards the end of the seventh century, offered 'his kin and his church to Patrick for ever'.[3] At this period Armagh, which had begun as a territorial diocese, was laying claim to early foundations and to churches free from obligations to an existing overlord.[4] Armagh, Kildare, Seir, Emly all succeeded in turning themselves into monastic *paruchiae*: it was the only way to survive. Other early episcopal foundations failed to compete, for they disappear for centuries from the ecclesiastical records.[5]

The legislation does not provide any complete answer to the crucial constitutional changes which took place in the Church. By the seventh century the monastic *paruchiae* were already launched, and our only sixth-century canons are about a Church governed by bishops, in the old style. Nevertheless, the canons show that bishops with jurisdiction survived into the seventh century, and other Irish legal institutions help to explain why the Irish Church diverged in its organisation from the main west European practice.

The canons show us two parties in the seventh-century Church. Other sources report a great struggle over the date of Easter. Various systems for calculating Easter had been current in the early Church on the continent and it was not until the very end of the

---

[1] Some late Lives speak of the transfer of druidic lands to the Church (Plummer *VSH*, I, 80 ff, II, 111), but I doubt if they can be trusted.

[2] This is what St Samson's family did, according to his early Life. Hughes, *CEIS*, 76-7.

[3] Stokes, *Tripartite Life of St Patrick* (RS, London 1887), II, 346.

[4] Hughes, *CEIS*, 87-8.   [5] *Ibid.*, 68.

sixth century that Irish peculiarities became troublesome. By the seventh century the date of Easter was a vital issue. The southern half of Ireland conformed to the general practice in the 630s, but the north held out until shortly before 704.[1] So much we should know anyway. But the legislation shows us these two parties, the 'Roman' and the 'Irish', in action, and reveals their other concerns beside the Easter controversy.

The 'Romans' were very much aware that they were part of a continental Church.[2] They were trying to secure uniformity with continental practice on issues where the Irish had failed to conform with changes introduced elsewhere. The Britons were the hard core of Celtic conservatism, and the Roman party warned its clergy against them as 'contrary in all things' and cut off 'from Roman custom and the unity of the Church'. Irish Romanists wanted the Petrine tonsure universally accepted, and they jeered at the Celtic tonsure, which they said was first worn by the swine-herd of king Lóegaire. They were also trying to introduce continental practice into the Irish law of contract, for they require not only witnesses and sureties, but a written document, and business transactions must be confirmed 'by signature, in the Roman manner'.

The Church for which the Romans legislated was a Church under the jurisdiction of bishops, and some of their canons were specifically aimed at supporting episcopal authority. Clerics from abroad were to come with letters of recommendation; bishops were to keep within their own dioceses and not trespass on each other's jurisdiction; priests and clergy, if they could not reach agreement in disputes, were to bring their cases to the synod. Although they legislated for the monastic life, the Church of the 'Romans' was still a diocesan Church under episcopal control.

The 'Irish' canonists, on the other hand, show very clearly that the administrative head of the Church is the abbot, often called *princeps*. Their main aim was not to bring the Church into line with continental practice, but to adjust it to the native law. The

---

[1] See Hughes, *CEIS*, 103–10, especially 109, note 2, for the date.
[2] *Ibid.*, 125–6, 130–1, for references.

Romans won the dispute on Easter and the tonsure, but everywhere else the Irish party in the Church triumphed.

Many books emphasise the changes which Christianity brought about in Ireland. Art and learning did indeed gain new dimensions. But many of the native institutions were little affected. The druids disappeared and were replaced by the clergy, who were accorded a position of honour in society, but the lawyers and poets were too well-entrenched to ignore.

The preface to Fiacc's Hymn shows the reluctance felt by a young man who was being trained in the secular schools to become a cleric. His tonsuring was secured by a kind of trick, for it was only when he saw his master Dubthach about to be tonsured that he submitted:

'What is attempted?' said Fiacc.
'The tonsuring of Dubthach,' said they.
'That is foolish,' said he, 'for there is not in Ireland a poet his equal.'
'You would be taken in his place,' said Patrick.
'My loss to Ireland is less than that of Dubthach,' said Fiacc.[1]

This is not exactly an enthusiastic response to Patrick's call to the priesthood.

Some people in the Church had a great respect for native learning. They saw that the Church's best interests would be served by accepting all that they could of the secular laws. The job of the seventh-century 'Irish' canonists was to apply the native law to the Church. In so doing they produced an Irish Church, with a unique constitution.

In the canons we can see a reconciliation between ecclesiastical and secular law. I think that some of the seventh-century canonists of the 'Irish' party may have had some training in the secular law, or at least have been advised by jurists. If not, then the educated Irishman must have understood the technicalities of the law very well.

They were interested, of course, in working out rules concerning Church property. One of the secular law tracts discusses funeral fees payable to the Church: a definite rate is laid down

[1] *Thesaurus Palaeohibernicus*, ed. W. Stokes and J. Strachan (Cambridge 1903), II, 307–8.

according to status, but if a man had added to his family's property he might make a larger grant, provided he left the inherited family land intact.[1] Irish law also required a woman heir to give legal guarantees that she would not alienate her land, which had to go back to her kin. The canonists were sufficiently in sympathy with the jurists to safeguard the right of the kin. Female heirs, they say, are to give sureties not to alienate their inheritance: if their kin make no objection the women may give part to the Church, but if the kin objects the grant is invalid.[2] The canons also legislate for the situation which may arise if an abbot is ejected from a church[3]—what is he allowed to take with him?—or if a man, having granted his property to one church then moves to another.[4] They lay down the size of bequest an abbot may make at his death,[5] but say that a monk may leave nothing without his abbot's consent. This is paralleled in the secular law tract which says that the *dóermanach* cannot make a valid contract unless it is authorised by the abbot.[6]

The Church was also interested in the law of liability, and sought to protect herself from injuries committed by those who had moved outside her responsibility—monks who had fled from their church, evil pilgrims, people who had been expelled from the Church.[7] The canons lay down penalties for those who abandon children on the Church without the knowledge of the abbot—if the parents give a fee for fostering the child he is to be brought up as their son, if not he is to be a slave of the Church.[8]

There are also canons on suretyship and on what constitutes valid evidence. The people whom the canonists forbid to act as

---

[1] *Corus bescna, ALI*, III, 42–52.

[2] *Collectio Canonum Hibernensis*, ed. H. Wasserschleben, *Die irische Kanonensammlung* (Leipzig 1885), XXXII, 20; Cf. *Studies in Early Irish Law*, 176–8.

[3] *Collectio*, XLIII, 6; Hughes, *CEIS*, 159.

[4] *Collectio*, XVIII, 6–7.

[5] *Ibid.*, XLI, 4.

[6] *Ibid.*, XLI, 8, Cf. *Corus bescna, ALI*, III, 10. On the *dóermanach* see Hughes, *CEIS*, 136–41.

[7] *Collectio*, XLII, 29.

[8] *Ibid.*, XLII, 22, 24.

surety are very similar to those who the secular law says may not make a valid contract.[1] They lay down how long the surety has to pay,[2] and expell from the Church any debtor who resists witnesses and sureties.[3] One rather surprising ruling says that 'the evidence (*testimonium*) of women is not to be accepted, as the apostles did not accept the evidence of women concerning the resurrection of Christ'. Since the apostles were so utterly mistaken in not accepting the women's testimony this sounds an absurd reason, until we remember that in early Irish law women were not competent to give eye-witness evidence.[4]

The Irish canonists, we can see, were trying to fit the Church into the native legal system. The secular jurists were working towards the same end. Each grade of the clergy was assigned his status with the relevant honour-price and privileges. Tithes, firstfruits and firstlings were to be paid to the Church.[5] Every firstborn son of the *manaig* (i.e., the lay-monks who farmed the monastic lands and married)[6] was to be offered to the Church and educated by the Church: later he inherited his share of the family land and farmed it as a free-client of the Church.[7] Society had thus not only accorded the clergy an honourable place but had made ample provision for their support. Canonists and jurists must have been on excellent terms.

There was one native institution which the Irish canonists could not stomach, and that was polygamy. Their marriage regulations were strict. They required considerable periods of continence from married persons and adultery brought heavy penance.[8] The canonists were not agreed on whether a man might re-marry if his wife had left him.[9] In demanding monogamy 'Irish' and 'Roman' canonists were in agreement.

There is still a lot of unexplored material in Irish canonical collections, though they have been in print for some time. The

---

[1] *Ibid.*, XXXIV, 3; Cf. *Corus Bescna, ALI*, III, 10.

[2] *Collectio*, XXXIV, 4; *ZCP*, XVIII (1930), 365–72; *St. Ir. Law*, 232 f.

[3] *Collectio*, XXXIV, 8.   [4] *Ibid.*, XVI, 3. Cf. Heptads, *ALI*, V, 284.

[5] *ALI*, III, 12–14.   [6] Hughes, *CEIS*, 136–42.

[7] *ALI*, III, 38–42.   [8] Bieler, *op. cit.*, 90–2, 264, 88.

[9] *Ibid.*, 90, 178, 194.

authors of many books on the Irish Church seem never to have read them. The canons certainly force a very considerable revision of the views widely held on Irish ecclesiastical history before 750.

II

The *cána* (except for the Law of Sunday) were laws attributed to particular saints.[1] We know about them partly from the annals, partly from two surviving texts, the Law of Adamnán[2] and the Law of Sunday. The annals suggest that they were promulgated over wide areas by ecclesiastical and secular authorities combined. The entries are not always explicit. Sometimes we merely have *lex Patricii* (*AU* 767), sometimes 'the law of Ailbe in force in Munster' (*AI* 784), sometimes 'The law of Columcille by Domnall (king) of Meath' (*AU* 753) or 'Nuadu abbot of Armagh went to Connacht with the law of Patrick' (*AU* 811). But sometimes all the details are given in the same entry, for example, 'The promulgation of Patrick's law in Cruachu (the plain of Connacht) by Dub-dá-leithe (of Armagh) and Tipraite son of Tadc' (king of Connacht). The kings mentioned are provincial kings and they are proclaiming the law in their own provinces, but a saint's law could have force outside the province in which his chief church lay: for instance the law of Patrick was proclaimed over Munster in 823 and over Connacht in 825. In one year (737), when there was a royal meeting between the chief kings of the north and south, 'the law of Patrick held Ireland.'

What was the purpose of these laws? The Law of Sunday was an attempt to enforce Sunday observance, but the other laws seem to have been aimed at keeping peace and order and protecting non-combatants from violence. A gloss on Colman's Hymn reads:

[1] R. Thurneysen, *ZCP*, XVIII (1930), 382–96, discusses them, with references to the texts in which they are cited.

[2] The Law of Adamnán was edited by K. Meyer (Oxford 1905) and discussed by J. Ryan, *St. Ir. Law*, 269–76. Thurneysen cites alleged excerpts from *Cáin Dáiri* found in unpublished legal MSS.

The four chief laws of Ireland, the law of Patrick, and of Dáire and of Adamnán and of Sunday. The law of Patrick, now, not to slay clerics; the law of Dáire, not to steal cattle; of Adamnán, not to slay women; of Sunday, not to travel.[1]

The Law of Dáire, promulgated in Munster in 810, in Connacht in 812 and 826, by the Uí Néill (so presumably throughout their lands in the northern half) in 813, seems to have been designed to prevent cattle raiding. The Law of Patrick, as defined in this passage, is no longer extant, but the Law of Adamnán has survived in a composite text of which the oldest part goes back to the end of the seventh or the eighth century.[2]

Its intention, it says, is to protect 'clerics and women and innocent children until they are capable of slaying a man'. These classes are taken under the protection of the saint, who thereby gains a right to profits from their injury. Fines are also imposed for violating a church's sanctuary. The usual procedures are followed to enforce the law. Pledges and sureties must be given for its performance—three sureties from every major church, one from every *derbfine* (the four generations family group), two from every over-king.[3] A secular law tract provides evidence of the king's part when it says that the Law of Adamnán is one of the four kinds of government which an over-king binds by pledge on his people, presumably at a public assembly.[4] Officials are to be appointed by the community of Adamnán to levy the fines for breaking the law, and are to be maintained while they are on circuit. These arrangements meant that a powerful institution had an interest in enforcing order and that the law would be a source of profit to the Church. The word *cáin* (sg.) has the double sense of 'law' and 'tribute'.

The function of the *cána* is a vexed question. It has been maintained that the *cáin* or *lex* was 'the technical term for the alleged right under which the relic tax was exacted' when a circuit of the

---

[1] W. Stokes and J. Strachan, *Thesaurus Palaeohibernicus*, II, 306.

[2] *Cáin Adamnáin*, ed. K. Meyer, especially 24–33.

[3] The word is *ard-fhlaith*.

[4] *CG*, lines 521–4, and p. 104; Mac Neill, *PRIA*, XXXVI (1923), 303.

saint's shrine was authorised within a given jurisdiction by the local king and abbot.[1] But the Law of Adamnán has a genuine early core, and it seems to me much more likely that originally the intention was to protect non-combatants and church property from violence. As time went on the material advantages the *cáin* gave to a church would emphasise its importance as a tax rather than as a law. Certainly the *Lex Patricii* seems in the annals to mean the formal acknowledgment of the overlordship of Armagh, and by the tenth century nobody knew what the *Cáin Patraic* was, so that the term was attached to various different texts.

All the laws belong to the period 697–842, though the Law of Sunday may have been revived later.[2] Their emergence demonstrates the co-operation between Church and secular government which had arisen in the seventh century.

Has the terminal date any significance? We have already seen that the secular laws atrophied in the ninth century and that the last great collection of canons was made in the early ninth century. The Vikings settled in the 830s. It would seem that the *cána* could not survive the Viking attacks. After the 830s the stable society needed to enforce the *cána* had for the time ceased to exist.

III

The Penitentials are one type of evidence with which the student of Irish history is better off than his English colleague. The Latin texts have been admirably edited and translated by Professor Bieler.[3] The Old-Irish Penitential was edited by Dr E. J. Gwynn[4] and has now been translated by Professor Binchy.[5] Professor

---

[1] F. O'Briain, *Féil-sgríbhinn Eóin Mhic Néill*, ed. J. Ryan (Dublin 1940), 457.

[2] *AU*, 887, reads: 'An epistle came with the pilgrim to Ireland, with the Law of Sunday and other good instructions.' The language of the text of the Law of Sunday belongs to the first half of the eighth century. See V. Hull, *Ériu*, XX (1966), 157–8.

[3] L. Bieler, *The Irish Penitentials*, SLH 5 (Dublin 1963).

[4] *Ériu*, VII (1914), 121–93; corrigenda *Ériu*, XII (1938), 245–9.

[5] In Bieler, *Irish Penitentials*, 258–77.

Binchy has also now re-edited and re-translated the Old Irish Table of Pentitential Commutations.[1]

They are early texts. The Latin penitentials drawn up in Ireland belong to the sixth and seventh centuries; one, which took its present form on the continent, is probably early eighth. The Old Irish Pentitential, in the vernacular but based on Latin sources, dates from the later eighth century. This text and the Irish tract on penitential commutations should both be associated with the reform movement of the later eighth century and may have been drawn up at Tallaght.

The texts were thus all composed before 800. Even the manuscripts in which they are copied are early. Professor Bieler lists twenty-three manuscripts for his edition of the Latin texts: of these, thirteen are as early as the eighth and ninth centuries and none are later than the twelfth. Only the Irish tracts are in later medieval manuscripts, and here the linguistic forms certify their early date.

The penitentials assign penances for particular sins. They are schedules drawn up for the use of a confessor. Look, for instance, at the first section of the Penitential of Cummean, on the subject of gluttony. This says that (i) a cleric who gets drunk is to fast forty days on bread and water, a layman seven days; (ii) anyone who encourages another to get drunk out of good fellowship is to suffer the same penalty, but (iii) if he does it out of malice, the sin is to be judged as if it were a killing; (iv) if a cleric is too drunk to sing the psalms, he is to perform a special fast; (v) if he eats before the canonical hour or seeks out some special luxury he is to go without supper or live two days on bread and water; (vi) if he gives himself indigestion with overeating, a day's penance; (vii) if he makes himself sick, a week's penance; and so on. Cummean's penitential deals like this with the eight deadly sins, gluttony, fornication, avarice, anger, dejection, languor, vainglory and pride, with three further sections added. There are variations between the schedules of penance set out in different penitentials.

[1] *Ériu*, XIX (1962), 47–72; also Bieler, *op. cit.*, 277–82.

Are the penitentials really worth the historian's attention at all? They are certainly not very congenial reading. Indeed, that great historian Charles Plummer wrote that

> The penitential literature is in truth a deplorable feature of the mediaeval Church. Evil deeds, the imagination of which may perhaps have dimly floated through our minds in our darkest moments, are here tabulated and reduced to system. It is hard to see how anyone could busy himself with such literature and not be the worse for it.[1]

I do not think that the penitentials are likely to have a morally harmful influence on anyone, but they could be extremely boring. They do not even tell you what sins were popular at the time— a fact which might be of interest to the social historian—since they attempt to list everything. What then is their interest?

The penitentials show that the system practised in the British and Irish Churches was one of private penance. The sinner confessed in private to a priest and the penance was performed in private. This is, in its essentials, the practice of the Catholic Church to this day. But in the early Church penance had been public. The New Testament shows that confession was also a community action: 'Confess your sins to one another and pray for one another, that ye may be healed,' is one of many similar exhortations. As time went on, confession was made to a bishop, but the penance was still public. The penitent wore special clothes and took up a special place at church worship. This public penance was at first allowed only once in a lifetime, though this was felt to be a harsh measure and some bishops came to allow it twice.

Exactly how, when and where private penance was first introduced is not clear, but the Celtic Church was certainly the first to make it a general practice, and it was through Irish and possibly British priests that it spread. The system of commuting penances was definitely Irish in origin. It was probably first worked out in Irish, for the word for commutation is an Irish word, and why

[1] Plummer, *HE*, I, clvii–clviii.

would anyone choose a native word to denote a system of commutations drawn up in Latin?[1]

The word, *arre*, Latinised *arreum*, means 'handing over on behalf
of another', 'paying over something in place of something else',[2]
and thus the meaning 'commutation' easily arises. The practice
was introduced to shorten the period of penance, which was
often impracticably long: sometimes it shortens and intensifies it,
sometimes shortens and moderates it. There is good evidence that
it was known as early as the seventh century, though it was
popularised by the reform movement of the later eighth century.

First, then, it seems to me of interest to find that disciplinary
practices of the medieval Church were introduced and popularised by the Irish. Moreover, the penitentials illustrate the theory
and practice of penance. Confession and penance were the 'medicine for souls'. They were intended to heal the hurt which a man
did by his sin; primarily to heal the hurt to himself, and also the
hurt to society. The confessor was a 'soul-friend': *anm-chara* is
his name in Irish. His job was to apply the appropriate cure to the
soul's disease.

> For doctors of the body also compound their medicines in diverse
> kinds; thus they heal wounds in one manner, sickness in another . . .
> So also should spiritual doctors treat with diverse kinds of cures the
> wounds of souls.[3]

The penitentials were to help them with their prescriptions.

Finnian, who wrote the earliest of the Irish penitentials, takes one
of the maxims of medicine and applies it to his remedies for souls.

> By contraries . . . let us make haste to cure contraries . . . Patience
> must arise for wrathfulness; kindliness, or the love of God and of
> one's neighbour, for envy; for detraction, restraint of heart and
> tongue; for dejection, spiritual joy; for greed, liberality.[4]

The seventh-century Cummean, in his 'prologue on the medicine

---

[1] Binchy, *Ériu*, XIX (1962), 50.   [2] *Ibid.*, 51.
[3] Bieler, *op. cit.* (Penitential of Columbanus).   [4] *Ibid.*, 84.

for the salvation of souls', states the same principle: 'The eight principal vices . . . shall be healed by the eight remedies that are their contraries';[1] and the Old Irish Penitential begins by listing the virtues which are 'to cure and heal the eight chief vices'.[2]

All the symptons of the individual case are to be taken into account by the wise confessor, for though the standard prescriptions are laid down in the penitentials it is recognised that 'Almighty God who knows the hearts of all and has bestowed diverse natures will not weigh the weights of sins in an equal scale of penance'. So the confessor must carefully note 'the length of time anyone remains in his faults; what learning he has received; by what passion he is assailed; how great is his strength; with what intensity of weeping he is afflicted; and with what oppression he has been driven to sin'.[3]

The penitentials must have been a support to the secular law. Occasionally we can see a close correspondence. For instance, Cummean lays down that a man who maims or injures another is to meet his medical expenses, compensate him for the deformity, provide for his work until he is well again *and* do penance for half a year.[4] The first three requirements are repetitions of the secular law; the penance is added. Columbanus requires that a murderer shall do penance as an unarmed exile as well as making satisfaction to the kin of the dead man: if he fails to make satisfaction he is to be a wanderer and a fugitive for ever.[5] Theft similarly requires restitution and penance. If a layman sins with a virgin he is to compensate her kin and do penance.[6] Some sins which earn heavy penances also carry penalties in secular law—kin-slayings, homicide and secret murder (for which commutations are not normally allowed), theft, bearing false witness, bringing a false suit or giving false judgment.

Nevertheless the concept of wrong-doing in the penitentials is quite different from that of the secular law. It is not an injury

---

[1] Bieler, *op. cit.*, 110.　　[2] *Ibid.*, 259.
[3] *Ibid.*, 132 (Cummean, concluding paragraph).　　[4] *Ibid.*, 120.
[5] *Sancti Columbani Opera*, ed. G. S. M. Walker, 172, 174.
[6] *Ibid.*, 176.

which must be paid for according to a fixed schedule, but a moral evil, a sin; so a man's motive, the degree of temptation he has experienced, what excuse his conditions offer, have all to be taken into account. For instance a killing which, viewed as an injury, would be the same whatever the motive, might be a sin of very different degrees. A layman who murders out of hatred, says Cummean, is to abandon the world for life; if he acts in unpremeditated anger he is to do three years' penance; if he kills by accident, one year.[1] Perjury for friendship's sake is a much less grievous sin than perjury for a bribe.[2] The penance of the cleric is heavier than that of the layman; a man in poor health is subject to less stringent fasts than a fit man, and a sick person may eat at any hour of the day or night. The penitentials are not, like the secular laws, considering how to compensate the injured party; their aim is to cure the sinner.

The secular lawyers were great schematisers and make one wonder if the penances, often laid down in such detail, were in fact performed. We know on good authority that some churches had groups of people undergoing penance. At Armagh the penitents formed a separate order who attended church every Sunday in the north quarter of the city[3] (the southern church was reserved for bishops, priests, anchorites and other religious). There were penitents living in Columcille's community on the island of Inba,[4] and the saint sent another penitent (who had killed a man and committed perjury) for seven years to Tiree.[5] Men who had committed major crimes were sent into exile. Columbanus requires ten years' exile for a man who has committed murder; when he returns home he must bring a testimonial from the bishop or priest under whom he has done penance. He must also make satisfaction to the relatives of the

---

[1] Bieler, *op. cit.*, 118–20.
[2] *Ibid.*, 267 (the Old Irish Penitential).
[3] Book of the Angel, Hughes, *CEIS*, 278. They worshipped with the virgins and 'those serving the church in legitimate matrimony'.
[4] *Adamnán's Life of Columba*, I, 21.
[5] *Ibid.*, II, 39.

dead man or, like Cain, be for ever a wanderer and fugitive.[1] Columcille gave a decision of twelve years' penitential exile for the combined sins of fratricide and incest.[2] Some of the continental complaints about Irish pilgrims may have had a real foundation, for penitential exile could be a way of getting rid of people who had committed major crimes against society.[3] The development of the practice of commutation is itself evidence that penances were being attempted.

The penitentials are one of the sources which illustrate Irish connections with Great Britain and the continent. There are Welsh and North British penitential canons, usually dated to the sixth century. The earliest of the Irish penitentials is that of Vinnian, dating from the second or third quarter of the sixth century. Vinnian, followed by later writers, accepts the principle of curing contraries by their contraries, and Cummean (in the seventh century) and others use the classification of the eight deadly sins.[4] Both these fundamentals of Irish penitential thinking come from Cassian, the founder of two monasteries near Marseilles and an influential writer of the early fifth century. The parallels between Vinnian and Caesarius, archbishop of Arles from 502 to 542, are less obvious,[5] but they show that Irish clerics knew of some of the opinions being disseminated in southern Gaul a generation or so earlier.

Irish influence on the penitential system of England is not in doubt. The old system of public penance never established itself in England. Theodore's penitential makes use of a *libellus scottorum*, which was either the Penitential of Cummean or a work very similar to it, and the Old Irish Penitential, in its turn, quotes from Theodore. Penitential practice must also have influenced some of the prayers of confession found in the Book of Cerne,

---

[1] Walker, *Sancti Columbani Opera*, 172.

[2] *Adamnán's Life of Columba*, I, 22.

[3] Hughes, 'The changing theory and practice of Irish pilgrimage', *JEH*, XI (1960), 145–6.

[4] Not seven, a classification which stems from Gregory the Great.

[5] They have been worked out by T. P. Oakley, 'Cultural affiliations of early Ireland in the penitentials', *Speculum*, VIII (1933), 494.

a manuscript which shows strong Irish influence. One such prayer to God as 'doctor of my soul' is particularly reminiscent of the penitentials, enumerating a long list of sins which it is most unlikely that any one person could have committed. Another confessional prayer here is elsewhere attributed to Patrick.[1] From such confessions it is only a short step to prayers for divine help. One in the Book of Cerne has an almost exact parallel in a later Irish poem:

> Guard my eyes for me, Jesus Son of Mary, lest seeing another's wealth make me covetous
> Guard for me my ears lest they harken to slander . . .
> Guard for me my tongue . . . that I revile no one . . .
> Guard for me my hands, that they be not stretched out for quarrelling, that they may not after that practise shameful supplication.
> Guard for me my feet upon the gentle earth of Ireland, lest, bent on profitless errands, they abandon rest.[2]

The penitentials affected the devotional expression of both Ireland and England.

They also spread the practice of private penance in continental Europe; for Irish pilgrims and English missionaries took their penitential discipline with them, and many of the texts survive in Frankish manuscripts. Brittany was clearly a centre of dissemination, for three manuscripts are in Breton hands and two others have Breton glosses. Other manuscripts are from *scriptoria* with Irish or Hiberno-Saxon connections. By the eighth century the Franks were drawing up their own tariffs of penance on the Hiberno-Saxon model, and the practice spread into Italy.[3] Irish influence, both direct and indirect, on France and Germany had far-reaching consequences, of which the history of penance provides one minor example.

[1] Hughes, *Studia Celtica*, V, (1970), 55–7.
[2] G. Murphy, *Early Irish Lyrics* (Oxford 1956), 54–7.
[3] The interpretation which P. Fournier puts on the evidence ('Études sur les penitentials', *Rev. d'hist. et de litterature religieuse*, IX [1904], 102–3) in opposition to the view of Schmitz.

IV

Anyone who tries to measure Irish monasticism by the standard of the Benedictine Rule will be impatient and bewildered. Irish monasticism had diverged from the common stock before the Benedictine Rule spread, and it is more enlightening to compare it with the very early monasticism of the desert; its asceticism, variety of practice and absence of clear legislation are all similar.

The Rule of Columbanus, who died in 615, is early.[1] It was drawn up for his monks on the continent, and is rather different from other Irish rules, most of which were drawn up during or after the reform movement of the later eighth and ninth centuries. Columbanus' *Regula Monachorum* has the teaching style and intellectual command of his sermons. He begins by reminding his monks that first comes the love of God and one's neighbour. 'Next,' he says, 'our works.' Then he begins with a chapter on obedience. This is not just bare legislation. 'Let this mind be in you which was also in Christ Jesus, who . . . emptied himself, taking the form of a servant, and being found in fashion as a man, humbled himself, being made obedient to the Father up to death, even the death of the cross. Thus nothing must be refused in their obedience by Christ's true disciples, however hard and difficult it be, but it must be seized with zeal, with gladness.' This Rule shows very well the joyous and positive committal of Irish asceticism, with its purpose constantly in mind.[2]

Columbanus' Monks' Rule states the philosophy which underlies Irish ascetic practice. There are three stages which must be followed. The first is 'nakedness and disdain of riches', to be

---

[1] See G. S. M. Walker, *Sancti Columbani Opera*, 122–42.

[2] The *Regula Coenobialis* which follows it in Walker's edition, though it is called a rule, is in fact a set of penitential rulings, dealing with punishments for such misdemeanours as talking while you eat, speaking with a shout, cutting the table with a knife, coughing or laughing during the offices, censuring the porter, back-answering, and a host of other daily offences, some less, some more important.

'satisfied with the small possessions of utter need'. The second, which emerges from the first, is 'the purging of vices', and the third 'the most perfect and perpetual love of God . . . which follows the forgetfulness of earthly things'. This is the aim of monastic life.

In the later eighth century there was a revival of asceticism in the Irish Church. It had never completely died out, but the monastic fervour of the late sixth and early seventh centuries was by this time not the prime preoccupation of a wealthy and powerful institution. Now groups of ascetics calling themselves *céli Dé* (anglicised culdees), meaning 'clients of God', were formed. The *céle Dé* was the man who took God as his lord, entering into a contract of service with him. Not only were new religious houses of culdees formed: the ascetics ('anchorites') attached to the old monastic houses, and supported by them, grew in number. A number of Irish monastic rules seem to have been drawn up as a result of this movement.

These rules are not so much legislation as precept: 'Make not a fire of fern', says one rule, advising perseverance. 'Advance a step every day; practise not the ways of a charioteer'. 'Be not hard and niggardly. Be not deaf to prayer to you. Refuse not, solicit not. Love not a man's wealth'. These are extracts from an Old Irish metrical rule.[1] The rule attributed to S. Columba is similar in tone: 'Fervour in singing the office for the dead, as if every faithful dead was a particular friend of yours'; 'Three labours in the day, prayer, work and reading'; 'Take not of food till you are hungry, sleep not till you feel desire, speak not except on business'.[2] Whereas Benedict is drawing up a code which embraces the whole of monastic life, Irish rules give moral advice with more or less detail about normal routine. The cleric may leave the ascetic life,[3] though several rules advise him not to. The soul-friend who receives confession from those in authority

[1] Ed. J. Strachan, *Ériu*, I (1904), 191–208.
[2] *Councils*, II, 119–21.
[3] Rule of Ailbe, ed J. O'Neill, *Ériu*, III (1907), 104.

in his own church has no power to enforce a penance.[1] All this is foreign to Benedictine monachism.

It would be impossible to draw up a full time-table for the monastic day from any one rule. Moreover, there is no uniformity of practice between houses. For example, we know quite a lot about the dietary regulations of the culdees. Two of their leaders in the late-eighth century, from neighbouring houses near Dublin, argued over whether beer should be drunk on festivals.

'As long as my injunctions are observed in this place,' said Máel-Ruain (of Tallaght), 'the liquor that causes forgetfulness of God shall not be drunk here.'
'Well,' said Dublitir (of Finglas), 'my monks shall drink it and they shall be in heaven along with yours.'

But Máel-Ruain had the last word:

'Anyone of my monks who hearkens to me and who keeps my rule, shall not need to be cleansed by the fire of Doomsday . . . Your monks, however, shall perchance have something for the fire of Doomsday to cleanse.'[2]

Thus even the practice of the culdees, who form a distinct group at this period, might differ from house to house.

Nevertheless we can see that some practices were common to clerics leading the religious life. The offices were the fixed points in the monastic day, and, according to Columbanus, the night offices lengthened in winter and shortened in summer, as they did elsewhere.[3] The brothers seem to have stayed silent in their cells until terce, in prayer or private work.[4] The main meal of the day was taken in the refectory after nones.[5] All the middle part of the day between terce and nones, except for the short office

---

[1] 'The Monastery of Tallaght', ed. E. G. Gwynn and W. J. Purton, *PRIA*, XXIX, C (1911), 128.
[2] *PRIA*, XXIX, C 129–30.
[3] Walker, *Sancti Columbani Opera*, 128.
[4] Rule of Ailbe, *Ériu*, III (1907), 100.
[5] *Ibid.*, 102.

at mid-day (sext), was given over to work,[1] which might be of various kinds. At Tallaght some of the culdees worked on the farm.[2] The Rule of Columba defines work as 'your own work and the work of your place, as regards its real wants; secondly, your share in the brethren's work; lastly, to help your neighbours, by instruction or writing or sewing garments or whatever labour they may be in want of'.[3] After the evening meal each one went to his own cell for private prayer or reading until vespers, which was followed by bed.[4] At Tallaght two monks stayed in the church saying the psalms until matins (the night office), while another pair relieved them from matins until lauds.[5] Prime and compline were probably said as prayers by the monks in their cells, not as choir offices. It looks, therefore, as if the Irish Church had six choir offices corresponding to those of the primitive eastern Church.[6]

The sources show us some monasteries where the whole community led an ascetic life; others where some men, supported by the monastery, lived a religious life retired from the main group. The ascetics seem usually to have been in orders, and they often provided the 'soul-friends' and the learned men of the community. The monastic administrators could belong to the ascetic group but need not. An Irish monastery was not just a place for the pursuit of the religious life: it was also a city, a place where hospitality was dispensed, a school, a penitentiary. And it had *manaig*, 'monks'.

The Irish word for monk (*manach*, pl. *manaig*) is confusing. Sometimes *monachus* in the documents means a man following a religious life, what we mean by a monk today.[7] Elsewhere *manach* means 'monastic client'. The *manach*, however, should not be equated with the tenant of a Benedictine monastery. He had

[1] Rule of S. Carthage, ed. Mac Eclaise, *IER*, 4th ser., XXVII (1910), 510.
[2] *Hermathena*, XLIV, second sup. vol. (Dublin 1927), 38.
[3] *Councils*, II, 120.
[4] Rule of S. Carthage, *IER*, XXVII (1910), 514.
[5] *Hermathena*, XLIV, 46.
[6] R. I. Best, *Ériu*, III (1907), 116.
[7] See Hughes, *CEIS*, 136–42.

certain rights in the church. Where the kin of the founder and donor had failed, the *manaig* provided a successor to the abbacy. They were married laymen; they supported the church by their labour and taxes. In return they received the spiritual ministrations of the church and a clerical education for their first born sons and every tenth son thereafter.[1] Some of them may be the layfolk under spiritual guidance whom the tracts speak of, who were committed to a strict regime of continence on Wednesday, Friday, Saturday and Sunday and fasting on Friday and Saturday.[2] This must have been a semi-ascetic regime very different from that followed by the majority of the population.

The Irish Church held asceticism in high esteem. Early monastic founders like Columbanus had pursued it with ardour, and the reformers of the later eighth and ninth centuries revived its standards within monasticism for a time. But the monastic clients are there in the background. When we speak of Irish monasteries we must not think only of small groups of brethren leading a religious life under a common rule. An Irish monastery was a community following its own independent practices, with abbot, men in higher orders, ascetics and scholars; officials like a steward and a cook. There were also the *manaig*, married laymen without whom it could not have survived in prosperity. The tenants of a Benedictine monastery were outside the monastic family, the *manaig* of an Irish monastery were within it. The rules relate mostly to the ascetics, but the *manaig* must not be forogtten, for they are an essential part of the constitution of the Irish Church.

v

The legislation is not the easiest of the sources, but it is absolutely vital to an understanding of the development of the Irish Church. Much of it is early, and it is the best evidence we have for eluci-

---

[1] Two versions of a tract, one called 'The Rule of Patrick', the other 'The Rule of the Céli Dé' discuss reciprocal obligations. See *Ériu*, I (1904), 216–24; *Hermathena*, XLIV (2nd sup. vol., 1927), 78–87.

[2] These regulations vary slightly according to the tract.

dating the peculiar, and changing, constitution of the Church. It lets us see the inner workings of the monastic life, the hierarchy of officials and their functions, the training in religion; it shows us the Church in contact with its own clients and in relation to secular society and law. It even illuminates some ecclesiastical concepts, such as the meaning of sin and sanctity. Legislation provides the framework of our knowledge of the men, the institutions and the ideas. It cannot be disregarded.

CHAPTER 4

The Annals

I

A book on the sources of Irish history must have a chapter on the annals. Three major works are forecast: Professor Gearóid Mac Niocaill's edition of the Annals of Ulster is soon to appear; Professor Kelleher of Harvard has promised a chapter on the annals in the *New History of Ireland*; and Professor Byrne has a history of the high-kingship which has now gone to press. I hope that what I have to say here is soundly based on the facts, but it will need to be re-examined if fresh evidence is produced.

'At first sight', said Mac Neill, 'the pages of our native chronicles appear as a sort of trackless morass to the inquirer after Irish history.'[1] The first stage of the way must be to see how the various versions of Irish annals inter-relate.

Apart from the Annals of the Four Masters, which are a seventeenth-century compilation, the most complete version of Irish annals is contained in the Annals of Ulster (*AU*). *AU* is recorded in late manuscripts, the most important being the fifteenth-century Trinity College Dublin MS H.1.8. This shows the text still in course of compilation. The annal entries are well spaced out, with gaps after each year, which have sometimes received additions. Stanzas have been added in the upper and lower margins, and the manuscript is interlineally glossed.

The Annals of Ulster were edited with a translation and notes for the Rolls Series by William Hennessy in 1887. The edition is not satisfactory, because the marginal and interlinear glosses are incorporated into the text without indication other than brackets sometimes (not always). Seán Mac Airt was working on a new edition of the Annals of Ulster before his untimely death, and

---

[1] *Phases of Irish History*, 178.

Dr Gearóid Mac Niocaill has now taken over this very important work. Years ago I went through photostats of the text of *AU* up to 740, marking the marginalia, additions and glosses into my own copy. Recently Professor Myles Dillon, with Professor Mac Niocaill's consent, most kindly sent me a xerox copy of Mac Airt's edition of the text up to 1056 (which was in proof when he died).

The second set of Irish annals which we must consider is called the Annals of Tigernach (*Tig.*). *Tig.* is in various fragments.[1] Fragment 1, which goes up to 160 in the reckoning of the Eusebian Chronicle, is in a twelfth-century Bodleian MS, Rawl. B.502. Fragment 2 runs from 322 BC to AD 360. Fragments 3 and 4 are the ones which concern us. They run from 489–766 and from 974–1178, and are both in a fourteenth-century MS, Rawl. B.488. It is unfortunate that 767–974 which, as we shall see, is a vital part, is missing.

The Annals of Tigernach get much less attention than they deserve. This is partly because they are in an almost unobtainable edition which is tiresome to use. Whitley Stokes printed them in several numbers of the *Revue Celtique* at the end of the last century.[2] Instead of putting the text on one side and the translation on the other he interspersed the text with sentences and phrases of translation in brackets.

In 1892 Charles Plummer, on the basis of an edition by Earle, issued his *Two of the Saxon Chronicles Parallel.* We badly need a parallel edition of *AU* and *Tig.* Since editing one set of these annals is a major work I have had to make do with a poor substitute. I have underlined in my copy of *AU* those passages which are not in *Tig.*, and I have underlined in *Tig.* those passages which are not in *AU*. Some interesting conclusions emerge from the comparison. If you want to test them you could very easily get

[1] E. Mac Neill, 'The authorship and structure of the Annals of Tigernach', *Ériu*, VII (1914), 30–113.

[2] *Revue Celtique*, XVI (1895), 374–419; XVII (1896), 6–33, 116–263, 337–420; XVIII (1897), 9–59, 150–303, 374–91.

xerox copies of a sample, say twenty years, of each and provide your own parallel version.

Anyone who does this very simple job of collating the two texts will realise immediately that both *AU* and *Tig.* go back ultimately to the same version. Let us call it the Chronicle of Ireland. On the other hand, it is not true to say that the two are 'almost identical'. Hardly a year passes without *AU* having entries not found in *Tig.*, and *Tig.* having entries which are peculiar to it.[1] For example, here are some of the *Tig.* entries not found in *AU*:

=718 Tonsura corona super familiam Iae datur.
=724 Clericatus Neactain reigis Pictorum. Drust postea regnat.
=726 Cillenus Longus, ab Ie, pausat.
=726 Dungal de reghno iectus est, et Druist de reghno Pictorum iectus et Elphin pro eo regnat. (Dungal son of Selbach was king of Scottish Dál Riada.)
=729 A hundred and fifty Pictish ships were wrecked at Ross Cuissine in the same year.
=732 Nechtan mac Derile moritur (he had been king of the Picts).

This is a tiny selection. I have chosen them because, on other grounds, we can be pretty certain that they were in the Chronicle of Ireland. That Chronicle, as we shall see later,[2] incorporated a Chronicle of Iona, and these entries about Iona, Scottish Dál Riada and Pictland must have come from it.

AU, on the other hand, has other entries which are not found in *Tig.* and which must have come from the same source, the Iona Chronicle:

664 Bellum Lutho feirinn .i. i Fortrinn. (Fortrenn was a province of Pictland.)
683 Obsesio Duin att, et obsessio Duin duirn. (Dunadd is a fortress in Scottish Dál Riada, Dundurn is in Strathearn. The *obsessio* entries are a feature of the Iona Chronicle.)

[1] Beginning with AD 487, one year must be added to that given in the nineteenth-century edition of *AU*. The *Tig.* date in Whitley Stokes's edition is that of *AU* and other sets of annals, which Stokes gives.
[2] *Infra*, 117–19.

691 Ventus magnus xvi. kl. Octimbris quosdam vi. ex familia Iae mersit. (Note the detail.)

698 Combustio Duin Onlaigh. Expulsio Ainfellaig filii Fercair de regno, et vinctus ad Hiberniam vechitur. (Dunollie is another fortress of Scottish Dál Riada, opposite Iona. Ainfellach was king of Dál Riada.)

In fact, in order to understand the history of Scottish Dál Riada and Pictland it is essential to take *AU* and *Tig.* together. A lot of entries are common to both. Some get dropped in one version or the other. We need both sets of annals to reconstruct the Chronicle of Ireland.

When *AU* and *Tig.* report the same event, *Tig.* often gives details which are missing from *AU*, the place where the battle was fought, the names of the persons who were killed, their rank. I will give one or two examples in English, underlining the information not found in *AU*.

635 *Ségíne, abbot of Iona* founded the church of Rechru. (*AU* merely says it was founded. This entry shows that it was part of the *paruchia* of Columcille.)

637 The battle of Mag Rath (Moira) *gained by Domnall son of Aed and by the sons of Aed Sláine—but Domnall ruled Tara at that time—in which fell Congal Caech king of Ulaid and Faelchu with many nobles, in which fell Suibne son of Colmán Cuar.* (*AU* merely says *bellum Roth.* I think the remark 'but Domnall ruled Tara at that time' is the comment of a later editor who remembers Cummíne of Iona's story that the battle was instigated by Domnall Brecc, who was king of Scottish Dál Riada. (See Adamnán's *Life of Columba*, III, 5, and Anderson, p. 49.) But Domnall Brecc seems to have taken Scottish forces to join Congal Caech,[1] who was opposed by Domnall son of Aed, the Uí Néill overlord. So this is not inconsistent with Cummíne's story. Moira is in Co. Down.)

638 The battle of Glen-morrison, *in which the household of Domnall Brecc was put to flight.*

[1] J. Bannerman, *Celtic Studies, Essays in memory of Angus Matheson*, ed. J. Carney and D. Greene (London 1968), 5, for references.

678 Destruction of the Cenél Loairn in Tirinn, i.e., *between Ferchar Fota and the Britons, who were the victors.* (Ferchar Fota was king of Dál Riada, of the Cenél Loairn.)

686 The battle of Dun-Nechtain was fought on Saturday, 20th May, in which Ecgfrid son of Oswy king of the Saxons, the fifteenth year of his reign being ended, was killed with a great multitude of his soldiers *by Bruide son of Bile, king of Fortrenn.* (This is the battle of Nechtansmere. Bruide was king of the Picts.)

One could, of course, argue that only the entries, or portions of entries, common to both *AU* and *Tig.* were in their exemplar. I do not think this is true. Both are, rather, independent versions of the same source, and a number of the references peculiar to one recension or the other were probably once in the Chronicle of Ireland. The much abbreviated text of the Chronicle of Ireland which is in the Annals of Innisfallen very occasionally gives entries which are in *AU* or *Tig.* but not in both. All the same *Tig.* and *AU* were both interpolated and glossed after the recensions divided. The passages peculiar to each are scattered right through the texts, but sometimes there is a little block of peculiar entries at the end of the year, which look suspiciously like additions. Since we have no early manuscripts of either text it will probably not be possible ever to say how much was in the Chronicle of Ireland and how much was later interpolation.

The Chronicle of Ireland was already itself glossed when the texts diverged. The H.1.8. manuscript of *AU* has a number of marginalia, including quatrains in early forms. In *Tig.* the quatrains start at 490 and they are especially frequent in both manuscripts until the end of the seventh century. Between 490 and 695 there are nineteen quatrains in the margins of *AU* which are copied into the text of *Tig.*[1] *AU* also has sixteen quatrains in these years (all in the margins) which are not in *Tig.* And *Tig.* has seventy-three quatrains (all in the text) which are not in *AU*. At least the nineteen quatrains common to both manuscripts are likely to have been in the exemplar, probably as marginalia. *Tig.* incorporated them into the text; a scribe went through *AU* after the

[1] I checked this against a photostat.

manuscript was written, copying them into the margins. (These quatrains might repay study.)

Some entries which are now part of the text of *AU* were added *after* the ancestor-copy of *Tig.* was made. *Tig.* has not a single reference to the Book of Cuana, which *AU* quotes quite frequently as a source between 469 and 629. The inference from this must be that the Book of Cuana references entered the text of *AU* after the families diverged. Even without the text of *Tig.* one would suspect that an editor of *AU* went through his manuscript quite late in its development with the Book of Cuana in hand, for he says at 603: 'All the things which are written in the following year I have found in the Book of Cuana to have happened in this.' *AU* also quotes the Book of Dub-dá-leithe for an entry of 629. It is worth noting that *Tig.* has very few duplicate entries after 585. Mac Neill thought that these were in the exemplar and that *Tig.* dropped them,[1] but it seems to me much more likely that *AU* added them in later editions.

One other very important point becomes clear in comparing *AU* and *Tig.* The Chronicle of Ireland had no *anno domini* dating. Mac Neill said this in 1914, not only of the exemplar of *AU* and *Tig.*, which he believed was compiled c. 712, but of the Irish annals down to the eleventh century.[2] It is certainly impossible to believe that an annalist would not copy *anno domini* dating, which made his task infinitely easier, if he found it in his exemplar. The texts themselves bear out its absence. Up to 585 there are very considerable discrepancies in the sequence of events given in the two texts. After this the basic order is similar, though, particularly in the late sixth and early seventh centuries, *AU* sometimes separates under successive years what is all one Kl. in *Tig.*[3] The few entries put in under completely different years are best explained as marginal glosses in the exemplar.

Before we come to the question of when the two families diverged it is necessary to note one other point about *Tig.*

[1] *Ériu*, VII (1914), 74.
[2] *Ibid.*, 92, 101.
[3] Kl. is used to denote a new year.

Someone made a copy of the Chronicle of Ireland for Clonmacnoise: if it was not made for Clonmacnoise the copy reached that monastery. For *Tig.* has a number of entries of Clonmacnoise interest which are not in *AU*. Many of the abbots of Clonmacnoise have notes added about their families (=*AU* 614, 628, 638, 694, 724, 740, 753). There are six other entries in *Tig.* (not in *AU*), before the lacuna at 766, which strongly suggest Clonmacnoise provenance:

=*AU* 610 Aed king of Airthir *died on pilgrimage at Clonmacnoise.* (*AU* merely has his death.)

=*AU* 649 A long account of an offering made to Clonmacnoise by Diarmait, Uí Néill overlord. He had marched to battle through Clonmacnoise, and the community had prayed for him. By reason of his grant the king demanded to be buried at Clonmacnoise.

=*AU* 663 Burial of Guaire Aidne at Clonmacnoise.

=*AU* 723 Indrechtach king of Connacht died *on pilgrimage at Clonmacnoise.* (*AU* has only his death.)

=*AU* 755 Burning of Clonmacnoise on 21 March.

=*AU* 758 Death of Gormán abbot of Louth, the father of Torbach heir of Patrick. It is he that lived for a year on the water of Fíngin's well at Clonmacnoise, and died on pilgrimage at Clonmacnoise.

I think that 649 must be an addition to the exemplar put in at Clonmacnoise. The note on Gorman at 758 also reads like a later comment. The other entries may have been in the Chronicle of Ireland, but it seems likely that they were added at Clonmacnoise.

When was that ancestor-copy of *Tig.* made? Up to 766 *AU* and *Tig.* are closely related. Then there is a gap in *Tig.* When *Tig.* resumes in 975 the two sets of annals are independent. The copy must have been made at some time between 766 and 975. We can tell the precise date from a study of *Chronicon Scottorum* (*CS*). This is a version of the annals contained in Trinity College Dublin H.1.18, a manuscript in the handwriting of the seventeenth-century antiquary Duald Mac Firbis. It has many fewer entries than either *AU* or *Tig.*, but its relation to them in some way unspecified has long been recognised. If you put this set of annals alongside your 'two sets of Irish annals parallel' comparing the texts before the lacuna in *Tig.* (at 766) you will find that it is not a copy of *AU* or of the Chronicle of Ireland, but a direct copy of *Tig.*[1] There are scores of entries not in *AU* but in *Tig.* which are copied in *CS*, including entries of Clonmacnoise provenance. There is in total very little indeed in *CS* which is not also in *Tig.*

CS is not taken directly from our MS of *Tig.*, but from some other copy. Occasionally *CS* allows you to reconstruct the ancestor copy of *Tig.*, for the scribe of our MS of *Tig.* inadvertently dropped a few entries when he was transcribing. The most interesting of these concerns the battle of Lethirbe (*CS* 630) which is omitted in *Tig.* and is reported more fully in *CS* than in *AU*. There are a few other very short entries in *CS* and in *AU* which must have been in the ancestor-MS of *Tig.* (*CS* 651, 661, 689).

There are a very few other entries in *CS* which are neither in *Tig.* nor *AU*, but which I think must have been in the ancestor-MS of *Tig.* The stanzas at 585 and 605 were probably copied from the Chronicle of Ireland. They would seem to have been there as marginalia, like all the others. At 661 *CS* says that Colmán Cas held the abbacy of Clonmacnoise one year and three days: the three days are omitted in our copy of *Tig.* And the long description of the battle of Allen in *CS*, though it follows *Tig.* closely, has one or two details not in our copy of *Tig.*, which were probably inadvertently dropped. There are also obits of the kings of Connacht at 664, 705 and 711 which may have been in the exemplar of *Tig.*

There are a few miscopyings in *CS*. For instance at 660 *CS* speaks of an earthquake *in Hibernia*, whereas *AU* and *Tig.* both have *in Britannia*. In other cases our copy of *Tig.* has made a slip, for example *Tig.* gives cxxii years since the mortality, whereas *AU* and *CS* give cxii years. Such things merely underline the relationship between the manuscripts.

[1] I have not compared these annals carefully in the later period, and so this conclusion relates only to early times.

We have, therefore, in CS an abbreviated copy of a manuscript of Tig. for the years 765–973 when our copy of Tig. is
defective. CS is itself defective between 718 and 804, but from
804 to 973 it helps us to reconstruct Tig. In particular, between 805
and 913 we can see that the Clonmacnoise entries go on. The following are missing from AU (I give the CS years): abbots and
bishops 876, 885, 889, 890, 901 (a change of abbots); other church
dignitaries, 823, 827, 838, 843, 847, 896, 904; a burning 832;
death on pilgrimage at Clonmacnoise 835; building of a stone
church at Clonmacnoise 908; a longish entry at 823 about the
profanation of Clonmacnoise by the king of Uí Maine and the
compensation adjudged; Feidlimid king of Cashel's plundering of
the city in 846 and Ciarán's revenge; the profanation of the shrine
of Ciarán and the wounding of the bishop in 899. These must
all have been in the MS used for CS, as original entries or as
glosses.

CS, as a faithful though much abbreviated, copy of a MS of
Tig. will tell us when the two families of Tig. and AU diverged.
After 913 (AU) the two texts separate. From 891 (AU) the differences become marked. Presumably the scribe who made the
copy was able to make additions or alterations over the last
twenty-three years, which might be covered by his own adult
lifetime.

To sum up, AU and Tig. represent a Chronicle of Ireland which
must have been drawn up at some time before 913, for at this
point the two families diverge. A copy was made then and was
subsequently taken to Clonmacnoise, where additions were
inserted.[1] In the seventeenth century Duald mac Firbis copied it,
or more probably a copy of it, as the text we now know as
Chronicon Scottorum.

So far we have been dealing with a group of annals concerned
mainly with the northern half of Ireland. But our earliest

[1] In 1088 Tig. reads: 'Tigernach wrote as far as this before he died' (see
Macalister, *Irish Historical Studies*, IV [1945], 44). This is the obit of a scribe.
He might be the same as the Tigernach, a monastic official (*airchinnech*) of
Clonmacnoise, who died in 1088 (AU). Macalister is doubtful.

manuscript of Irish annals is Rawl. B. 503,[1] which contains a set of Munster annals known as the Annals of Inisfallen (*AI*). The entries down to the middle of 1092 were copied at that time, and then continued in a number of contemporary hands. There is an excellent edition by Seán Mac Airt.[2] Between 433 and 1092 *AI* is the transcript of an exemplar which was abbreviated. Up to 969 the entries are mostly of battles and obituary notices. From 972 (the years 970 and 971 are missing) the annals become an O'Brien document.[3]

I have put *AI* alongside my 'two sets of Irish Annals parallel', underlining the entries which are not in *AU* or *Tig.* Some interesting facts emerge. First, up to the late-eighth century there is no doubt whatever that *AI* is closely related to *AU* and *Tig.* Most of the *AI* entries are in both the other texts, but a few are in *AU*, while a very few are in *Tig.* only.

Like *Tig.*, *AI* has no *anno domini* dating, and up to 721 the sequence of events is not always the same as that of *AU* and *Tig.* Mac Airt, in his edition, has given the dates for the corresponding events in *AU* up to 704 and a glance at his book will show the discrepancies. If we continue for another ten years in *AI*, the *AU* sequence is 704, 708, 706, 707, 710, 709, 710, 711, 713. Up to the year 720 *AI* separates in different years what are the same years in *AU*, or puts entries which are under different years in *AU* under the same year. From 721, on the other hand, the dating of *AI* (though it is indicated by Kl. and not by the year of the incarnation) fits in with *AU* almost exactly. I infer from this that *AI* was following a different MS of the Chronicle of Ireland from the exemplar of *AU*, and that there was not agreement on the sequence of events before 721 between the two manuscripts.

There are a few entries peculiar to *AI* in the seventh century, but after about 717 they increase in number. Between 717 and 790 there is a total of 134 entries, of which 48 are peculiar to *AI*.

---

[1] *The Annals of Inisfallen*, facsimile with introduction by R. I. Best and E. Mac Neill (Dublin, London 1933).
[2] *The Annals of Inisfallen* (Dublin 1951).
[3] *Infra*, 297–8.

Between the end of the eighth century and the beginning of the tenth century the proportion of entries not in *AU* substantially increases. From 790 to 904 there are ninety-three entries which *AI* has in common with *AU*, ninety-five entries which are peculiar to *AI*. These figures hardly do justice to the original element in *AI*, because I have noted as 'common' entries a number which are very differently reported. It may be best to put a few of these side by side:

AI	AU
818 The shrine of Mochta of Louth in flight before Aed son of Niall, and it came to Lismore.	Cuana, abbot of Louth, went in exile to the land of Munster, with the shrine of Mochta.
851 Repose of Ólchobar son of Cinaed, abbot of Emly and king of Cashel.	Ólchobar (*interlined*, i.e., son of Cinaed) king of Cashel died.
854 Indrechtach grandson of Fínnechta, abbot of Iona, suffered martyrdom at the hands of Saxons when on his way to Rome.	The heir of Columcille, *sapiens optimus*, was martyred by Saxons on 12 March.
887 Anealoen the pilgrim came to Ireland and the wearing of the hair long was abolished by him and tonsures were accepted.	An epistle came with the pilgrim to Ireland with the Law of Sunday and other good instructions.

I think such entries ought probably to be regarded as independent. If they are, there is a substantial independent element in *AI* after 790, quite considerably more than half the total number of entries.

AU and *AI* seem to diverge completely at 905, but only briefly. Up to this date nearly all the *AI* entries are of battles or obituary notices; at 905 for four years the entries become much more discursive. After 909 there are once again a lot of entries which have parallels in *AU*, although events in *AU* are occasionally given in a different order[1] and there are considerable differences in the reporting. Here are some of the more notable instances:

AI	*AU*
922 Tomrair son of Elgi, a Jarl of the Foreigners, on Luimnech (the lower Shannon) and he proceeded and plundered Inis Celtra and Muicinis and burned Clonmacnoise, and he went on Loch Rí and plundered all its islands, and he ravaged Meath.	The fleet of Luimnech, i.e., of the son of Ailche, on Loch Rí, so that they destroyed Clonmacnoise and all the islands off the lake and carried off a great spoil, between gold and silver and other treasures.
929 Repose of Tuathal, learned bishop of the Northern Half.	Tuathal son of Óenacán, scribe and bishop of Duleek and Lusk and steward of the household of Patrick from the mountain southwards, died alas at an early age.
930 A naval encampment (made) by the Foreigners of Luimnech at Loch Bethrach in Osraige, and Derc Ferna in Osraige was ravaged by them.	Gothfrith grandson of Imar, with the Foreigners of Dublin, demolished Derc Ferna, a thing that had not been heard of from ancient times.

The entries in *AI* are still very laconic, and there are many which could be interpreted as a precis of the *AU* entries.

After 969 two years are missing in *AI*. Though there are still entries comparable with *AU* there is great interest in the activities of Mathgamain and Brian and some of the entries become fuller. From this time on *AI* is certainly an independent O'Brien chronicle.[2]

There is no problem about the early entries in *AI*. They are definitely based on a version of the Chronicle of Ireland. But *AI* also represents another set of annals of mainly Munster interest.

---

[1] There are not enough common entries in one year to draw reliable conclusions from such comparisons.

[2] *Infra*, 297–8.

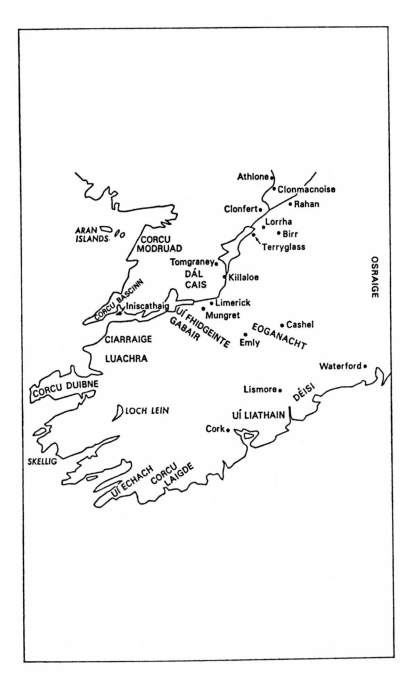

Sketch map 1

These are well in evidence before 790. Particularly noticeable are a series of Lismore entries missing from *AU* and *Tig*. (638 foundation [*sic*], abbots at 701, 760 and 778); a sequence of abbots of Terryglass from 677 to 784 (677, 717, 740, 784) and the drowning of more than a hundred of the Connachta at Terryglass in 777; and four Emly entries (720, 760, 771, 787). Various kings are also mentioned: of Iarmumu (west Munster) at 633, 700, 717, 734; of Gabair and Uí Fhidgeinte (in Co. Lim.) at 706, 732, 751; of Ciarraige Luachra (in N. Kerry) at 741; of Corcu Duibne (in W. Kerry) at 785; of Corcu Bascinn (in S.W. Clare) at 723, 725, 788; and of Déisi (in Waterford) at 632, 645, and 731.[1] These entries cover a wide area of Munster, and three religious houses, Terryglass, Emly and Lismore are more or less equally represented.

After about 790 *AI* becomes a predominantly Munster Chronicle. An indication of Munster interests is provided by the following list of entries, ecclesiastical and secular, which are not in *AU*.[2]

Cork 816, 825, 828, 836, 863
Clonfert 838, 850, 866, 891, 895
Emly 819, 825, 848, 851, 858, 872, 898
Inis Cathaig 863, 901
Lismore 814, 816, 818, 825, 833, 863, 867, 883, 894
Skellig 882
Terryglass 884
Aran 886
Cashel 821,[3] 848, 852, 856, 859, 861, 873, 889, 896, 901
Ciarraige Luachra 796, 850, 853, 857, 873, 878, 890
Corcu Bascinn 853, 864, 898
Corcu Duibne 793
Corcu Laigde 815
Déisi 828, 897
Gabair 829, 832, 848, 860

[1] See sketch map 1.
[2] The period considered here is 790 to 904 inclusive.
[3] Feidlimid is not actually mentioned as 'king of Cashel'. There are entries about him at 830, 836, 838 and 840 which are peculiar to *AI*. His death is reported at 847.

It is not easy to see from this where the chronicle was drawn up. Lismore has the most entries.[1] There is obviously a solid block of entries in the south and east of Munster—Lismore, Emly, Cashel and, to a lesser extent, Cork. But there is also considerable interest in kingdoms which lie on either side of Shannon harbour—Ciarraige Luachra, Corcu Bascinn and Gabair. Inis Cathaig might be expected to have taken an interest in these kingdoms, but there are only two entries for Inis Cathaig.

The annals between 905 and 969 show a similar concern in the south-east and in north Munster. In the following table I have given all the entries from *AU* and *AI* referring to the places stated, but I have italicised those which are only found in *AI*. This is because I am uncertain whether there is any relationship now between *AU* and *AI*, or whether *AI* is independent.

Emly 913, *914*, *935*, *942*, *942*, *947*, *954*, *957*, *968*
Cork *928*, *951*, *961*
Lismore 912, *920*, *938*, *953*, *954*, *958*, *959*, *961*, 965
Ciarraige Luachra *909*, *929*, *948*, *963*
Corcu Bascinn *920*
Uí Fhidgeinte 962
Gabair *969*
Corcu Modruad 919, *936*
Dál Cais *934*
Inis Cathaig *958*
Tomgraney *934*
Clonfert 916, *922*, *946*, *951*, *954*, *958*

Emly and Lismore have exactly the same number of entries, nine each. The Lismore entries are, however, much more conventional in style. Seven are obits of abbots, one the obit of a bishop, one of king Cormac who was vice-abbot of Lismore. Emly has four obits of abbots, the obit of a bishop, the obit of a lector (which is unusual). It also notes that one man 'took the abbacy' in 914. And at 947 'a leaf from heaven (descended) upon the altar of Emly, and a bird spoke to the people'. This is one of a class of *mirabilia* entries, a type rather unusual in *AI*. So Emly has

[1] For Lismore, see *infra*, 141–2.

the less conventional entries. Only one of the Emly entries is to be found in *AU*.

Tomgraney, later an important Dál Cais monastery,[1] appears for the first time since the mid-eighth century. Bishops of Tuadmumu are mentioned at 927 and 952: this is Thomond, an area mainly in Co. Clare. A king of Dál Cais is mentioned at 934 (he is the abbot of Tomgraney), and Cennétig's obituary notice is given at 951 as *rígdamna Cassil*.[2] The death of a son of Cennétig is reported at 953. It looks as if O'Brien influence is being exerted, probably retrospectively, on the annals of this period.

The Annals of Innisfallen leave a lot of unsolved problems.[3] When and where were the Munster entries peculiar to *AI* put together? When and where were these conflated with a text similar to *AU*? We have an excellent modern edition of *AI*, but the problems raised by the entries up to 969 have not yet been adequately discussed.

A comparison of *AU*, *Tig.*, *AI* and *CS* shows that there was a Chronicle of Ireland in existence at the beginning of the tenth century. This was conflated with Munster annals (possibly after 972) and was later savagely abbreviated. The abbreviated version is our *AI*. About 913 the texts of *AU* and *Tig.* diverge. One copy of the Chronicle of Ireland reached Clonmacnoise, where it was interpolated and became our *Tig.* In the seventeenth century Duald mac Firbis made a copy of a MS of *Tig.*, which is now known as *Chronicon Scottorum*. Another copy of the Chronicle of Ireland, after a series of interpolations, became our *AU*.

How do these conclusions compare with those which Professor Kelleher mentioned in 1963, when discussing 'Irish History and pseudo-history'? He said then: 'Apart from interpolations, it would appear that up to 910 all the annals are but selective versions of one common source, a text very likely composed in that year and both fuller and more national in its purview than any recensions derived from it.'[4] I find myself in agreement with his

---

[1] See *infra*, 297.   [2] One eligible for the kingship.   [3] See *infra*, 146.
[4] *Studia Hibernica*, III (1963), 126. See now *Ériu* XXII (1971), 107–27.

view about when the texts of *AU* and *Tig.* diverged (whether it is 910 or, as I have suggested, 913, really makes little difference). I am not certain when *AI* becomes an independent text. Whether or not the Chronicle of Ireland was 'composed' in 910 has still to be considered.

There are other recensions of annals relating to early Ireland which I have not discussed here. The opening section of *The War of the Gaedhill with the Gaill* relates to Irish affairs from the early ninth century to the time of Brian.[1] The Cottonian Annals[2] are very brief: Professor Kelleher refers to them as of the Uí Néill group. The *Annals of Clonmacnoise*,[3] an English translation of Irish annals, are related to Clonmacnoise. Then there are the *Three Fragments of Irish Annals*, copied by Duald Mac Firbis.[4] The *Annals of the Four Masters*[5] are a seventeenth-century compilation. It may be seen that we are not short of material for Early Christian Ireland.

II

The work to establish the stemma of these four texts was exciting to do (probably much more interesting to do than to read) and most of it was comparatively easy. We now have to turn to the much more difficult task of trying to sort out the native sources which go to make up the compilations. Unless we do this we cannot know how reliable the annals are as historical records.

On this latter point various scholars have expressed contrary opinions. Professor Byrne, writing most recently, says: 'My own reading of the annals inclines me to the view that the entries begin to be contemporary in the second half of the sixth century.'[6] Professor Kelleher, on the other hand, has claimed that everything

---

[1] See *infra*, 294–7.
[2] Ed. A. M. Freeman, *Revue Celtique*, XLI (1924), 301–30; XLIII (1926), 358–84; XLIV (1927), 336–61.
[3] Ed. D. Murphy (Dublin 1896).
[4] Ed. J. O'Donovan (Dublin 1860).
[5] *Ibid.* (Dublin 1856).
[6] *Irish Ecclesiastical Record*, CVIII (1967), 164–82.

in the annals up to 590 and a large number of entries between 590 and 735 were either freshly composed or wholly revised not earlier than the period 850–900.[1] Does this mean that Professor Kelleher thinks that a contemporary chronicle was kept from 735 on, or does he mean that a chronicle was not compiled, but actually composed, in 910?

In Eoin Mac Neill's view, the exemplar which lies behind *AU* and *Tig.* (which he calls the 'Old-Irish Chronicle') was compiled c. 712.[2] T. F. O'Rahilly called the common source of *AU* and the other annals up to c. 740 the 'Ulster Chronicle'. He maintained that it incorporated an 'Iona Chronicle', that it was compiled in east Ulster, probably at Bangor, c. 740 and was thereafter continued from year to year.[3] Thus there seems to be some support for the view that contemporary annalistic records were being kept at least as early as 740.

What criteria of criticism am I to use in forming an opinion on this question? I shall argue that if a particular area has a concentration of entries over a considerable period there is a strong likelihood that local records were being kept there. I do not believe that later writers made up a lot of entries from nothing[4] (though they may have edited them or fitted them into a time sequence largely by guess-work). Where a sequence of entries refers to kingdoms of comparatively minor importance we may feel fairly confident in postulating some early record.

This method means, first of all, finding the English equivalents of the places mentioned. I have used the index to Seán Mac Airt's *AI* (very simple to use) and when this fails Edmund Hogan's *Onomasticon Goedelicum*.[5] The places have then to be located on a map. Then the people have to be identified. The annals often give a man's name and ancestry, but not his address, so he has to be looked up in the genealogies to find out his family, which it

[1] *Studia Hibernica*, III (1963), 122.

[2] 'The authorship and structure of the Annals of Tigernach', *Ériu*, VII (1913), 30–113, especially 73–90.

[3] T. F. O'Rahilly, *Early Irish History and Mythology*, 253.

[4] Neither does Professor Kelleher, *op. cit.*, 122.

[5] Dublin 1910.

is often possible to locate. Here M. A. O'Brien's *Corpus Genealogiarum Hiberniae* is an indispensable work of reference.[1] I must admit that my efforts to do this petered out as the annals went on: even in the early period I often abandoned one identification and went on to the next. Nevertheless, I hope that some acceptable conclusions will emerge.

I am starting with the Iona Chronicle, because this is the group of entries in our present annals which stands out most clearly with separate identity. I shall discuss the entries before 585 in a later part of this chapter. Here I am considering the entries between 585 and about 740. Mac Neill and O'Rahilly were aware of an Iona Chronicle, but the fact that we can now speak of it with confidence is due to Dr John Bannerman, in the most important work on the annals which has appeared recently.[2] Professor Byrne, writing in 1967, said: 'It has long been obvious that one of the most important strands in the annals is an Iona Chronicle.' Nevertheless the evidence was not satisfactorily demonstrated until Dr Bannerman's paper was published in 1968.

Scottish Dál Riada (the area of south-west Scotland north of the Firth of Clyde) was settled by Irish from Dál Riata in Ulster. Iona was founded by Columcille in 563. The annals between this time and 740 contain a solid core of entries about the politics of Scottish Dál Riada and Pictland, with some references to England (mainly Northumbria) and the Britons. There is a continuous sequence of abbots of Iona. Some of the entries were incontrovertibly composed in Scotland, for we hear of people going to Ireland (*ad Hiberniam*) and coming from Ireland (*de Hibernia*). Some events from the later seventh century onwards are recorded with precision, suggesting a local chronicle. There are characteristic features, such as the frequency with which forts and strongholds are mentioned, and the taking of prisoners. This Chronicle seems

---

[1] Dublin 1962. On the genealogies, see the appendix to this chapter.
[2] 'Notes on the Scottish entries in the early Irish annals', *Scottish Gaelic Studies*, XI (1968), 149–70. Cf. I. Henderson, *The Picts* (London 1967), 165–8; O'Rahilly, *op. cit.*, 235–59; Mac Neill, *Ériu*, VII (1913), 80. Now see *infra*, 146, note 1.

to come to an end about 740, for after 740 the Scottish entries become shorter and fewer. We now hear of abbots of Iona coming to Ireland (*in Hiberniam venit*) so that these entries must now have been composed in Ireland.

Were these Iona entries contemporary? From the 670s the entries are more frequent, from the 680s some become much fuller, from 686–740 there is a series of precisely dated entries. All this suggests to me that the Iona Chronicle is contemporary from about the 680s and that records were kept before this, even if they were not written up as formal annals until the later part of the century. It is worth remembering that the abbot of Iona between 679 and 704 was Adamnán, a man who took a lively interest not only in scholarship but in political affairs. He may have encouraged the development of an Iona Chronicle.

The Iona Chronicle is now embedded in Irish entries, but occasionally we have a year in the annals which is almost confined to Scottish events. Take 729 in the Chronicle of Ireland which reads:

1. Ecbericht, a soldier of Christ, rests on Easter day (*AU* the second day of Easter). (Ecgbert was an Englishman who went to Ireland as a youth and stayed there. Later he wanted to go as a missionary to Germany, but was instructed by a vision to go to Iona and convert that monastery to the Roman observance. He succeeded in this, and died there, Bede says at the age of ninety. See all the references in Plummer, *HE*, II, 456.)

2. The battle of Monith-carno near Loch Loegdae, between the host of Nectan and the army of Oengus; and the *exactatores* of Nectan were killed, that is Biceot mac Moneit and his son, Finguine mac Drostain, Feroth mac Finguine and many others; and the *familia* of Oengus triumphed.
   (The place is unidentified. Nectan is Nectan son of Derilei. Oengus is Oengus son of Fergus. Both are named in the Pictish King Lists. Nectan had been king earlier, but according to *Tig.* had become a cleric in 724 while Drust took over the kingdom. *AU* at 726 says 'Nectan son of Derile was put in fetters by king Drust'. Drust was subsequently expelled and Oengus, after a fight with a rival, took the throne. According to *Tig.* Nectan came back into power. In 729 Nectan and Oengus were fighting it out.)

3. The battle of Druim-Dergblathug in the territory of the Picts, between Oengus and Drust king of the Picts, and Drust fell.
(Here Oengus met another rival claimant, Drust, who had already been recognised as king for a time and who appears in the Pictish King Lists. *Tig.* says the battle was on 12 August. The career of Oengus was eventful. He died in 761.)
AU and *Tig.* then each have one short entry not apparently from the 'Iona Chronicle'.

This short extract shows the kind of coverage which the political history of Scotland was getting in the Iona Chronicle. No one later on in Ireland would bother to make all this up: indeed, it is astonishing that it was all copied so faithfully. I think that the Iona Chronicle can be taken as an accurate contemporary record certainly from the later decades of the seventh century, and very probably using contemporary notes to compile the earlier entries.

It is worth noting the place of these entries in each year. Either Scottish or Ulster entries very often come at or near the beginning of each year. It looks as if a Scottish/Ulster chronicle formed the basis of our present annals. They were probably the oldest stratum of entries. This was the view put forward by O'Rahilly.

The entries from north-eastern Ireland are a problem. There are a number of entries about the internal politics of Ulster, especially the Dál-Fiatach (or Ulaid), who occupied the Down seaboard, and the Dál-nAraide (called the Cruithin) who occupied the interior of county Down and much of Co. Antrim. There are also a number of entries about the peoples of Airgialla, especially the Airthir, in whose territory Armagh stood. Is it correct to look at these Ulster and Airgialla entries as a solid block?

The Airgialla sub-kingdoms before 827 seem to have been in political alliance with the Uí Néill overlord. This is the situation indicated by an Old Irish poem edited by Mrs O'Daly, to whose significance Professor Byrne has recently drawn attention.[1] The entries concerning them should perhaps therefore be regarded separately from the Ulster entries. Their records are most likely to have been kept at Armagh, which lay in this area.

[1] 'A poem on the Airgialla', *Ériu*, XVI (1962), 179–88. Cf. J. Byrne, *The Rise of the Uí Néill and the high-kingship of Ireland* (Dublin, 1969), 20.

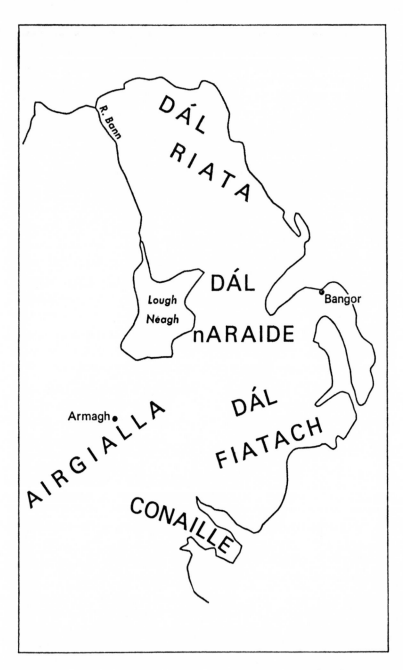

DÁL
RIATA

R. Bann

DÁL
nARAIDE

Lough
Néagh

Bangor

Armagh●

AIRGIALLA

DÁL
FIATACH

CONAILLE

Sketch map 2

Iona must have been interested in the affairs of Ulster. Until after the battle of Mag Rath in 637 the king of Scottish Dál Riada was also king of Irish Dál Riata. In the first half of the seventh century Dál nAraide was allying with Irish Dál Riata against her rival Dál Fiatach.[1] So the politics of Ulster might well find a place in the Iona Chronicle. All the same, the emphasis in the annals rests on Dál Fiatach and Dál nAraide: Comgall of Bangor was patron of the Dál nAraide and his monastery lay in Dál Fiatach territory. In the report of the battle of Mag Rath,[2] the annals never mention the participation of Dál Riada, though we know from Cummene's Life of Columcille that the Dál Riadans were involved. This passage was entered in the 713 MS of Adomnán's Life, but it seems that it may not have been in Adomnán's original text.[3] We could therefore argue that the Iona Chronicle would have reported Dál Riadan participation at Mag Rath, and that the entry in the annals, with its emphasis on Congal Caech, king of Dál nAraide as opponent of the Uí Néill, is from a Bangor Chronicle. On the other hand it would be possible to argue that the Iona Chronicle had deliberately not reported an incident discreditable to Scottish Dál Riada.[4] On the whole, I am inclined to believe in a Bangor Chronicle. We have that very rare thing, a complete seventh-century list of abbots,[5] and we know that Bangor had a *scriptorium* in the seventh century.

It should be noted that the Ulster entries form quite a small proportion of the whole. There are many years which do not mention Ulster. For example 634 tells of: the murder of two sons of Aed Sláine (Brega) by Conall son of Suibne (of the Clann Colmáin of Meath); the killing of this Conall by Diarmait, the murdered men's brother; Diarmait's victory over another

---

[1] J. Bannerman, 'The Dál Riata and Northern Ireland', *Celtic Studies*, ed. J. Carney and D. Greene, 1-11.

[2] *Supra*, 102.

[3] A. O. and M. O. Anderson, *Adomnán's Life of Columba*, 474-5 (III, 5).

[4] I believe that Mr Alfred Smyth has an article now in the press opposing the existence of a separate Bangor Chronicle, but I do not know what his arguments are. See *PRIA, LXXII* (1972), C 1-48.

[5] *Infra* 122-3.

grandson of Colmán Mor (i.e., all Brega-Meath events). Then we go on with the founding of Rechru (a church of the *paruchia* of Columcille); snow in Mag Breg; the death of two southern Irish saints; the death of the king of the Picts of Scotland; the death of a cleric of Lismore. Finally we have the battle of Seguis, in which two of the Eoganachta fell and the king of the Picts. (This last reference to the king of the Picts looks as if it has been misplaced.)

In the earliest stages, a chronicle of mainly Scottish (with some Northumbrian and British) affairs must have been kept at Iona; I am inclined to think that a separate chronicle was kept at Bangor dealing with Ulster affairs, in particular with the two kingdoms of Dál Fiatach and Dál nAraide to which Bangor was nearest. The list of seventh-century abbots of Bangor in the annals is supported by independent seventh-century evidence. There is a poem in honour of the abbots of Bangor in the Antiphonary of Bangor. If we put the entries in *AU* and *Tig.* together (neither *AU* nor *Tig.* alone will do it) we can see that the Chronicle of Ireland recorded the obits of all the abbots plus the foundation and a burning.

Antiphonary of Bangor	*Chronicle of Ireland (AU dating)*
	559 Ecclesia Benncair fundata est.
1. Comgillus	602 Comgoll ab Bendchair, xci anno etatis sue, principatus autem sui l. anno et iii. mense et x. die. vi idus Mai quievit (*Tig. AU* just records *Quies Comghaill Bennchair*, and also gives his *pausa* the year before).
2. Beognus	606 Quies Beugnai abbatis Bennchoir.
3. Aedeus	610 Mors Sillani moccu mMinn abbatis
4. Sinlanus	Bennchoir et mors Aedain ancoritae Bennchoir.
5. Fintenanus	613 Quies Finntain Oentraibh abbatis Benncoir.
	616 Combustio Benncoir.
6. Mac Laisreus	646 Mc Lasre, abb Bennchair, quievit.
7. Seganus	663 Quies Segain moccu Chuind, abb Bencoir (*AU* only).

8. Berachus	664	Berach ab Bennchair.
9. Cumenenus	⎧ =667	Mortalitas in qua quattuor abbates Benn-
10. Columba	⎨	chair perierunt, Berach, Cumine, Colum,
11. Aidanus	⎩	Mac Aedha (*Tig.* only).
12. Baithenus	=666	Baithine abb Bennchair (*Tig.* only).
13. Critanus	669	Obitus . . . Critani abbatis Bennchair.
14. Camanus	680	Colman, abbas Benncair, pausat.
15. Cronanus	691	Cronan moccu Chualne, abb Bennchuir, obiit.

This looks like a Bangor Chronicle. The chronology seems to be a little confused during the years of the great plague, 664–7, but this is what one might expect.

There also seem to be a lot of early entries about Airthir (in which kingdom lay Armagh) and other Airgialla peoples, with entries of Armagh events. Whereas Bangor rather fades out of the annals later, Armagh comes to take a very prominent place; so it is much more difficult to be confident about the early history of Armagh. Nevertheless, I think it very likely that an early chronicle of chiefly local events was kept here, and was incorporated with our annals.

I think (with O'Rahilly) that an Iona/Ulster Chronicle formed the earliest stratum in the Chronicle of Ireland. One has, however, to note that the Iona/Ulster entries are completely swamped by the rest. This is true even of the seventh century in many years, and increasingly true in the eighth century, as the records become fuller. Entries range all over the northern half of Ireland, with references to Leinster and Munster. For instance the years 751 and 752 contain (besides two entries which I have not identified) references to Uí Fhailghi (from which the present Co. Offaly is named), south Brega (the area north of Dublin), Clonard (in Co. Meath), Kiltoom (in Co. Westmeath), Devenish (on L. Erne), Slane (in Co. Meath), Clones (in Co. Monaghan), Leckan (in Co. Meath), Aughrim (west of the Shannon in Co. Galway), Iona, Kildare, Egg (one of the islands of western Scotland), Inishmurray (off the west coast of Ireland), Leamakevoge (in Co. Tipperary), Clonfert, the Cenél-Coirpri, the Conaille-

Muirtheimne(north Co. Louth), Iona, Terryglass (Co. Tipperary), Clooncraff (Co. Roscommon), Tomgraney (just west of Loch Derg), Clonmacnoise, the north-west of Co. Westmeath, the Uí Briuin of Connacht. This shows the range of entries. Even if we allow that a number of these entries were interpolated in later editions, I still think that, had the Chronicle of Ireland been drawn up in Ulster (as O'Rahilly implies), one would expect it to have a more localised look.

The structure of the annals is undoubtedly provided by the activities of the Uí Néill. A continuous history of the Uí Néill overlords could be written from the annals: it is they who provide the coherent and continuous thread. This is true for the seventh century as well as for the eighth. It therefore seems more sensible to look for the place where the annals were compiled not in east Ulster but in the territories of the Uí Néill.

Fortunately we can be more precise than this. The early annals are interested in the Uí Néill overlords, but they are especially interested in the descendants of Aed Sláine. They were part of the southern Uí Néill, some of them were among the overlords, but some were minor kings of Brega, the area which is now Co. Louth and the east of Meath.

Here it is useful to see which religious houses are named in the annals for the period between 741 and 790. During the eighth century references to monasteries become more frequent and it might be expected that the political and ecclesiastical coverage would bear some relation to each other. It does. Two main areas are represented by the monasteries. One is the central east of Ireland (see sketch map).[1] The compiler of the Chronicle probably had access to Kildare records (thirteen entries between 740 and 790) and to Clonard records (fourteen entries), but the main scatter of houses is further north, in the area which later[2] came under the interests of Patrick's steward. There are several houses on or near the Slighe Assail, along the Boyne–Blackwater valley. Louth

---

[1] The other area which emerges very clearly is that of houses on or near the Shannon.

[2] *Infra*, 133–4.

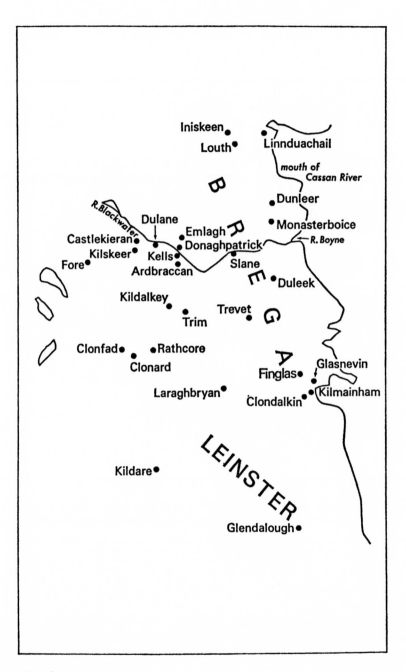

Iniskeen

Louth

Linnduachail

mouth of
Cassan River

B

R

Dunleer

R.Blackwater

Dulane

Emlagh

Monasterboice

R. Boyne

Castlekieran

Donaghpatrick

Kilskeer

Kells

Fore

Ardbraccan

Slane

E

Kildalkey

Trim

Trevet

Duleek

G

Clonfad

Rathcore

Clonard

A

Finglas

Glasnevin

Laraghbryan

Clondalkin

Kilmainham

Kildare

LEINSTER

Glendalough

Sketch map 3

has the obits of six abbots during this fifty years.[1] Are we now beginning to see why Professor Kelleher suggested Louth in Brega as the place of composition for the annals? This area undoubtedly receives considerable emphasis.

We need to consider when the annals were compiled. Ó Máille, when he studied the name forms of *AU*, concluded that the bona fide contemporary language started about 740 or 750.[2] This was before the work of either Mac Neill or O'Rahilly. There is one very noticeable characteristic of the annals between 749 and 790 which may be relevant here, that is, the frequency of entries about burning, each with an identical formula, *combustio* followed by the place name. Between 598 and 740 only eight burnings are recorded. Between 749 and 757 there are eight, between 775 and 790 there are sixteen. They are Uí Néill entries, ranging over the northern half of Ireland (with one reference to Clonfert in north Munster, and two to Leinster churches) and do not seem to have come from a local Ulster chronicle. In the years immediately following 790, a few burnings are noted, but with a different formula (except in one case). Now we have *Cell Achaid cum oratorio novo ardescit* (805), *Tir-da-glass ardet* (806) and later, in the 830s, *loscud* (burning). I infer that a contemporary annalist between 749 and 757 decided to put these entries in. His successor left them out. Between 775 and 790 someone else resumed the practice and after 790 the fashion in which the burnings were recorded changed. I suppose this variation could be due to a series of later compilers, but a contemporary annalist seems to me more likely. Incidentally Mac Neill mentioned that the *Cruithin* occur for the last time at 774: thereafter the term used to describe them is Dál nAraide. This also points to a change of annalist or compiler at 775. The characteristics and stylistic peculiarities of the annal entries need much further attention.

---

[1] From *AU* and *Tig.*

[2] T. Ó Máille, *The Language of the Annals of Ulster* (Manchester 1910). This book unfortunately starts from the assumption that the annals are contemporary, but it does set out the evidence. Philologists may want to revise some of its conclusions.

It might be worth noting also one other type of entry which suggests contemporary records, that is the exactly dated entry. I have used both *AU* and *Tig.* to list these, until *Tig.* ends in 766. There are very few exactly dated entries before 670. Between 670 and 750 there are twenty-three. Three of these are events of national importance, where dates might have been put in any-where, or perhaps even added later (671 the assassination of the king of Tara, 703 the battle of Corann, 722 the battle of Allen). Six are natural portents or disasters (comets, etc., and a mor-tality); again we do not know where these were entered. One concerns the north of Ireland, one concerns Ulster, and no less than ten relate to Scotland. I think that there is a very strong likeli-hood that these precisely dated, contemporaneously recorded, entries came from the Iona Chronicle. Between 741 and 773 only four precisely dated entries are given (lower than the previous average). Then they start up again in 773, about which time we have already seen reason to think that there was a new chronicler.

I will set out the precisely dated entries for the 770s and 780s (abbreviating some of the wording):

773 A dark moon on 4 Dec.
774 The death of the abbot of Trevet on the sixth day between the two Easters.
778 Burning of Clonmacnoise on 10 July.
779 Burning of Kildare on 11 June. A great wind at the end of autumn.
780 Burning of Dumbarton on 1 Jan. Great snow in April.
781 Confusion in Armagh at Shrovetide.
782 Death of the abbot of Aghaboe on 10 May. Battle of the Curragh near Kildare on Tues. 27 Aug.
783 Terrible lightning during the entire night of Saturday and thunder on 2 Aug.
786 A very great storm in January.
788 Moon red like blood on 18 Feb.
789 Burning of Clonard on Easter night. Great snow in April.

Allowing for the fact that we are dealing with an interpolated text, this looks to me like contemporary chronicling.

Though I think that an Uí Néill chronicle, incorporating earlier material, was compiled in the second half of the eighth century and that contemporary entries were made from this time on, this does not mean that *all* the entries are contemporary. *AU* is a heavily interpolated text. Take the year 743. This gives us (amongst other things) an account of four battles. The entry ends: 'These four battles took place almost in one summer.' An entry about Rechru has been interpolated between the first and second battles. Or look at the year 772, where we have two separate accounts of the same thing, plus an interpolated entry, thus:

1. 'The fair of the clapping of hands' (*oenach inna lam-comarthae*) in which was fire and thunder like the day of judgment. (In Latin except for the first three words.)
2a. 'The clapping of hands' on the feast of Michael, of which was said 'the fire from heaven'. (In Irish.)
3. Death of Suibne, abbot of Iona. (In Latin.)
2b. The Irish fasted two three-day fasts together and one meal between them through fear of the fire. (In Irish.)

2a and b were inserted from some other source, for Irish is an unusual language in the annals as early as 772. To make matters more complicated we have the same entry again, in the same wording as 2a, at 799. Among the few entries in Irish before 811 there were two concerning the profanation of Armagh (789 and 793) and a series concerning the aggressive activities of Aed, king of Cinél Eogain and Uí Néill overlord. In 802 he went on a hosting to Meath, in 804 to Leinster, in 805 to Dun Cuair and in 809 plundered Ulster. I think that these may all have been inserted into an existing text. There were probably many more interpolations which cannot now be detected. We have already seen that interpolation had taken place in the Chronicle of Ireland before it was copied after 913. So that 'some evidence for a contemporary chronicle from the second half of the eighth century' is not an answer which solves all the historian's problems.

III

Let us now turn to the ninth century. In the last decade of the eighth century and the beginning of the ninth century some substantial changes come about in the character of the entries of *AU*. We have already seen that changes occur in *AI* round about this time. I should now like to consider first the ninth-century Uí Néill record, as it is contained in *AU*, then the ninth-century Munster record.

The most obvious change in *AU* is in the language. Until about 810 the language of *AU* is Latin, save for prepositions and the odd word like *slógad* (a hosting) and very occasional entries. (I think, therefore, that the entries in Irish before this date may be interpolated.) Between 811 and 818 some entries at or near the ends of the years are in Irish, except for 817, where a block of entries in the middle is in Irish. After 818 the Latin and Irish entries are intermixed. The obits, abbatial circuits, some battles are in Latin. On the whole the less conventional entries are in Irish; hence this is the language used for nearly all the Viking entries. By the 830s the entries are roughly half in Irish and half in Latin. After 810 I cannot see that the language has any significance for detecting the date of the entries. Irish at this period was a suitable language for use in the monastic schools, so it is not surprising to find it being used in the annals.

The first of the major changes in time concerns Armagh. Up to 780 the annals have recorded the deaths of clerics of Armagh and three burnings. With 781 they begin to show a much greater interest in the affairs of Armagh,[1] an interest which becomes intimate and compelling from 793 onwards. We still get obits, but often accompanied by descriptive phrases like *subita morte*, *immatura morte*, or two *in una nocte*. The *cáin* entries are still there, but in each case we are told who was responsible for the promulgation.[2] (Before this there are only two *lex Patricii* entries in *AU*.)

---

[1] e.g., 781 and 789, as well as obits, a burning and the *cáin Pátraicc*.
[2] 799, 806, 811, 818, 823, 825, 836. Cf. 738, 768.

We are now told, in detail, about disturbances at Armagh,[1] opposition to abbots and other officials (sometimes involving political interests),[2] the replacement of one abbot by another[3] (perhaps rather discreditable episodes, for they could not be known from the list of heirs of Patrick).[4] We also hear of affairs concerning the honour of Patrick outside the city of Armagh.[5] And, of course, there are records of the city plundered by Vikings,[6] and of the capture of monastic officials.[7]

Often quite a lot of detail is given. In 893 we have: 'A disturbance at Whitsuntide in Armagh, between the Cenél Éogain and the Ulstermen, wherein many were slain.' This is from *AU*. *CS* goes on to name the participants, to say that Máel-Brigte (who was the abbot) separated them, and to give details of the compensation which was paid for the insult to Patrick's honour. *CS*, of course, is here following *Tig.*, unfortunately defective for this period. This sort of material must have come from Armagh itself. After 793 the annals show the liveliest concern with Armagh, which is in marked contrast to the conventional character of the entries before 781.

The second feature of interest in the annals of the ninth century is the union of interests between Armagh and the kings of the Uí Néill, either with the Uí Néill overlord or with the king of the Cenél Éogain, the leading people of the Northern Uí Néill. Armagh was part of Airgialla. Dub-dá-leithe, the abbot who died in 793, and his son, abbot Condmach, were of the Clann Sínaich, one of the leading families of Airgialla. It is possible that the Northern Uí Néill were already giving their support to Armagh abbots in Dub-dá-leithe's day, for a poem in the 'Ancient List of Heirs of Patrick' says: 'Dub-dá-leithe, son of Sínach, is at hand with kings from the north.'[8] This is not in *AU*. But the

---

[1] 819, 893.   [2] 827, 831, 863.   [3] 835. Cf. 839, 848, 877.

[4] Ed. H. J. Lawlor and R. I. Best, *PRIA*, XXXV (1919), C 316–62.

[5] 810, 831, 836, 851, 859.

[6] 832 (first plundering, three times in one month), 869 (1,000 captured or slain), 895 (710 captives), *CS*, 899.   [7] 845, 879.

[8] *PRIA*, XXXV (1919), 322. Two entries in the annals at 737 may presage this. They read: 'A meeting between Aed Allán and Cathal at Terryglass (in

annals make it clear that in 827 Niall, king of Cenél Éogain, was definitely interesting himself in the affairs of Armagh. There was a quarrel then in Armagh between the lector Éogan and the abbot Artrí who was brother or half brother to the king of Airgialla. A battle was fought at Leth Cam between Niall (supporting Éogan) on the one hand, and Artrí, the king of Airgialla and the king of Ulaid on the other. Niall won, and secured the recognition of Éogan as abbot of Armagh. This seems to have been a decisive battle in the expansion of Cenél Éogain power southwards.[1]

In 859 we again see Armagh identifying her interests with the Uí Néill, this time in the person of the Uí Néill overlord, Máel-Sechnaill, king of the Southern Uí Néill. A royal assembly was held at Rahugh (in present Westmeath) where Máel-Sechnaill, Fethgna abbot of Armagh and the abbot of Clonard were all present. Its purpose was to establish peace. 'And it was in that assembly', the annal goes on, 'that Cerball king of Osraige[2] made complete submission to the community of Patrick and to his successor, and thereat Osraige was permanently alienated to Leth Cuinn (the northern half of Ireland) and Mael-guaila king of Munster warranted (i.e., give sureties for) this alienation.' This must have been a major political event. It meant the renunciation of the traditional claim that Osraige owed allegiance to the king of Munster, and it shows Armagh in full support of the Uí Néill.[3]

The annals for the ninth century also show us a clear claim by Armagh to be the chief church in the north, where her abbot had a position corresponding to that of the Uí Néill overlord. As early as 804 there was a great Uí Néill assembly at Dún

Irish). Lex Patricii tenuit Hiberniam.' If these entries are connected they suggested that, at a royal meeting between the overlord of the Uí Néill and the king of Munster, the *cáin Pátraicc* was promulgated in both provinces.

[1] T. Ó Fiaich, 'The Church of Armagh under lay control', *Seanchas Ardmhacha*, V (1969), 80-2.

[2] Almost co-extensive with the diocese of Ossory (Cos. Kilkenny and Leix).

[3] The Uí Néill king either had a house at Armagh or was staying there in 870, for a man was killed 'before the door of the house of Aed king of Tara'.

Cuair, on the borders of Meath and Leinster. The annals clearly say that the leader of this assembly was Condmach, abbot of Armagh. In the next year the annals report a hosting of Aed (king of the Cenél Éogain and Uí Néill overlord) to Dún Cuair. The writer of the Preface to the Martyrology of Oengus fused these two events, for he says that Aed went on a hosting to Dún Cuair taking Condmach and the clerics of Ireland with him. An agreement was reached on this hosting (reported in Irish in the annals and possibly an addition to the original entry) that the clergy were to be exempt from expeditions and hostings.[1] The annals are here naming the abbot of Armagh as leader of the clergy of the Uí Néill, though it was not he who gave the judgment.

In 851 they report a deliberate drowning which took place 'in spite of the guarantees of the nobles of Ireland and of the successor of Patrick *specialiter*'.[2] Here again the abbot of Armagh is accorded a leading place in the account of an event of public importance. But the most outstanding instance comes in 859[3] when Cerball's submission to the Uí Néill was made to 'the community of Patrick and his heir'. When we read later in the century (874) that bishop Fethgna, heir of Patrick, died on 6th October 'head of the religion of all Ireland', the annalist is making an assertion quite in accord with his report of ecclesiastical politics during the century.

Another of the political developments of the ninth century which the annals emphasise is the concern of the Cenél Éogain in Brega. Perhaps mutual interests brought Brega and the Cenél Éogain together, for both were the natural rivals of Meath, now the leading power of the Southern Uí Néill. In 822 Murchad of the Cenél Éogain came on a hosting as far as Ardbraccan. The

---

[1] *The Martyrology of Oengus*, ed. W. Stokes (London 1905), 4; cf. *AU*, 804.

[2] This was a drowning of the king of Brega by the kings of Meath and Lagore. He really deserved it, for he had joined the Vikings the year before in plundering Meath and sacking Lagore. Why should he have been under the protection of the abbot of Armagh? See below for linking of Armagh and Brega interests.

[3] *Supra*, 131.

men of Brega went secretly to him and gave him hostages. Brega was then plundered by Conchobar, king of Meath and Uí Néill overlord. He plundered the south of Brega again with extensive damage on 1 November and the Uí Cernaig (one of the Brega families, descendants of Aed Sláine)[1] submitted 'through compulsion'. This sounds as if the sympathies of the annalist are with the men of Brega and against Meath. Brega had recognised Cenél Éogain power.

In 862 and 864 Aed, king of the Cenél Éogain (now Uí Néill overlord), and the king of Brega were joining forces, first to plunder Meath, then to win a victory over the Ulstermen.[2] It is not altogether surprising to find that Aed actually died in Brega, at Dromiskin, on Friday, 12 December 879, according to the annals.

I have shown that the ninth-century annals were concerned with Armagh as never before; with Armagh as head of the clergy, with Armagh as representative of the Uí Néill. But there is still a lot of interest in Brega. The annalist thinks it worth while to record not only the obits of kings[3] but the obits of some heirs to the kingship.[4] He also gives us entries about the internal politics of Brega, which would have been of interest mainly to someone living there,[5] and details about Viking raids.[6]

How then are we to explain this combination of a strong Armagh–Uí Néill interest and the concern in the local affairs of Brega? I think that the clue lies in the entries about Patrick's steward (*maer*) in Brega. In 814 the annals record the death of Feidlimid, abbot of Kilmoone and steward of Brega on the part of Patrick. In 888 we have Máel-Pátraic, *scriba et sapiens optimus*, abbot of Trevet and steward of the household of Patrick 'towards the mountain from the south', and another steward is mentioned with the same descriptive phrase at 894. This mountain may mean the Fews in the south of Co. Armagh (though Slieve Bregh is another possibility, since Kilmoone and Trevet both lie to the

---

[1] *CGH*, 144 b 1.
[2] This trend of co-operation between Aed and Brega was reversed in 868.
[3] 815, 826, 838, 849, 868, 869, 888, 896.
[4] 887, 893, 895, 896.   [5] 817, 839.   [6] 836, 837, 840, 852.

south of these hills). At 921 the steward was abbot of Dunleer, and his territory was defined as 'from Belach-duin to the sea and from the Boyne to the Cassan'. *If* Belach-duin should be identical with Castlekieran (it is doubtful), this area would take in a number of houses along the Boyne–Blackwater valley which are well represented in the annals.[1] The steward collected the revenue due to Armagh. Presumably Patrick had stewards in other areas:[2] if so, it is significant that the Brega steward is the only one mentioned. If, on the other hand, Brega was the first area in which Armagh managed to establish a steward, this would suggest close ties between Armagh and Brega.

If there were a connection between Armagh and Louth, one would expect to find evidence for it in the *Vita Tripartita*, the Life of Patrick compiled during the period 895 to 902. A note appended to the Life, which probably dates from the time of abbot Joseph (died 936), names twenty-four persons who were in orders with Patrick.[3] The first and second are bishop Sechnall and Mochta (patron of Louth). These twenty-four, it concludes, should all form part of abbot Joseph's unity. The Life also tells how Patrick wished to set up a community at Ardpatrick, just to the east of Louth. He and Mochta met daily until Patrick, at an angel's guidance, moved on to Armagh.[4] It looks as if links existed between Armagh and Louth in the ninth and tenth centuries.

I think that contemporary Uí Néill annals were being kept at least as early as the last quarter of the eighth century. These *may* at first have been kept at Louth.[5] But the overwhelming weight of evidence from the late eighth century onwards points to Armagh. There are fifty-eight entries in *AU* between 780 and 900, eight Louth entries in the same period. When Armagh

[1] See sketch-map *supra*, 125. Henry, *Irish Art*, II, 19, accepts the identification.

[2] The *Vita Tripartita* suggests interests not only in Brega and Meath and the Uí Néill lands, but also in Connacht, Ulster, Munster and Leinster.

[3] *Vita Tripartita*, ed. W. Stokes (London 1887), I, 264–6.

[4] *Ibid.*, 226.

[5] See Kelleher, *Studia Hibernica*, III (1963), 126.

revived in the second half of the seventh century the kings of Brega had been the dominant Uí Néill power. Muirchú not unnaturally sited Patrick's great conquest with Lóegaire in the plain of Brega,[1] and perhaps Armagh's early expansion was in this area. In the eighth and ninth centuries she retained a close interest in Brega; the annal entries from that area may be best explained by Patrick's steward south of the mountain.

IV

When people talk about the 'high-kingship' at this period they mean the Uí Néill overlordship. The northern annals show us the Uí Néill overlords gaining authority, and the interest of historians tends to concentrate on them. But the Munster annals are making rather similar claims for certain of the kings of Cashel. Of course the Munster annals are so abbreviated that all we have is a series of attenuated notes; but this makes the claims which are made the more remarkable.

The ninth-century story has an eighth-century prologue. In 721 Cathal son of Finnguine, king of Munster, harried Brega. So much was in the Chronicle of Ireland. *AU* says that Cathal had an ally, Murchad son of Bran, king of Leinster, whom the Munster annals do not mention. *AI* goes on to relate that Cathal of Munster and Fergal of the Uí Néill made peace, 'and Fergal submitted to Cathal'. This submission may have had no long-term significance, but an eleventh-century editor[2] saw it as part of a pattern and adds: 'For these were the five kings of the Mun-stermen who ruled Ireland after the (introduction of the) Faith, viz., Aengus son of Nad Fraich (who was supposed to have died in 492) and his son, i.e. Eochaid who ruled Ireland for seventeen

[1] *Infra*, 230–1.

[2] It is possible that the note about Fergal's submission may be part of the eleventh-century addition. If so, Cathal's obit in 742 *AI* as 'King of Ireland' is presumably another addition. It is worth remembering here that one seventh-century story-teller referred to Corc of Cashel as 'King of Ireland'. See B. Ó Cuív, *PBA*, XLIX (1963), 242.

years, and Cathal, son of Finnguine, and Feidlimid, son of Crim-
thann, and Brian, son of Cennétig.'

Feidlimid, named here, was an aggressive ruler who was
determined to expand the power of Munster. In 830 he inflicted
a defeat on the combined forces of Uí Néill and Connacht. *AU*
does in fact record this, but without emphasising the damaging
effect on the Uí Néill: 'Burning of Fore by Feidlimid. Follamain
son of Donnchadh was slain by the Munstermen. Destruction of
the southern Uí Briúin by Feidlimid.' The crucial entry comes at
838, when *AI* reads:

> A great assembly of the men of Ireland in Clonfert, and Niall, son
> of Aed king of Tara, submitted to Feidlimid, son of Crimthann, so
> that Feidlimid became full king of Ireland that day (*lanrí hErend*).

This is a claim to be supreme overlord of the northern half as
well as of Munster. *AU* gives no hint of the claim, merely recording a royal meeting in Cloncurry between Feidlimid and
Niall. In 840 Feidlimid ravaged the northern overlordship from
Birr to Tara.[1] *AU* records his ravaging in Meath and Brega with
a stanza, but adds that Niall also plundered, and, according to *AU*
only, a further hosting into Leinster in 841 was met by Niall,
who would seem to have had the best of it.

Thus the southern annals are definitely putting up a claim that
Feidlimid was recognised by the north as her overlord, a claim
about which *AU* says nothing at all, unless it is disguised in an
epigrammatic quatrain at the year 839 or in Feidlimid's obituary
notice as *optimus scotorum*.

Cormac, king of Munster, took the hostages of the Uí Néill
in 907, according to the Munster record. When in 908 he was
defeated and killed by the Uí Néill overlord Flann Sinna he was

---

[1] According to *AI* on this expedition he seized Gormlaith daughter of
Murchad. Professor Mac Cana suggests (*Études Celtiques*, VIII [1958], 62–3)
that this might be a symbolic seizure of the sovereignty of Ireland, since
Gormlaith was the wife of Niall Caille, king of Tara. This would mean
identifying the Gormlaith, daughter of Murchad, entered here with Gormlaith,
daughter of Donnchadh, who died in 861 (*AU*). Gormlaith, daughter of Murchad, was wife of Brian.

invading Leinster. The issue, as Mac Neill points out,[1] concerned sovereignty over Leinster: should it go to the Uí Néill or to Cashel? The king of Osraige (whose allegiance *AU* claimed for the Uí Néill in 859) was fighting on the side of Munster. It looks as if Munster ambitions had been once more revived.

AI and *AU* present very different claims in the ninth century. If we had a set of annals for the south as full as the Annals of Ulster we might be as impressed by Munster's claims to overlordship in the ninth century as we are by the expanding power of the Uí Néill. At least we can see that such claims were being made, and that Munster's reading of political events was very different from that of the north.

In the northern annals we saw Armagh entering into close alliance with the Uí Néill overlords. The Munster annals show us some of the kings of Cashel joined to the abbacy of Emly. Feidlimid, whom *AU* describes as 'scribe and anchorite', had taken over the abbacy of Clonfert in 830 and the abbacy of Cork in 836. *AU* says nothing about this, but has a rather sinister entry in 836 to the effect that 'Dúnlang son of Cathasach abbot of Cork died without communion in Cashel'. Feidlimid's successor Ólchobar was already abbot of Emly when he took the kingship of Cashel in 848 and he died in 851 as abbot of Emly and king of Cashel. *AU* merely says 'king of Cashel'. We find that Cenn Faelad, king of Cashel from 861–72, died as abbot of Emly (again a detail which *AU* omits). Cormac, who became king in 901, was a bishop and celibate. These very laconic Munster annals tell us of the union of the kingship with the abbacy of Emly in the middle years of the century and show us a series of kings who were distinguished ecclesiastics.[2] Again, we can only regret that we have not the equivalent of *AU* for the southern half; yet in spite of their brevity, the Munster annals show us a province with somewhat different traditions of kingship from the north.

[1] *Phases of Irish History*, 260–1.
[2] Some of the minor kingdoms also seem to have had kings who were ecclesiastics; see *AI*, 929, a king of Ciarraige Luachra who was 'chief anchorite of Ireland', and 934 Rebachán, abbot of Tomgraney and king of Dál Cais.

v

What I have said so far may have given the impression that the Chronicle of Ireland was almost exclusively concerned with the Uí Néill and Ulster provinces. This would certainly not be true. I thought it might be worth while to extract the entries of Connacht and Munster interest from the annals, in an attempt to see what sources the Chronicle of Ireland drew on. Let us begin with Connacht.

The Chronicle of Ireland had a lot of entries about Connacht; not only about the Uí Briúin, whose lands lay along the upper Shannon, but also about the Uí Maine further south and about the Uí Fhiachrach. Many of the entries are about the internal affairs of Connacht, even down to such matters as 'a little battle' (*belliolum*) in 803 between the Sogen and the Maenmagh (both Uí Maine peoples).

The overwhelming majority of entries in the period, where we have the evidence to see, are in both *AU* and *AI*. Of the Clonmacnoise and Connacht entries I have counted between 741 and 766 (when *Tig.* stops), five are in *Tig.* alone, two in *AU* alone, the rest common. We can therefore be confident that the Chronicle of Ireland carried a lot of Connacht entries.

It was also interested in the houses of the Shannon–Brosna basin. When discussing the annals between c. 740 and 790 I said above that two main areas stood out among the entries on religious houses. One was the central east. My sketch map 4 shows the other main area. One notices immediately that all the houses on it are within easy reach of Clonmacnoise. Clonmacnoise is, moreover, one of the very few houses for which we have a continuous sequence of abbots.

If we take the entries for Clonmacnoise and Connacht, a steady rise in number begins c. 740. In the thirty years between 740 and 770 there are twenty-eight entries, evenly spread over the period. They increase in the 770s, rising to twenty in the 780s and sixteen in the 790s. The number of entries stays fairly high until about

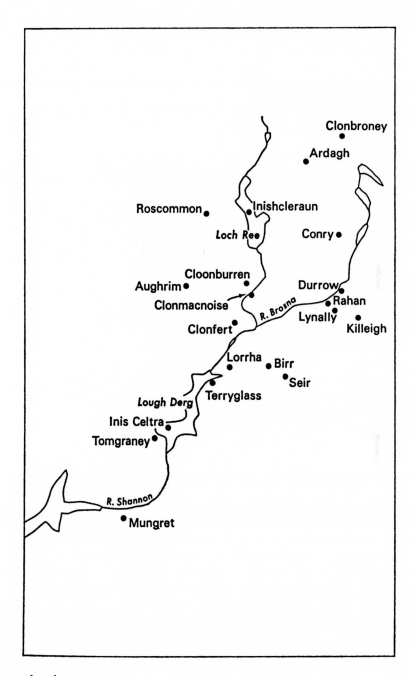

Sketch map 4

820. Then the position is confused by finding some of the entries only in *CS*. Was *Tig.* adding Connacht entries or was *AU* dropping them? Even with the *CS* evidence there is a fall-off in Connacht entries after 850.

Some of the entries from the mid-eighth century have a fair amount of detail, for example:

$=AU$ 755 The burning of Clonmacnoise on 21 March.

758 The battle of Druim Robaigh between the Uí Fhiachrach and the Uí Briúin, in which fell Tadhg son of Muirdebar and three grandsons of Cellach, Cathrannach, Cathmug, Artbran. Ailill, grandson of Dunchad, was victor.

764 The battle of Argaman between the family of Clonmacnoise and (the family of) Durrow, wherein fell Diarmait Dub, son of Domnall, and Dighlach, son of Dublis, and 200 men of the family of Durrow. Bresal, son of Murchad, remained victor, with the family of Clonmacnoise.

766 The battle of Sruthair between the Uí Briúin and the Conmaicne where great numbers of the Conmaicne fell and Aed Dub, son of Taichlech, was slain. Dubindrecht, son of Cathal, was victor.

778 Burning of Clonmacnoise on 10 July.

I am reluctant to express conclusions about Clonmacnoise, because a study of the *Annals of Clonmacnoise* (which I have not made) might alter the whole picture. But from *AU* and *Tig.* it looks as if regular annals were being kept for Clonmacnoise from the mid-eighth century.

Munster presents an even worse problem than Connacht. The trouble here is that a number of entries are found only in *Tig.*, some only in *AU*, and one cannot be certain whether or not these were in the Chronicle of Ireland. And the Munster entries peculiar to *AI* were almost certainly put in from some separate source. So in the tables below I have omitted entries only in *AI* and italicised entries which were definitely in the Chronicle of Ireland. It must be remembered that *Tig.* breaks off in 766, so that entries after this date, though they are not in italics, may have been in the common source.

Let us take first the period from 590–790. I want to see if the Chronicle of Ireland had access to Munster records. So I have left out of account all the entries which might reasonably find a place in an Uí Néill chronicle, i.e. all those affecting the houses of the lower Shannon, the kingdoms of Uí Fhailgi, Osraige and Uí Fhidgeinte and any references to kings of Munster. We are left with the following:

Cork *682*
Emly *781*
Lismore *592, 635,* 700 (*AU*), *703, 718, 746, 751* (*Tig.*), *753, 757, 760,*
    768 (*AU*), *781,* 783 (*AU*)
Ciarraige 742 (*Tig.*)
Corcu Laigde 751 (*Tig.*)
Déisi 667 (*Tig.*), 700 (*Tig.*) or 701 (*AU*), *732, 744, 751* (*Tig.*)
Iarmumu *690*
Uí Liatháin 750 (*Tig.*), 765 (*Tig.*)

The Lismore entries are impressive. We seem to have that uncommon thing, a complete list of eighth-century abbots. And there are a considerable number of references to the Déisi, in whose kingdom Lismore lay, plus two entries about the adjacent kingdom of Uí Liatháin. The late Père Grosjean, in a delightfully ingenious paper, showed that Lismore had a flourishing scriptorium in the seventh century.[1] The affairs of that monastery seem to have reached the records of the north.

If we take the period 790 to 913 in the northern annals, and again omit the Munster entries which an Uí Néill chronicler might readily have made, we have some coverage for Cork and Lismore throughout the period. Cork has nine entries, of which three are from *CS*; Lismore has five entries, including one from *CS*, Emly has four entries, beginning in 887. There are political entries at 804, 812, 823 (*CS*), 833, 836, 838, 848, 848 (*CS*), 850 (*CS*),

[1] 'Sur quelques exégètes irlandais du viie siècle', *Sacris Erudiri*, VII (1955), 67–98.

857 (*CS*), 864 (*CS*), 873 (*CS*), 876 (*CS*), 894 (*CS*), 907 (*CS*). It is noticeable that all the political entries after 848 are from *CS*. This means that they must have been in *Tig.*: a lot of them come at the ends of years. *AU*, though it retains an interest in the Shannon houses and in some north-Munster kingdoms after 850, is becoming a more local chronicle from about that date.

This evidence makes it likely that annalistic records were kept at Lismore at least as early as 700. The Chronicle of Ireland seems to have had access to Lismore records.

I would therefore offer the following tentative interpretation of the sources of the Chronicle of Ireland. The bases were an Iona Chronicle, probably contemporary from the later seventh century, and a Bangor Chronicle. These were incorporated into an Uí Néill chronicle, which I think started between 740 and 775. It was certainly contemporary by the end of the eighth century when the Brega-Uí Néill emphasis becomes fused with the interests of Armagh. Meanwhile Lismore had been keeping local annals from at least as early as 700. Clonmacnoise also had a chronicle, probably in the form of contemporary annals from the mid-eighth century. These were both incorporated into the Chronicle of Ireland. (If the fall-off of Connacht and Munster entries in *AU* about 850 has any significance, they may have been incorporated about then.) The Chronicle of Ireland was prefaced by some notes on the period before 585 (see below). I can hardly stress too strongly that the evidence for the sources of the Chronicle of Ireland is difficult to interpret, and interpretation, I am afraid, will always depend to a considerable extent on individual judgment. The views I have expressed are not final and may have to be revised as further work is published.

VI

You may wonder why I have left the entries before 585 until so late. It is because I think that many of them are late. If you compare *AU* and *Tig.* you will see that after 585 there is fairly close agreement between the two texts. Before 585 there is much greater diversity. If you take the period 488 (when *Tig.* begins) to 585 you will see that there is a common core of entries between *AU* and *Tig.*; but that, even in this common core, the texts are not in agreement about the order of events. Let us compare a few years in *Tig.* with similar entries in *AU*:

Tig.	*AU*
kl.	495
kl.	496, 498
kl.	497
kl.	—
kl.	501, 502
kl.	499
kl.	504
kl.	504
kl.	509
kl.	506, 507
kl.	512
kl.	506
kl.	512

This looks as if the scribes of the two recensions had little guidance in their exemplar about where to put the entries. I think that the Chronicle of Ireland must have had a series of notes and marginalia for the period before 585, not proper yearly annal entries.

Moreover, *AU* and *Tig.* seem each to have added a lot of entries after the recensions divided. Let us compare the entries of 650–700 with the entries of 500–585. In the later period just under two-thirds of the total entries are common to both manuscripts, just under one-sixth are peculiar to *Tig.*, a little over one-sixth are peculiar to *AU*.[1] In the earlier period just under half the total entries are common, about one-quarter are in *Tig.* and just over a quarter (some of which are duplicates) in *AU*. *AU* and *Tig.* are much less interdependent texts in the period before 585 than in the period after.

I am not sure how justifiable it is to regard *AI*'s evidence here,

[1] This hardly does justice to *Tig.*, since though it has fewer entries than *AU* it often gives more detail. The total sum of material peculiar to *Tig.* is probably greater than that peculiar to *AU*.

since it is such an abbreviated text. It may, however, be worth mentioning that between 488 and 585 *AI* has 98 entries of which only five are found in *AU* but not *Tig.*, and three in *Tig.* but not *AU*. There is very little in this early period in *AI* which is not also in both *AU* and *Tig.*

My conclusion is that the Chronicle of Ireland had notes and marginalia on the period before 585; that a lot of the material before 585 in our present annals was added after 913 when the texts of *AU* and *Tig.* diverged. The entries common to *AU* and *AI* and *Tig.* (when it begins in 491) were in the Chronicle of Ireland c. 913.

Here it is worth remembering Ó Máille's work on the language of *AU*. Before the late-sixth century, he said, the orthography of the entries is comparatively late, and can be shown in some instances to belong to the late-ninth century.[1] If my interpretation is correct some of it may be even later, though of course the compilers might have incorporated entries from some early source now lost.

The Annals of Ulster start at 431, but *AI*, after the loss of some leaves at the beginning, starts with God's promise to Abraham and goes on (with a further loss between c. 219 and 19 BC) down to the Council of Ephesus in 431. Then there is a list of high-kings compiled in the eleventh century (it ends with a king who died in 1022) followed by annalistic entries for the years 430–2. A different recension of the text is presented by *Tig.* I have not compared the texts in the pre-Patrician section. Professor Kelleher hopes to show 'that the apparent division at 430–1 is merely editorial and is quite late'.[2]

VII

What, then, is the historical value of the annals? The preceding sections should to some extent have cleared the ground. About half the total entries in *AU* and *Tig.* relating to the period before

---

[1] T. Ó Máille, *op. cit.*, 9.

[2] *Studia Hibernica*, III (1963), 125. R. A. S. Macalister discussed 'The sources of the Preface of the Tigernach annals', in *Irish Historical Studies*, IV (1945), 38–57.

585 were added after 913. I would hesitate to attach any importance to the dating even of the common core of entries before 585, for I think that the separate copyists after 913 fitted those entries in where they thought best. *AI* probably gives an impression closer to the Chronicle of Ireland for this early period than either *AU* or *Tig.* It records the conversion at 433, the death of Patrick at 496 and the obit of Iarlaithe, third abbot of Armagh, at 481. The difficulties of the Patrician dates are very well known.

H. M. Chadwick and T. F. O'Rahilly long ago pointed out the serious chronological dislocation in the fifth-century entries.[1] The death of Niall of the Nine Hostages is recorded at the beginning of the fifth century; the activities of his sons are at the very end of the fifth and the beginning of the sixth. Subsequent generations of Niall's family are chronologically consistent among themselves, but they require that Niall should be put considerably later.[2]

This does not mean that even before 585 the annals are useless. There were traditions of fifth-century battles. The men of learning probably memorised lists of kings in the right order. But chronology is a concept foreign to oral literature, and later historians had the job of fitting the information into a time sequence. As they came to the period when written records became more plentiful the reliability of their guesses would increase.

From 585 onwards the situation greatly improves. There were probably no contemporary annals until late in the seventh century, but there must have been earlier material to draw on. For instance, I would place a good deal of confidence in the Iona Chronicle and in the Bangor Chronicle after 585. Ó Máille showed that there were a lot of early forms among the names from 590 on, and this is what one would expect on other grounds.

I think that between 740 and 775 a set of Uí Néill annals becomes contemporary, and that from about 780 or 790 they were kept at Armagh. The chronicler had to provide an Uí Néill history for

---

[1] *Early Scotland* (Cambridge 1949), 135-6; O'Rahilly, *op. cit.*, 209 ff.
[2] There are similar problems about the Patrician dates, divided, as Mr Dolley points out to me, by a generation.

the seventh century. No doubt he had genuine records to draw on, for monastic *scriptoria* were flourishing in the seventh century. Our texts were subsequently interpolated. The interpolations may have been made from other early sources.

At about 913 *AU* and *Tig.* diverge. I am not sure when *AI* becomes independent. I am inclined to think that an early edition of *AU* and a Munster set of annals may have been conflated to provide the pre-972 section of the O'Brien annals, at some time after 972. But this whole question remains open.

We shall do well to remember that, while the jurist, the genealogist, the poet and storyteller all belong to a native Irish tradition of learning, the chronicler was following a completely foreign form. Pre-christian Ireland had no chronology. In the earliest stratum of the laws (as Professor Binchy points out to me) there is no trace of the week or of week-days; days are reckoned in tens, and were presumably counted on fingers. The whole idea of annals and chronicles was imported from outside, as was the Julian Calendar which made them possible. The language for a long time was Latin, and the conventions of reporting which the chroniclers follow are different from those of indigenous Irish scholarship.

I am afraid that there is no short cut to estimating the historical reliability of the annals. The method stated by Professor Kelleher and Professor Byrne, i.e., putting them alongside other contemporary material, is the only one. The trouble is that these scholars have both come to different conclusions. Their promised works will surely set out the evidence by which they reach their conclusions.[1] We need a lot more research into short periods of Irish history in which all the early evidence is put alongside.

In case at this point you are overwhelmed by scepticism, I shall conclude by looking briefly at the Anglo-Saxon Chronicle, for it presents comparable problems which have been much more thoroughly investigated.[2] The Anglo-Saxon Chronicle as it now

[1] See now Kelleher on the Uí Maine, *Celtica*, IX (1971), 61–112.
[2] Here I am indebted to Professor Whitelock. See the introduction to her translation of *The Anglo-Saxon Chronicle* (London, 1961).

exists was first compiled in the reign of Alfred, i.e., in the later
ninth century. Versions A, B and C are West-Saxon. The compiler
drew on annals for the first half of the eighth century for the
reign of Egbert and for the earlier part of Aethelwulf's reign. In
Stenton's view the annals on which the West-Saxon chronicle
were based began, at the earliest, in 670.

A version of the Chronicle reached the north in the later tenth
century, where it was conflated with a set of northern annals,
before it came back to Canterbury (after 1031) and in the twelfth
century reached Peterborough. This is version E. Another text of
this conflation received further additions in the late tenth or very
early eleventh century. This is version D. These two versions D and
E, and the twelfth-century *History of the Kings*, attributed to Symeon
of Durham, were using a fullish set of eighth-century northern
annals, which scholars agree were written contemporaneously.

The Anglo-Saxon Chronicle, though it was not compiled
until the late ninth century, allows us to reconstruct annals for
south-western and northern England which were contemporary
records for the later seventh and eighth centuries respectively.
This situation is not unlike that presented by the Irish annals.
The versions C, D and E of the Anglo-Saxon Chronicle, which
deal with eleventh-century affairs (A and B stop before this), show
a different political bias. We have already noticed the very considerable differences between the Uí Néill and Munster views of
ninth-century events. Anglo-Saxon historians are fortunate in
having an early manuscript of the Chronicle, the Parker manuscript of version A. This was written up to 891 in a hand of the
late ninth or very early tenth century and permits one to see the
interpolations made in the eleventh century. We may be certain
that comparable interpolations were made in the Irish annals
before the manuscripts of *Tig.* and *AU* were transcribed in the
fourteenth and fifteenth centuries.

The annalistic records for England are less full than they are for
Ireland.[1] The earliest traceable contemporary annals begin about

[1] We have clearly not talked about Irish annals nearly enough, when so
distinguished a medievalist as Professor Southern can say (*Medieval Humanism,*

the same time (the later seventh century) and the compilation which represents the existing annals can be seen with certainty at about the same date (the late ninth and early tenth centuries). Yet the most reliable English historians use the Chronicle for the period before the ninth century. Although Ireland has no Bede, she is rich in early source material. Professor Binchy rightly describes the annals as 'the most copious and reliable sources for the history of native Ireland for over a thousand years'.[1] Of all our historical sources they are the ones which most urgently need study.

VIII

I wanted to take one subject of importance in Irish history and discuss what the annals have to say about it. The obvious subject to choose would be the development of Uí Néill power, since this provides the connecting thread through the maze of the northern annals. The development of Uí Néill power in the pre-Viking period is also contemporaneous with the society laid down in the laws, and would almost certainly show us whether there is any substantial divergence between the theory and historical practice of kingship in this period. But it would be silly to try to give a very brief and impressionist sketch here of what Professor Byrne is about to do solidly and at much greater length; so I have decided instead to discuss the evidence which the annals offer about Viking raids and settlements.

This is now a subject of dispute. One point of view was put by Professor Binchy to the First International Congress of Celtic Studies, held in 1959. He believes that 'the Norsemen had a profound—one might even say a shattering—effect upon native Irish institutions', that most, if not all, of the 'radical transformations' which took place in tenth-century Irish society may be ascribed to the impact of the Norse invaders on the traditional

161) that the Anglo-Saxon annals are unique in western Europe as a vernacular record of contemporary events, and that to find a parallel we must go as far afield as *Russia*!

[1] In *Seven Centuries of Irish Learning*, ed. B. Ó Cuív (Dublin 1961), 59.

order.[1] With these views he entitles his paper 'The Passing of the Old Order'.

Professor Peter Sawyer's book on *The Age of the Vikings* (London 1962) has disputed many of the traditional viewpoints. His material is taken mostly from Scandinavian and English sources; nevertheless, he does not omit a preliminary consideration of Irish evidence and many of his conclusions apply to the Vikings in general. He believes that the Vikings, 'at least for some', were 'little more than a complication, an additional factor in the already confused world of quarrels and disputes'. The real difference in the violence of the Viking and pre-Viking age is that the Vikings regarded the Church as their main source of wealth, whereas the Irish or English had respected the Church in their wars: 'Churchmen apart, in the eyes of most men the Vikings were but a complication and for some a welcome one.' This explains why our view of the Vikings is so distorted. The contemporary writers were churchmen, and extremely hostile to the Vikings. 'The bias is often obvious and the exaggerations blatant'; we must beware of accepting their estimates on the size and destructiveness of Viking armies for want of anything better. What the Vikings desired most of all was land for settlement, land which, after the first raids, they were prepared to buy.[2] Our views on the character of the Viking occupation have in the past thus been seriously mistaken.

More recently Dr Lucas, Director of the National Museum of Ireland, has written two articles on the Vikings in Ireland.[3] Dr Lucas has not only seriously discussed his evidence, but has set it out in detailed indices. He argues convincingly that some of the acts of violence which took place within church enclosures were violations of sanctuary, when men who had sought protection there were 'taken out of' the monastery or killed at the door

---

[1] *Proceedings of the International Congress of Celtic Studies* (Dublin 1962), 119–32.   [2] *The Age of the Vikings*, 196, 143–4, 9, 198–9.

[3] A. T. Lucas, 'The plundering and burning of churches in Ireland, 7th to 16th century', *North Munster Studies*, ed. E. Rynne (Limerick 1967), 172–229; 'Irish-Norse relations: time for a re-appraisal?', *JCHAS*, LXXI (1966), 62–75.

of the church. He concludes that, between 600 and 1163, the Irish and the Norse shared an 'equal guilt and partnership in guilt' in the plundering and burning of churches. This contradicts Professor Sawyer's claim that Irish armies spared the churches and, unlike Professor Sawyer, Dr Lucas accepts the evidence of the annals as substantially accurate.

There are thus fundamental differences about how the evidence should be interpreted. There even seem to be differences between Professor Sawyer and Dr Lucas about what it says and how far it is reliable, even though these two scholars agree in opposing the traditional view. We have therefore to decide whether any significant change came about in the character and extent of violence in society with the Viking age. But first we need to consider whether the annals are distorted and biased accounts, for they provide most of our evidence about the Viking attacks.

By the Viking period I think that the annals were contemporary, though there must have been later interpolations. They were certainly kept by churchmen, but the interests of churchmen and laity were closely interlocked. We have already seen how Armagh identified herself with Uí Néill interests; how the ninth-century kings of Cashel were often abbots, how one was a bishop. Would king and abbot think very differently? According to the annals, the Viking attacks hit the monasteries extremely heavily; but this is very likely to be true.

What did the Vikings want? They wanted plunder, valuables. Some of these took the form of metalwork, with which the churches were well stocked. But, as Dr Lucas says, this was by no means all they looked for. Dr Lucas claims that laymen deposited their property, food, seed-corn, armour, for safekeeping in the church. There is good medieval evidence for this custom, though the early evidence is less clear.[1] The annals leave us in no doubt that there was one very valuable kind of plunder which the Scandinavians looked for, and that was people. The Vikings

---

[1] In the time of Edward the Confessor when war was imminent, the Welsh 'took their goods to the sanctuaries of the saints'. Life of Gwynllyw, ed. Wade-Evans, *Vitae Sanctorum Britanniae et Genealogiae* (Cardiff 1944), 186.

were slave traders, and the monasteries were centres of population. We read of 'a great prey of women' taken from Howth in 821, great numbers of the family of Armagh taken captive in 831, a great many captives from southern Brega in 836, the plundering of Louth from Lough Neagh in 840, when bishops, priests and scholars were carried off. These are the only people the annalist thinks worth mentioning, but presumably there were also more humble prisoners. In 964 Kildare was plundered by the Norse, but nearly all the clerics were redeemed by Niall Ua hEruilb; i.e., they were made captive and subsequently ransomed.[1] According to the annals the Vikings during their most violent period of aggression were looking for plunder; in particular, metalwork and prisoners were both of them valuable and portable.

Professor Sawyer claims that the figures given in the annals are exaggerated. We had better look at these. In:

837 there was a victory by the men of Brega over the Norse, in which 120 were killed;

848 a battle by the Uí Néill overlord, Máel-Sechnaill, over the Norse, in which 700 were killed;
A battle by the combined forces of Munster and Leinster against the Norse, in which 1,200 were killed;
A victory by the Eoganacht of Cashel over the Norse, in which 500 were killed;

866 Aed, king of Cenél Éogain and Uí Néill overlord plundered all the 'longports' where the Vikings had settled along the coast of north-eastern Ireland, carrying off spoils and flocks and herds. He won a victory over them at Loch Foyle and brought away 240 heads;

867 Another victory against the Norse with 100 heads;

868 A great host of Vikings is described as 300 or more;

869 In the plundering of Armagh by the Vikings 1,000 were lost between captives and slain;

917 In a battle between the Northern and Southern Uí Néill and the Vikings 100 men fell between them, mostly of the Vikings.

The figures go on in these dimensions. They are obviously round numbers, and there is a natural human tendency to exaggerate.

[1] All these references are from *AU*.

Nevertheless, the numbers are commensurate with the losses given for pre-Viking age battles on the rare occasions when these are quoted. In 764 there was a battle between Durrow and Clonmacnoise, when Durrow lost 200 men. The king of South Leinster supported Taghmon in a battle against Ferns in 817, when 400 were killed. The annalist regarded the Viking attacks as devastatingly violent, yet he quotes the slain in hundreds rather than in thousands.[1]

I would agree with Dr Lucas in thinking that the Irish annals are substantially accurate accounts. The figures may be somewhat exaggerated, but not wildly so. The Vikings had to eat, so they needed meat and corn; but according to the annals they were mainly looking for portable plunder, trading commodities such as metalwork and prisoners.

Are the Viking attacks significantly different from earlier violence? Dr Lucas says that they were not; Professor Binchy thinks that they were. According to the annals, what characterised the Viking attacks was their wholesale, universal aspect. No quarter was given, no respect paid to rank. When the Vikings had taken as much as they could, they would set the place on fire. It was a practice of deliberate destruction. Was this the case in warfare in the pre-Viking period?

Violence involving the Church is very much better documented than violence in lay society, so let us take the Church first. I do not think that the entries about burnings in the pre-Viking age tell us much that is relevant. As Dr Lucas says, these were sometimes accidental. For example, Armagh and Mayo were burned in 783, probably in the terrible lightning on Saturday, 2 August, which is recorded immediately afterwards (so the Four Masters understood); and Clonbroney was destroyed in the same storm. But sometimes the burnings were deliberate, as in 757, when Kilmore was burned by the Uí Cremthainn. On the vast majority of the occasions noted we do not know whether the burning was

---

[1] Compare the numbers of slain in mythological battles; see, for example, the 87,806 (not counting the common people) who fell in the Second Battle of Moytura!

accidental or an act of violence. Moreover these entries, as we have seen,[1] are recorded in spurts, not consistently, and there were probably many others which we know nothing about.

There are a number of occasions reported when monastic houses went to war with each other or took part in secular battles. I have already mentioned the battle between Clonmacnoise and Durrow in 764, and the battle between Taghmon and Ferns in 817. There was also a battle between Clonmacnoise and Birr in 760, another between Clonfert and Cork in 807, and in 824 (*AI*) a plundering of Tallaght by Kildare. One can hardly argue that both sides were the victims of violence. It also seems likely that monasteries occasionally took part of their own will in secular battles. Cork was involved in a major battle in 828 (*AI*); in the same year the king of South Leinster and Taghmon together fought the Vikings.[2] In 776 Durrow had been involved in fighting between the Uí Néill and the Munstermen; this may have been difficult for a border monastery to avoid. The majority of these battles look like deliberate acts, and, though the defeated side must have found them destructive (the nobles of the family of Cork were killed in 807), they do not seem to have had any major effect on culture or institutions.

There were also some monastic quarrels, like the battle in Ferns between the abbot and the steward (783), or the killing of a bishop by a priest in the oratory of Kildare (762). Sometimes these assumed larger proportions. In 793 it is possible that Dub-dá-leithe, abbot of Armagh and Faendelach, another claimant, may have been supported by secular powers, for a poem in the list of coarbs of Patrick says that Dub-dá-leithe 'is at hand with kings from the north'.[3] In 826 Éogan Mainistrech was driven from Armagh by the lord of Airgialla who set up his half-brother as abbot. Niall, king of Cenél Éogain, supported Éogan.[4] There

---

[1] *Supra*, 126.
[2] They had fought Ferns together in 817, so there may have been some link between king Cathal and Taghmon.
[3] Ed. H. J. Lawlor and R. I. Best, *PRIA*, XXXV C (1919), 322.
[4] *AFM*, 825, Cf. *AU*, 827.

was a major battle at Leth Cam between the Airgialla and Ulstermen on one side and Niall on the other. Éogan afterwards assumed the abbacy 'through the power of Niall'.[1] This did not protect him from profanation in 831 by Conchobar, king of the Southern Uí Néill, when his family were made prisoners and his herds carried off. Abbots clearly sometimes got involved in secular politics, and violence might result.

Of course it is not by chance that Armagh, Clonmacnoise and some other houses near the Shannon are mentioned so often in these reports of disturbances. Though such events are already fairly frequently reported in the annals, there must have been similar situations in other monastic houses which are not covered. Yet it is likely that they were all similar in character, and none of those I have mentioned is the kind of total devastation made by a Viking sack.

We also hear about attacks on individual clerics. Presumably this was in pursuit of some private quarrel. For example:

744 The slaying of the abbot of Seir. The slaying of Colmán, bishop of Lessan, by the Uí Tuirtri.

805 The killing of Cormac, abbot of Baslick, and the devastation of Ciarraide afterwards by Muirgis (king of Connacht).

Sometimes such actions met with revenge. In 809 Dúnchú, abbot of Telach-liss, was killed beside the shrine of Patrick in the abbot's house. Aed son of Niall (king of Cenél Éogain and Uí Néill over-lord) afterwards plundered Ulaid in revenge for the profanation of the shrine of Patrick. When the abbot of Rathboth was killed in 818 the family of Columcille went to Tara to curse king Aed, who must have been responsible for the killing. Monastic sanctuary might be violated in pursuit of revenge. Aed Roin was taken out of the oratory of Faughart to be killed in 735 (*Tig.*); Down-patrick was profaned and six prisoners tortured in 746. Churches might, however, succeed in obtaining compensation for violation of their sanctuary, as Tallaght did in 811 when the monks obtained many gifts from the Uí Néill.

[1] *AFM*, 825.

There is no shortage of entries like this before 831, but there are only five examples in *AU, Tig.* and *AI* of the plundering of monasteries which could compare in destructiveness with a Viking sack. In 780 Donnchad, king of Meath and Uí Néill over-lord pursued two Leinstermen and 'wasted and burned their territories and churches'. This looks like indiscriminate plunder. In 815 Cloncrew was plundered and a man killed there by the Síl-Cathail and the men of Breifni. In 779 there was a conflict in Clonard between Donnchad and the monastic family of Clonard. And in 822 and 830 Feidlimid, king of Cashel, burned Gailinne and Fore. In all these cases the churches were unwilling victims of secular violence. But such instances are very rare before 831.

We have to conclude that the monasteries were quite often involved in violence before 831. Sometimes they were willingly involved, taking a deliberate part in battles, presumably for their own advantage. Sometimes quarrels arose unexpectedly. Some-times clerics were hunted down and killed. Sometimes sanctuary was violated. A certain amount of damage must have been done in such incidents, but they seem to have had little effect on learning or art: scribes and craftsmen must have got their work out of the way. Institutions were unaffected: no one felt that these incidents dislocated normal life on a wide scale.

The annalists clearly felt that the Norse attacks were different. They were much more frequent, and they were wholesale. The Vikings were not hunting down individuals; they were rounding up the inhabitants, killing indiscriminately, sacking places. As against all the Viking attacks, between 831 and 880 (when the attacks of the Norse are easing off) there are five entries in *AU* about the deliberate plunder of churches by Irishmen. In:

> 833 Cellach son of Bran king of Leinster gained a battle over the church of Kildare, in which many were slain.
> Feidlimid king of Cashel killed the family of Clonmacnoise and burned its termonn[1] to the door of the church. He did the same to Durrow.

[1] The termonn is the area of inviolable sanctuary about the church.

850 Cináed king of Ciannachta joined the Norse against the Uí Néill
   and wasted their churches and territories from the Shannon to
   the sea. He burned the oratory of Trevet with 260 men in it.

874 Aed, Uí Néill overlord, on a hosting against the Leinstermen,
   profaned Killashee and other churches.

882 Flann, king of Meath and Uí Néill overlord, plundered Armagh
   when on a hosting to the north.

Although such cases may compare in destructiveness to Viking
attacks, they do not compare in extent. There are also occasional
reports after 831 about quarrels within the monastery, about
violation of sanctuary and violence against individuals. The battles
between monasteries apparently cease.

My conclusion would therefore be that there were very few
wholesale and indiscriminate attacks on churches by Irishmen
before 831, few even before 880. I agree with Professor Sawyer
that in the pre-Viking period Irishmen normally respected the
Church. This is in apparent contradiction to Dr Lucas's true
statement: 'On the 309 occasions on which ecclesiastical sites were
plundered between AD 600 and 1163, when the nationality of the
plundering party is known, the Irish were responsible on 139
occasions and the Norse on 140, while on nineteen occasions the
plundering was carried out by Irish and Norse in combination.
When the burners can be identified on the 313 occasions on which
churches or monasteries were burned during the same period, the
Irish were responsible in fifty cases, the Norse in thirty-seven and
a combination of Irish and Norse in five. Of the twenty churches
said to have been both plundered and burned in the same span of
years, twelve were maltreated by the Irish and seven by the
Norse.'

As everybody knows, figures have a way of proving different
things according to the way they are arranged. If we break these
figures down into periods, we can see certain developments taking
place. For this purpose I have used Dr Lucas's indices, where the
relevant figures include entries from *AU, Tig., AI, CS,* the *Annals
of Clonmacnoise, Three Fragments of Irish Annals,* the annals at the
beginning of the *War of the Gaedhill with the Gaill* and the *Annals of*

the Four Masters. The last text provides a large number of entries. I have tried to break the whole period down into round numbers. First comes the half century from 830 to 880. This is a period of intense Viking pressure. The raids get heavier in 831, and the Vikings put their fleets on the Boyne and the Liffey in 837. In the late '70s the pressure eases and there is about forty years of comparative calm, so my second phase is 880 to 920. During this period, in 902, the Dublin Vikings were heavily defeated by a combined army from Brega and Leinster, and 'escaped half-dead, having been wounded and broken'. In 914 a new fleet put in at Waterford. In 917 Sitric came to Dublin and in 919 Niall Glundubh, the Uí Néill overlord, was killed there in battle by them. There was now another period of about sixty years of Norse activity. All the same, the position had changed. The Norse had trading centres and warehouses which were vulnerable to Irish attack. And Uí Néill overlords now had behind them a century of increasing power. In 980 Máel-Sechnaill II, king of Meath, and Uí Néill overlord won a great victory over the Norse. 'Their power was banished from Ireland,' *AU* says, rather prematurely perhaps, and *AI* reports a great spoil, 'a measuring rod being required everywhere'. From this time on the Irish were definitely in the ascendant, though there were colonies of Norse still in Ireland. So my final period is 980 to 1170, since the Anglo-Normans arrived in 1169.

The figures from Dr Lucas's indices, arranged in these four periods, look like this:

	Plundering or burning (or both) by Irish	*Plundering or burning (or both) by Norse*	*Plundering or burning (or both) by Irish and Norse together*	*Plunderings and burnings by unidentified persons*
830–880	10	83	3	3
881–919	6	27	1	2
920–980	28	43	10	4
981–1170	152	37	13	162

We see here that Irish respect for Church property was gradually broken down. Until 880 the Vikings were by far the more destructive. By the tenth century Irish kings were often plundering monasteries in enemy territory. For example in 971 Domnall (king of Cenél Eogain and Uí Néill overlord) went on a hosting into Meath, when he spoiled all their churches and forts; in 984 (*AI*) Munster devastated Osraige and its churches and the churches of Leinster, in 993 (*AI*) the king of Osraige devastated the churches and forts of Meath. Most of the unidentified burnings and plunderings in the period 981–1170 must have been by the Irish. By this time the Norse were fairly quiet; at the end of the century they started to strike their own coinage, and they now had a great deal to lose. The evidence for Dr Lucas's statement comes mainly from the period after 980.

The evidence I have quoted so far relates mainly to churches, though some of the entries concern the plundering of whole areas, *etir cella ocus tuatha*. Warfare was endemic in early Irish society. Nevertheless, the Viking kind of warfare was more 'total' than the Irish of the earlier period. As Professor Binchy says,[1] pre-Viking warfare 'followed a curiously ritual pattern'. Various rules were observed: territory was normally not annexed, nor were lands confiscated, tribal dynasties were not dethroned, neutral zones were usually observed and the king's death ended the battle. Viking warfare had no such taboos.

The physically destructive character of attacks by the Vikings themselves on the Irish kingdoms must not be overestimated. The worst period lasted only fifty years. Ireland was so decentralised that she could not be conquered by a few; and the Norse, who had already settled in the Northern and Western Isles of Scotland, would have needed far greater numbers than they possessed to colonise Ireland *tuath* by *tuath*. There is no evidence that in Ireland they wanted land for settlement. They wanted, and secured, trading bases, and their settlements were confined to a few great ports and to coastal strips.

Certain changes were occurring in Irish society at this period,

[1] *Proc. of the International Congress of Celtic Studies*, 128.

which the historian has to account for. We have seen how, in the tenth century, Church property ceased to be regarded as a neutral zone, and the Irish took to waging war *more gentilico*. Development in the secular law ceases; the tracts become fossilised. In the field of ecclesiastical law the *cána* come to an end in 842; laws aimed at protecting non-combatants and Church property from violence must by then have seemed hopeless. There is a decline in manuscript art and metalwork after the mid-ninth century: the major advances of the later ninth and early tenth centuries are in stone building and sculptured crosses, both media more or less impervious to damage by violence. As Professor Binchy says, a revolution in the ownership of land began in the tenth century, which finally resulted in the dispossession of many hereditary families.[1] A great development in overlordship took place: small *tuatha* were further weakened and only overlords could usually raise forces powerful enough to defeat the Vikings in major battles. In this same period a few very powerful monastic *paruchiae* emerge head and shoulders above the rest. Their climb to eminence had started before the Vikings arrived, but it was probably helped by the elimination of competitors.

You need some major sociological impact to account for all these changes. The Viking depredations do account for them, and are the only thing I know of which does. So I think that we are right in seeing the ninth and tenth centuries as 'the Viking age'. It is however true that in the eleventh and twelfth centuries violence to churches by the Irish did not prevent the production of fine books and metalwork. This needs explaining.[2]

[1] *Proc. of the International Congress of Celtic Studies*, 128.
[2] Were the centres of production now confined to a few great houses?

Appendix: The Genealogies

There are genealogies of thousands of Irish families in a number of big manuscript compilations. Genealogical material includes not only the pedigrees and kindreds ('branching relationships') traced back to a common ancestor, but also king-lists, origin legends, poems and other anecdotes. A ninth-century poem on a Leinster prince named Aed shows that it was proper at a feast to recite panygyrics and genealogies in honour of the patron. The last stanza reads:

'At ale poems are chanted: fine (genealogical) ladders are climbed: melodious bardisms modulate through pools of liquor the name of Aed.'[1]

The genealogies must have been originally the preserve of the secular men of learning, but monastic *scriptoria* came to be interested in them also. The Psalter of Cashel (now lost), written at the beginning of the tenth century, contained genealogical lore, and the twelfth-century monastic compilers included such lore in their collections.

The first half of the present century saw the edition of several genealogical papers, but the real breakthrough came in 1962 with M. A. O'Brien's edition of the genealogies from Rawl. B 502 and the Book of Leinster.[2] He also provided variant readings from the Book of Lecan (early fifteenth century), the Book of Ballymote (fourteenth century) and Laud Misc. 610 (fifteenth century). This edition has over 300 pages of indices, but no introduction or translation.[3] It is a mine of source material which very few people know how to use.

---

[1] Stokes and Strachan, *Thesaurus Palaeohibernicus*, II, 295.
[2] For these two MSS, see *infra*, 274–6.
[3] *Corpus Genealogiarum Hiberniae*, I (Dublin 1962).

Appendix: The Genealogies

Mac Neill,[1] Miss Dobbs,[2] and more recently Professor Byrne,[3] Professor Kelleher[4] and Dr Ó Corráin[5] have provided some historical criticism of the genealogies. Some very important points emerge from their work. There is some ancient material in the genealogies. Scholars in the eighth century seem to have been busy compiling a genealogical scheme from earlier written sources. We can recognise that these existed because the scheme they produced has discordances and anomalies, and, had they been inventing without regard for tradition, they would presumably have drawn up a more coherent account.[6]

Professor Kelleher shows that the way in which the genealogies are arranged in Rawl. B 502 reflects the dominance of the Uí Néill kings. He suggests that the scheme was drawn up about the mid-eighth century, or a little earlier. Miss Dobbs argued that the Dál Fiatach genealogies were compiled in the second decade of the eighth century;[7] Professor Byrne proposes c. 730 or a little earlier as the date for the Dál Fiatach tract in LL and Laud.[8] This is also a period of activity in annalistic writing. There seems to have been a re-working of some earlier genealogical plan towards the end of the eighth century.[9] Again, this is precisely the period when the annals were taking shape under the influence of Armagh.[10] The early article by Mac Neill also argued that at the close of the tenth century someone at Armagh compiled genealogies which included mainly eighth-century material. That text, with later additions, was the source of the Laud tract.

It looks, then, as if the annals and the genealogies took shape at

[1] 'Notes on the Laud genealogies', ZCP, VIII (1912), 411–19. See also Celtic Ireland (Dublin, London 43–63), and T. F. O'Rahilly, EIHM, 266–9, 412–18.
[2] ZCP, XIII (1921), 308–59; XX (1935), 1–29; XXI (1940), 307–18.
[3] ZCP, XXIX (1964), 381–5 (review of M. A. O'Brien); 'Tribes and Tribalism', Ériu, XXII (1971) 128–66.
[4] 'The Pre-Norman Irish genealogies', IHS, XVI (1968), 138–53; 'The rise of the Dál Cais', NMS, 230–41.
[5] Éigse, XIII (1970), 226.   [6] Kelleher, IHS, XVI (1968), 144.
[7] ZCP, XIII (1921), 312.   [8] ZCP, XXIX (1964), 383.
[9] Kelleher, IHS, XVI, 147: 'During or not long after the reign of Donnchad mac Domnaill, c. 770–97.'
[10] Supra, 129 ff.

the same period, both using earlier written sources. After this there were attempts every now and then to bring large portions of the genealogies up to date. They became cumbersome and were abridged. As Ireland moved towards territorial kingships ruled by a single family, a genealogy with many 'branching relationships' became less necessary: what people now needed was chiefly a pedigree of the royal line.[1] This means that the genealogies are much more useful for the elucidation of the annals in the earlier period than they are in the later. By the twelfth century the genealogies seem to have comparatively little relationship to historic facts: people who are important in the annals often do not figure in the genealogies, while some unimportant tribes are given quite a full record. It was antiquarian, not political, interests which dictated the recording of the genealogies in the twelfth century.

At periods when the genealogies were being composed or rewritten they often reflect contemporary political conditions. Dr Ó Corráin has cited a number of examples of how the genealogy of a subject people might be attached to that of the people ruling over the territory in which they were resident.[2] Professor Kelleher indicates the importance of the genealogies in demonstrating the declining fortunes of the Eoganachta and the rise of the Dál Cais in the tenth century.[3] This kind of enquiry needs to be pursued.

A book like this ought to have a chapter on the genealogies comparable to the one I have just written on the annals. But the subject needs a lot of preliminary research, which I have not done. When that has been completed we shall know more about some of the people named in the annals, and much more about how political alignments changed during the period which we are considering. Professor Byrne says: 'Next to the annals, the great genealogical collections represent one of the most important primary sources for early Irish history.'[4] It may be a true claim, but it has not yet been demonstrated.[5]

[1] Kelleher, *IHS*, XVI, 151-2.   [2] *Éigse*, XIII (1970), 226.
[3] *North Munster Studies*, 234.   [4] *ZCP*, XXIX (1964), 381.
[5] See now Kelleher, *Celtica*, IX (1971), 61-112.

CHAPTER 5

Secular Literature

I

They were clerics who drew up the ecclesiastical legislation and annals, who composed the varied works of ecclesiastical learning and the hagiography which I shall discuss in the next two chapters. But Ireland had another class of learned men, the *filid*, usually translated as 'poets', though this is very misleading, since much of their literature is in prose. Etymologically the word probably means 'seers', and they were analogous to the *wātes* whom we see through Roman eyes in Celtic Gaul. The pagan priests in Ireland were replaced by Christian clerics, but the *filid* survived. In the Early Christian period they were still respected;[1] in the seventh and eighth centuries they enjoyed a high status, for one law tract divides them into seven grades, the highest grade (the *ollam*) having an honour price equal to that of the bishop and petty king. Their long education was separate from that of the monastic schools and their learning belonged to a different tradition. They were the guardians of Ireland's past, its 'historians', the men who remembered, recited and taught genealogies, lore of various kinds, mythological and heroic tales, antiquarian tradition. The bards, of lower status, sang praise-poetry or satire; though it seems that as time went on their functions were taken over by the *filid*.[2] The secular men of learning thus provide some of the sources of Irish history.

The panegyrics, 'history' and tales which have survived from our period were, until the end of the twelfth century, recorded in

---

[1] *Supra*, 77.

[2] See G. Murphy, 'Bards and *filidh*', *Éigse*, II (1940), 200–7. Professor Caerwyn Williams has recently argued that the *filid* may have composed praise poetry in the early period (in a British Academy lecture, not yet published).

the monastic *scriptoria*. Between the twelfth and seventeenth centuries the recording of the tradition passed to the great bardic families, under the patronage of lay lords. Most of the manuscripts they wrote are still in Ireland, and many of the separate texts have been edited and translated. We have to examine the claims of some of this literature to be considered as history. It may be easiest to consider first the place-lore, then the various cycles of tales; for it is said that Irish mythology tells us about pagan gods and prehistory, that the Ulster cycle is a window on the Iron Age, that the legends relating to the historical period throw light on the origins of peoples, on battles and historical characters. The *filid* have preserved a mass of literature about the past. What did their title of 'historian' amount to?

II

The Irish have always had an intense interest in actual places. The *dindshenchus*, 'tradition about places', tells how places got their names. There are pseudo-etymological explanations, but many of the stories are folk-lore, tales of the heroes of the mythological cycle of the People of the Goddess Danu.[1] It is now generally agreed that these People are the gods of pagan Ireland, who, legend says, when the ancestors of the present inhabitants arrived, retired underground into mounds, tumuli, caves and deep waters. So it is not surprising that the place-lore should be built up around them.

When I first went to the Dingle peninsula twenty years ago I was astonished and impressed by the remarkable knowledge of place-lore which some of the local farmers possessed. Every hill, cave, and bay had its legend, whether mythological, heroic, early Christian or sixteenth century (for one of the ships of the Spanish Armada came to ground here). This is the survival of the *dindshenchus* of the early period. Place-lore was once part of the common stock of knowledge of which the learned man, the *fili*,

---

[1] There is an important essay on 'The Metrical Dindshenchas' by Mrs M. O'Daly in *Early Irish Poetry*, ed. J. Carney (Cork 1965), 59–72.

was master, and which he had to be able to produce for instruction and entertainment.

The place-lore is in various versions. The prose *dindshenchus* appears to belong to the earliest part of the Middle Irish period, perhaps between 950 and 1000.[1] The metrical versions[2] are mostly of the tenth, eleventh and twelfth centuries.[3] There are a few legends about what seem to be pseudo-historical persons, like that trader Breccán who gave his name to Breccán's Cauldron near Rathlin Island, who was drowned here with fifty ships.[4] There is a long (and unique) eleventh-century account of one of Ireland's great fairs, the fair of Carman in Leinster, which began on 1 August (the feast of Lugnasad) and continued for a week. The place-lore tells what went on there; about horse-races, promulgation of law and judgments, discussion of the tribute due from the provinces, the recitation of stories, royal genealogies and panegyrics, entertainment of all kinds.[5] This sounds like an idealised picture, which may not bear a strict relation to the *oenach* of fact,[6] but it at least tells us what the poet thought a great fair ought to be like. Mrs O'Daly draws attention to the reference, 'perhaps the earliest we have', to the poet's practice of composing lying in the dark.[7]

Sometimes the *dindshenchus* allows us to see what antiquities were visible round about the tenth century and later. There is a list of 'Tara's remarkable places', with a considerable amount of topographical detail.[8] It is difficult to fit the archaeological evidence together with the written account. From the air a multitude of sites may be seen. The Rennes *dindshenchus* names forty-

---

[1] Ed. and trsl. W. Stokes, 'The Bodleian Dinnshenchas', *Folklore*, III (1892), 467–516; 'The Edinburgh Dinnshenchas', *ibid*. IV (1893), 471–97; 'The Prose-tales in the Rennes Dindshenchas', *Reveu Celtique*, XV (1894), 272–336, 418–84; XVI (1895), 31–83, 135–67, 269–312.

[2] Ed. and trsl. E. Gwynn, *The Metrical Dindsenchas*, 5 vols, Todd Lecture Series, 8–12.

[3] M. O'Daly, *op. cit.*, p. 62.

[4] *MD*, IV, 80 ff.   [5] *MD*, III, 2–25.

[6] See Binchy, *Ériu*, XVIII (1958), 125.   [7] *MD*, III, 110.

[8] *Revue Celtique*, XV (1894), 280–9.

two of these, and seems to move roughly from south to north. Ó Ríordáin's discussion locates only some, and there is disagreement about some identifications.[1] But at least the *dindshenchus* shows how Tara and its legend appeared to an early compiler.

Since the placelore provides us with a great many names, this is perhaps a suitable place to mention place-name studies, so important a tool for the historian. I have done no work at all on place-names and speak only at second hand. Early in this century the late Canon Power collected thousands of place-names of the baronies of Decies (modern Co. Waterford) from local speakers and translated them into English.[2] Many of the names from manuscripts and printed texts were collected by Edmund Hogan, with some references to his own sources, and identified with modern place-names.[3] This book is an indispensable work of reference, but it is what it claims to be, an index with identifications. Modern scholarship may be said to begin with Liam Price,[4] but a lot of preliminary work has still to be done. Early forms of names must be assembled before it is possible to see whether these fall into clearly defined groups, or how they are distributed on the map. Mrs Flanagan is at present working on the *domnach* names, which Armagh in the late seventh and early eighth centuries was claiming as Patrician foundations.[5] She has very generously allowed me to use her unpublished distribution map of *domnach* names, based on Hogan. This shows a very heavy concentration in the north and in Brega, with a few outliers in Leinster, Munster and Connacht. It proves conclusively that the *domnach* names are to be associated with the church of Armagh, which the eighth-century annals showed to be interested in Brega,[6] and that they cannot be connected with any (hypothetical) pre-Patrician Christianity entering from the south. The majority of these names in the north

[1] S. P. Ó Ríordáin, *Tara* (Dundalk 1957), 10–13.
[2] *The place-names of Decies* (Cork 1952, 2nd edition).
[3] *Onomasticon Goedelicum* (Dublin 1910).
[4] See especially *The Place-names of Co. Wicklow* (Dublin 1945–58).
[5] D. Flanagan, 'Ecclesiastical nomenclature in Irish texts and place-names: a comparison', *Tenth International Congress of Onomastic Sciences*, 379–88.
[6] See *supra*, 124–6, 132–5.

are to the west of Lough Neagh. This looks like an early Church in the heart of ancient Ulster, in modern Londonderry, Tyrone, Armagh, with further foundations in modern Meath, Co. Dublin and north Kildare. Did the influence of ancient Ulster extend south of the Boyne? When Muirchú was determined to have Patrick accepted by the Uí Néill in Brega,[1] it looks as if he had good grounds for his interests in that area. Although since 1964 there has been an Irish place-name society journal,[2] no one has yet been able to undertake any general study of Irish place-names. Mrs Flanagan's work on the *domnach* names shows how much historical evidence may be hidden in studies of separate name-forms.

The traditional literature on place-lore contains scraps for the historian, but at present it is mainly a quarry for the anthropologist. Here we meet the fertility goddesses. All the great meeting places of Ireland were under their protection. Taill-tiu cut down a wood so that it became a plain of blossoming clover and her heart burst at the effort: the games are held in her honour on the feast of Lugnasad.[3] Tlachtga bore three sons at one birth and was buried at the assembly place.[4] Macha, pregnant, was forced to race the king's horses outside Emain Macha, bore a boy and girl thereafter, and died:[5] she was buried at Armagh.[6] There are also sacred trees, like the tree of Tortan near Ardbraccan, which fell in the time of the sons of Aed Sláine (seventh century).[7] This tree is mentioned by Tirechán in the late-seventh century.[8]

Sacred trees and fertility goddesses leave their reflections in the historic period. Some monastic sites are associated with sacred trees. The Dál Cais had their sacred tree at Mag Adair, which was cut down by Máel-Sechnaill overlord of the Uí Néill in 982, an action which may have been a deliberate violation of the rival

[1] *Infra*, 231.   [2] *Dinnshenchus*.
[3] *MD*, IV, 146 ff., slightly differently in *Revue Celtique*, XVI (1895), 50–1.
[4] *MD*, IV, 186–90. Also *Folklore*, IV, 490–1, *Revue Celtique*, XVI, 61.
[5] *MD*, IV, 308 f., *Folklore*, IV, 480–1. This is one of the explanations.
[6] *MD*, IV, 130.
[7] *MD*, IV, 240 ff. See also tree of Mugna, *Revue Celtique*, XV, 419–20.
[8] Stokes, *Vita Tripartita*, II, 330.

monarch's attributes.[1] Even in the historic period the inauguration rite of a king may have retained some of the elements of fertility ritual. It is called his *banfheis rígi*, his 'wife-feast of kingship', and in it he was wedded to the goddess.[2] As late as 1310 the inauguration of a king of Connacht is described as 'the most splendid kingship-marriage ever celebrated in Connacht'.[3]

III

The tales of the mythological cycle tell us comparatively little about fertility goddesses, much more about the chieftain gods and the goddesses of war. You can meet many of them in The Second Battle of Moytura,[4] Nuada, Lug, Ogma, the Dagda and the goddess Morrígan. That story, in its present form, is a composite work, put together by an eleventh- or twelfth-century redactor, mainly from ninth-century material. It is a good story in its own right, though it loses impetus towards the end and tails off into a series of incidents.

The Christian Irish euhemerised their pagan gods, turning them into previous inhabitants. When the People of the Goddess Danu arrived, Ireland was already occupied by two peoples: the Fomorians, those native powers who had been driven to the limits of the land by successive invaders, and the Fir Bolg. The People of the Goddess fought and defeated the Fir Bolg (that is what the First Battle of Moytura is about), and they made an alliance with the Fomorians. From it were born Bres and Lug (the latter descended on his father's side from the leech of the People of the Goddess, on his mother's from Balor, whom O'Rahilly saw as a

---

[1] *AI, AFM*, 982. See P. Mac Cana, *Études Celtiques*, VIII (1958), 62–3.

[2] See O'Rahilly, *Ériu*, XIV (1940), 14; J. Carney, *Studies in Irish Literature and History* (Dublin 1955), 334 ff.; Binchy, *Ériu*, XVIII (1958), 133–5. Cf. Gerald of Wales account of the inauguration rite of a king of Cenél Conaill, *PRIA*, LII (1949), C 168, trsl. J. O'Meara, *Topography of Ireland* (Dundalk 1951), 93–4.

[3] For references see M. Dillon in *Mediaeval Studies presented to Aubrey Gwynn*, ed. J. A. Watt, J. B. Morrall, F. X. Martin (Dublin 1961), 186–202.

[4] Ed. and trsl. W. Stokes, *Revue Celtique*, XII (1891), 52–130, 306–8.

sun-god). As Bres grew up they made him their king, but he proved an oppressor, and the Second Battle of Moytura saw the defeat of the Fomorians.

Its theme is the fight between the forces of chaos and the gods. The chieftain-gods figure prominently, as the champions and protectors of their people. Mlle. Sjoestedt argues very persuasively that the Irish gods do not seem to have had specific functions.[1] The Dagda, the 'good god', is good at everything, Lug is the 'Many Skilled' (*Samildánach*). Nevertheless one cannot help noting that Lug secures entrance to Tara precisely because he is the *only* one of the chieftain gods who possesses all the arts together: the rest are a smith, a brazier, a wright, a leech and so on. Some of the gods are craftsmen. In the historic period the possession of an art gives status: in the mythological tale it is, in some cases, an attribute of divinity.

The mythological cycle tells us who were the pagan gods and a little (not much) about their attributes. Dr Anne Ross's work on *Pagan Celtic Britain*[2] has provided material illustration for some Celtic deities, while Dr Máire Mac Neill's study of the *Festival of Lughnasa*[3] (at the beginning of harvest) shows the continuity between pagan and Christian rituals. But there are still plenty of possibilities for differing interpretations, and this evidence provides us with nothing like a statement of pagan belief. To appreciate even such material as it does provide demands the training of an anthropologist rather than that of a historian.

The late O'Rahilly was interested in Irish mythology and legend primarily as a source for pre-history. Early Irish historians wrote of the various invasions of pre-historic Ireland in the 'Book of the Taking of Ireland'.[4] O'Rahilly's *Early Irish History and Mythology* provides a reconstruction of the successive invasions of pre-historic Ireland.[5] According to O'Rahilly the first recorded invasion was

[1] M-L. Sjoestedt, *Gods and Heroes of the Celts*, trsl. M. Dillon (London 1949), 14 ff., 38 ff.
[2] London 1967.   [3] Oxford 1962.   [4] *Infra*, 281–3.
[5] See the review by M. Dillon, *Speculum*, XXII (1947), 652–5. It is quite true that many of O'Rahilly's theories about pre-historic Ireland are not

by the Priteni, who spread over Britain and Ireland, and whose name survives in the Cruithin. The second was by the Fir Bolg who, 'there cannot be any doubt', were an offshoot of the Belgae,[1] and who invaded Ireland from Britain. O'Rahilly dates this invasion to about the fifth century BC. These people were also called the Érainn, and spread widely over Ireland. The third invasion was by the Laginian peoples and their kindred the Domnainn and Gálióin. The Domnainn 'it is hardly open to doubt' were a branch of the Dumnonii of Devon and Cornwall.[2] The Laginian tribes came from Amorica, invaded Ireland and Britain more or less simultaneously,[3] and in Ireland settled mainly in Leinster and Connacht. This invasion seems to have occurred in the third century BC. All these, according to O'Rahilly, spoke a p-Celtic language. The last invaders, the Goidels, were q-Celtic speakers. They came directly from Gaul. O'Rahilly seems to suggest three different dates for their arrival: early in the second century, not long before the beginning of the Christian era or between 150 and 50 BC. The latter date seems to be his ultimate conclusion.[4] It took centuries to complete the Goidelic conquest, and it was not until 516 that the plain of Meath was wrested from the Laigin (the date is from the annals). The changes in the Irish language which took place in the fifth and sixth centuries were probably accentuated by the adoption of the Goidelic speech by the native inhabitants.[5]

This provides us with an ingenious guide through a mass of legend. But for all its expertise and erudition, the historian remains unconvinced. For instance, though archaeologists are not in

taken seriously by scholars, but I find that the book is a stumbling-block to undergraduates, so I shall set them out briefly here.

[1] O'Rahilly, *op. cit.*, 54. This is because of the forms of the names. But Professor Dillon (*op. cit.*) regards this as one of O'Rahilly's 'not always fortunate' excursions into linguistics.

[2] *Ibid.*, 93–4.

[3] *Ibid.*, 419. O'Rahilly recognises that the Irish colonists who came later to the Dumnonian peninsula were from the south. Some were of the Uí Liatháin, not a Laginian people.

[4] *Ibid.*, 154, 207, 208, 420.   [5] *Ibid.*, 495.

agreement about when the Belgae invaded Britain, it would seem to be somewhere around the first century BC, not the fifth century, and they never got beyond south-east England. There are distinctive elements in their culture which can be clearly recognised in Southern Britain at sites like Aylesford and Swarling. O'Rahilly dismisses this,[1] saying that 'the much earlier occupation of Ireland by Builg from Britain suggests plainly that there were Belgae in northern Gaul' (and presumably in Britain) 'centuries before Caesar's time'. But the presence of the Belgae in Ireland is what he is attempting to prove. We should expect to find archaeological evidence of their settlement, cremation burials, well-equipped with gravegoods, including wheel-made pottery. There is none of this in Ireland, no known *oppida* of the Belgic kind. We have only a few isolated objects of about the turn of the Christian era which suggest contacts with southern Britain, such as the Keshcarrigan bowl and the mirror handle from Ballymoney, Co. Antrim. These are not enough to support the theory of a Belgic invasion.

O'Rahilly sees evidence for the Laginian invasion in the story of The Destruction of Da Derga's Banqueting House.[2] The site is in north Leinster. 'When we subtract from the tale its obvious mythological accretions', O'Rahilly interprets this as an account of an attack by a force of Laginian invaders on a king of the Érainn. But, in the story, the attacking army of the British prince Ingcél is almost annihilated, and Ingcél *goes back to Britain*. If there is any factual basis to this story it could have been provided by any British raid on Ireland.[3] 'As spectators before a dimly-lit stage,'

[1] In his Additional Notes, 456–9. He says that the British Brigantes belonged 'beyond question' to the Belgic section of the population of Britain (p. 34). This is contradicted by the archaeologists.

[2] Edited by E. Knott, *Togail Bruidne Da Derga* (Dublin 1936). For translation see W. Stokes, *Revue Celtique*, XXII (1901), 9–61, 165–215, 282–329, 390–437.

[3] O'Rahilly's claim that 'The Destruction of Dind Ríg' is another account of the Laginian invasion has the support of a postscript that Labraid went into exile, gained a kingdom as far as the Ictian Sea, and returned with 2,200 warriors with spears (*cosna laignib*), from which the Laigin are named. But this is just an ingenious explanation to which no historical weight can be attached.

says O'Rahilly, 'we have been able to discern, through the mists of the centuries, the actors in the drama of the Laginian invasion of some 2,000 years ago'.[1] The story of Da Derga's banqueting house was compiled in the eleventh century from two ninth-century manuscripts. O'Rahilly puts the Laginian invasion in the third century BC. We are therefore being asked to believe that the memory of the invasion lasted orally for twelve centuries.

O'Rahilly dates the Goidelic invasion very late. Here one must take into account that by the fifth century Ireland seems to be thoroughly Goedelicised. The people who went from north-eastern Ireland to Scottish Dál Riada spoke a Goidelic, not a p-Celtic, language. Ogam inscriptions, in a script brought by the Goidelic invaders, are most thickly scattered in the southern territories of the Érainn. Is 450 years a long enough time to allow Goidelic culture to spread throughout Ireland?

O'Rahilly's reconstruction involves a highly selective use of sources which a historian could not possibly apply to any normal historical evidence. When he detects Mac Neill in comparable actions, O'Rahilly scathingly condemns his 'arbitrary excisions'. Perhaps the only way to make *historical* sense out of Irish mythology is to reject what does not fit a hypothesis, but this cannot be a proper use for a historian to make of his material. If the historian turns to mythology as a source for Irish pre-history he will inevitably find himself in a Celtic twilight.

IV

With the Ulster Cycle we come into a society with a definite political context. There are certainly still mythological elements, less pronounced in the longest tale, The Cattle Raid of Cooley (*Táin Bó Cualnge*), than in some of the other tales, such as Bricriu's Feast.[2] O'Rahilly viewed the characters as euhemerised

---

[1] p. 140.
[2] Ed. and transl. G. Henderson (London 1899). One MS, written about 1100, has a scribal gloss: 'For at that period among the Ulstermen Conchobar was a god upon earth.'

deities.[1] Professor Jackson, though he makes no claim that the characters are historical, argues that the Ulster cycle depicts a real, not a mythical, society, which is pagan and heroic. Military prowess, courage, and honour are the primary requirements; the warriors, armed with spears and javelins, sword and shield, are driven to battle in their chariots by their charioteers. It is similar to the society we can see in pre-Roman Gaul.[2]

The Cattle Raid of Cooley shows us institutions with which we are familiar in the historic period such as clientship and fosterage, but the political situation of Ireland is quite different. In the story the four provinces of Ireland, led by Connacht, are ranged against Ulster.[3] The Ulster of the saga is a very much bigger province than the Ulster we know. Its capital, Emain Macha or Navan, lies in historic Airgialla. Conaille Muirtheimne, Cú Chulainn's own homeland (which is part of Ulster), is in modern Co. Louth, with its border on the Boyne. It is the men of Brega who provision him in his battle. The Uí Néill, who dominate the northern half of Ireland in the historic period, are not on the scene yet. It seems incredible that a later story-teller should have invented this setting to the story, a setting both unfamiliar and consistent: it must represent the situation at some period before our earliest historical records.

The story of the Cattle Raid of Cooley is early. Thurneysen thought it might have been recorded in the mid-seventh century.[4] It was known in the first half of the eighth century, and our earliest recension is a conflation of two ninth-century versions. This is version I, contained in a manuscript written about 1100 (*Lebor na hUidre*). Version II, the later version, is in the Book of Leinster.[5]

[1] *Op. cit.*, 271.

[2] See K. Jackson, *The Oldest Irish Tradition* (Cambridge 1964).

[3] O'Rahilly identifies the original Connachta with the midland Goidels (*op. cit.*, 172 ff) and would have it that the real struggle was between Ulster and Tara. But Cruachain in the west is the capital of Connacht in the saga, and the four provinces of Ireland are said to be attacking Mag Breg in which Tara stands.

[4] *Die irische Helden- und Königsage* (Halle 1921), 99–112.

[5] Ed. C. O'Rahilly, *ITS*, 49 (Dublin 1967).

The scribe who copied it added: 'A blessing on everyone who shall faithfully memorise the *Táin* as it is written here and shall not add any other form to it.' How far beyond the seventh century does the tradition go back? Oral tradition will only last a certain length of time, but, in Ireland, where there was no Roman conquest, the Iron Age lasted into the Christian period. Professor Jackson would put the formulation of the story (and of course the political set-up which it envisages) as not demonstrably earlier than about the fourth century AD.[1] The traditional date is about the turn of the Christian era.

The archaeological evidence relating to conditions depicted in the *Táin* needs to be considered. The use of chariots in war went out on the continent before the time of Caesar, though when he landed in Britain in 55 BC he met the custom there. The Caledonians used chariots against Agricola in AD 84 and the Picts were still using them early in the third century. These are all references from Roman literary sources.[2] There is some evidence for paired-draught in Ireland, very tenuous from the third century BC to the first century AD, more substantial between the first and fourth centuries.[3] The horse-bits show that horses were being used in pairs to draw a wheeled vehicle, though there is no evidence for war-chariots. The fine metalwork of the La Tène period, particularly the sword scabbards, could fit the context of the sagas, but the descriptions there are not sufficiently scientific to use this evidence with much assurance.[4]

A fairly recent interpretation of the archaeological finds emphasises the difference between the northern third of Ireland (roughly the old Ulster) and the rest.[5] Mr Etienne Rynne shows

[1] Jackson, *op. cit.*, 43–54.

[2] See Jackson, *op. cit.*, 33–5 for references.

[3] E. M. Jope, 'Chariotry and paired-draught in Ireland during the early Iron Age', *UJA*, XVIII (1955), 37–44.

[4] E.g., Will a sword two feet long, weighing little more than a pound, cleave a man in two from the head down with one stroke? See Jope, *op. cit.*, 39.

[5] E. Rynne, 'The introduction of La Tène into Ireland', *Bericht über den V. Internationalen Kongress für vor- und frühgeschichte, Hamburg, 1958* (Berlin 1961), 705–9.

that La Tène objects with British affinities are found in the north and in east central Ireland, though with a few outliers. La Tène objects with continental affinities would seem to have entered Ireland via the west and perhaps south-west. There is a group of them in Connacht. The objects with continental affinities seem to date to the late-third century BC, those with British affinities mainly to the late-first century BC and the first century AD. Even in the historical period the archaeological scene in the north differs from that elsewhere in Ireland, for in the north they cooked in hand-made, flat-bottomed pots known as 'souterrain ware'. These are absent from the rest of Ireland. When the tales distinguish between Ulster and the four other provinces of Ireland they are marking a difference which seems to have solid archaeological support. It is a constant feature of parts of the *Táin* and of the general Ulster hero tradition that 'the men of Ulster' are on one side and 'the men of Ireland' (i.e., the rest of Ireland) are on the other. This language would be natural in the mouths of people whose ancestors had come from outside Ireland, and who still remembered in some sort that they were not 'men of Ireland'.

Mr Dudley Waterman's excavations at Navan have provided new material of great interest, but have added to the puzzles of the historian.[1] The Iron Age phases at Navan begin with fairly modest houses. These were succeeded by a massive circular timber structure made of four concentric rings of posts, definitely not domestic but probably ritual in purpose. Round about 265 BC (the dating is by radiocarbon process) this was buried under a cairn and the timber of the outer wall destroyed (probably deliberately) by fire. This site therefore looks like the ceremonial centre of the kings of Ulster. But the *Táin* speaks of Emain Macha as a residential centre, a place where the king lived surrounded by his court and where the boys played on the green. Of course the whole of the eighteen acres of enclosure has not been excavated. Another site within it (site A) has been uncovered, but turned out to be a couple of ordinary houses. The Loughnashade trumpet from the foot of Navan hill may be part of a ritual deposit. The

[1] See *Current Archaeology*, No. 22 (Sept. 1970), 304–8.

fine brooches previously found on Navan hill may belong to either a ritual or a royal site. So far archaeology has revealed the House of the Red Branch as a sanctuary, and the domestic site which the tales also suggest has received no support.

It is possible, on present evidence, that before Ard Macha became a religious city it was a secular site. It is named, like the sanctuary two miles away, after the pagan goddess Macha. A ditch has recently been excavated here to the south of the grave-yard wall.[1] This ditch round the hilltop of Armagh seems to have been in existence by the end of the third century AD, for the date found by radiocarbon from the ditch bottom is AD 290.[2] It was out of use by the sixth century.

Presumably the siting of the ecclesiastical city of Armagh is significant, for it must have been near the secular capital or the ceremonial centre of Ulster.[3] After it was founded Ulster contracted, and that contraction is probably reflected in the fate of Patrick's relics. Whoever compiled the Book of the Angel (in the late seventh or early eighth century) maintained that Patrick was buried at Armagh (now no longer in Ulster).[4] But in the appendix to Muirchú's Life there is some embarrassment about who has his body. As the day of his death drew near Patrick desired to go to Armagh, but the angel Victor ordered him to return to Saul. He was buried in Downpatrick (i.e., in Ulster). But there was strife between the Ulstermen and the Uí Néill about his relics. The trouble was settled by a delusion, for the Uí Néill thought that they had carried off the body.[5] The obscurity which surrounds Patrick's cult between the fifth and the seventh centuries may well be due to a period of dislocation in the history of northern Ireland.

In the historic period we find the Uí Néill and their kinsmen

[1] Mrs Cynthia Gaskell Brown and Mr A. Harper are publishing a monograph on this subject.

[2] *Current Archaeology*, No. 24 (Jan. 1971), 29.

[3] Cf. Binchy, *Studia Hibernica*, II (1962), 149–50.

[4] See Hughes, *CEIS*, 278 for translation.

[5] Ed. W. Stokes, *Vita Tripartita*, II, 295–300; translated N. J. D. White, *St Patrick, his writings and Life* (London 1920), 104–9.

settled in the northern half of Ireland, with Ulster confined to Antrim and Down and the extreme north of Co. Louth. According to the genealogies, the Uí Néill derived their descent from Niall of the Nine Hostages, the Connachta from brothers of Niall, the Airgialla from three Collas, who were cousins of Niall's grandfather, Muiredach.[1] They were thus all of common stock. Legend says that it was the three Collas who made sword land of central Ulster. They lived for a time in Tara as champions of their cousin the king Muiredach, but as their children increased in number they foresaw rivalry with Muiredach's descendants. So Muiredach sent them north into Ulster, where, with the alliance of the Connachtmen, they conquered and settled Airgialla. O'Rahilly would have it that the three Collas were really the three sons of Niall of the Nine Hostages,[2] i.e., the great-grandsons of Muiredach. These three, Éogan, Conall and Énda are said to have conquered and settled the lands of the Northern Uí Néill. How much confidence can be placed in such origin legends is one of the many problems which await scholars who will work on the genealogies. Uí Néill origins involve the vitally important historical question of the date when Ulster ceased to be the dominant power in the north, a process in which the fall of Emain Macha must have been a crucial event. The Irish men of learning put it at various dates between AD 281 and 450. Professor Binchy pointed out that Emain must still have been flourishing when Armagh was founded. There are also indications that the conquest took much longer than later historians would have us believe, for the Cruithin seem finally to have lost their lands west of the Bann in 629. Professor Byrne thinks that until the battle of Mag Rath in 637 Ulster remained a serious threat to Uí Néill supremacy.[3] It seems likely that the political context so consistently indicated in the Ulster cycle survived into the beginning of the historic period, and that the Uí Néill conquest took considerably longer than later Irish historians believed.

---

[1] For a genealogical tree making this clear see M. A. O'Brien, 'The Oldest account of the raid of the Collas', *UJA*, II (1939), 170–7.

[2] *Op. cit.*, 228–30.   [3] F. J. Byrne, *Studia Hibernica*, IV (1964), 84.

V

The legends about historical characters would all need to be examined individually to see if they add anything to our historical knowledge.[1] Some are obviously late, at any rate in their present form. For example, the story of how Niall (in the fifth century) won the sovereignty of Ireland finishes with a reference to king Máel-Sechnaill, who died in 1022. This story is based on a mythological theme—the hideous old hag who, when she is not disdained by the young warrior (Niall), turns into a beautiful woman, the personification of the sovereignty of Ireland, which she grants him.[2] In another story Niall's name 'of the Nine Hostages' is explained: he holds five hostages from Ireland, and one each from Scotland, the Saxons, the Britons and the Franks.[3] This seems to represent a political situation later than Niall's day. He is seen raiding not only in Leinster but as far away as the Alps, though this may mean, by confusion, *Alba*, i.e. Britain. He was killed by a Leinsterman, among the Picts according to one tradition, and his body was brought back to Ireland. I just do not know whether there is any historical core in such legends. But the fact that legends gather around certain people almost certainly is significant.

The people who composed these 'historic' sagas were not writing history as we understand it. There were certain things they had to explain to their audience—names, proverbial phrases, ties of kindred and so on. But they cared very little about chronology. For example the Tale of Cano son of Gartnan makes Cano, who died in 688, the nephew of king Aedán who had died eighty years previously.[4] This Aedán in the story attacks Cano and Cano

[1] For the historical cycle see M. Dillon, *The Cycles of the Kings* (Oxford 1946), where a number of the stories are summarised and translated.

[2] Ed. and transl. W. Stokes, 'The Adventure of the sons of Eochaid', *Revue Celtique*, XXIV (1903), 190–207.

[3] 'The Slaying of Niall of the Nine Hostages', ed. and transl. K. Meyer, *Otia Merseiana*, II (1901), 84–92.

[4] *Scéla Cano meic Gartnáin*, ed. D. Binchy (Dublin 1963). For chronology see pp. xviii ff. It is translated into German by Thurneysen, *Zeit. für romanische Phil.*, XLIII (1924), 385–402.

flies to Diarmait and Bláthmac kings of Tara. These two kings died in 665 and the annals give Cano's voyage to Ireland in 668. Cano is supposed to have joined Diarmait in a battle against Guaire of Connacht which took place in 649. These are the kinds of anachronisms which one must expect to meet in 'historical' sagas.

Even when the story-teller is recounting a famous historical event he is not much interested in royal policy. The battle of Allen may have been a decisive event in the fight for supremacy between Cathal, king of Munster, and Fergal, overlord of the Uí Néill. Cathal had harried Brega (*AI*, 721, *AU* and *Tig.*), Fergal harried Leinster (*AU*, *Tig.*, 721), the saga says 'to injure Cathal'. According to *AI* (not *AU*) Fergal then submitted to Cathal. The battle of Allen took place the next year and the saga says it was an attempt to impose submission on Leinster by Fergal.[1] But this is almost all the saga tells us of politics. The hero of the story is Donn-bó, the king's bard. The king asks for entertainment from him the night before the battle, but Donn-bó does not feel in the mood to give it. However, he promises that whatever place the king is in on the next night he will entertain him.

In the battle next day Fergal and Donn-bó were both killed. That night the Leinstermen were feasting and king Murchad sent a warrior out to fetch an enemy head from the battlefield. When he came to the battlefield the warrior heard Donn-bó making music for his lord. He took Donn-bó's head instead of Fergal's, for the bard would save his lord from this indignity. It was put up on a pillar, and the Leinstermen demanded music. Then Donn-bó turned his face to the wall so that it might be dark to him and he sang so that all the host were weeping and sad. Later the warrior returned Donn-bó's head to his body and the bard was restored to life. According to the saga Cathal was angry with the Leinstermen for breaking his peace with Fergal and he subsequently marched against Leinster and defeated her. The annals say that this was in 735, i.e., thirteen years after the battle of Allen. Although we have here a fairly early account (probably going

[1] Ed. and trsl. W. Stokes, *Revue Celtique*, XXIV (1903), 41–67.

back to the ninth century) of a fairly late event which must have been of national importance, the story-teller shows very little interest in the historical implications of his tale. The relationship between Donn-bó and his lord, the singing of the severed head, were what would grip the fancy of his audience.[1]

The historical sagas have received comparatively little attention.[2] Professor Ó Cuív has suggested that much of the pseudo-historical literature of the eighth, ninth and tenth centuries was composed to support Uí Néill claims. Further study of the sagas might throw light not so much on the events they relate as on the interpretation which Irish historians put on those events in the context of their own day.

VI

The Irish story-teller was trying to entertain an audience, to tell a good story. He might claim to be reciting history, that is, events which had happened in the past; but he was not attempting to weigh up the pros and cons of a situation, assess his material critically and reach an unbiased conclusion. He was reciting within certain conventions, and one of these was exaggeration. He also had to give his audience what it liked to hear of—deeds of prowess—for he told stories for the aristocracy, who admired the heroic virtues of honour, courage and generosity. So the literature will provide a social history of Ireland. If you have been disappointed by the amount of direct historical information which emerges from the place-lore and tales, consider now what they tell about the audience.

One of the most successful of the tales is about the boyhood deeds of Cú Chulainn. It begins like this:

[1] For the cult of the severed head see A. Ross, *Pagan Celtic Britain*, 121 ff.
[2] For some illuminating comments see B. Ó Cuív, 'Literary creation and Irish historical tradition', *PBA*, XLIX (1963), 233-62. Professor Ó Cuív thinks that the task of isolating fact from fiction in the historical tales would be long and tedious, but rewarding.

The stories of the boys in Emain were told him, for there are a hundred and fifty boys there at play ... Now Cú Chulainn begged his mother to let him go to the boys. 'You shall not go,' said his mother, 'until you have an escort of the champions of Ulster.' 'It is too long, I think, to wait for that,' said Cú Chulainn. 'Tell me in what direction Emain lies.' 'Northwards yonder,' said his mother, 'and the journey is difficult,' said she, 'Sliab Fuait lies between.' 'I'll make an attempt at it so,' said Cú Chulainn.[1]

So, in spite of his mother's attempts to put him off, Cú Chulainn set out with his playthings, his toy shield and spear, his playing-club and ball. He joined the boys without realising that he should first have his protection guaranteed, and they all set on him. They threw their spears and balls and hurling-clubs, but he warded them all off and was seized with a hero's contortions, and the hero's light rose from his head. He overthrew fifty of the boys and pursued others into the fortress of Emain, leaping over the chess-board of Conchobar as the king sat at play. Conchobar asked what the trouble was about, and himself undertook the protection of Cú Chulainn; but the little boy insisted that the youths should also be placed under *his* protection! In Version II this all happened when the child was five.

Later (in Version II when Cú Chulainn was six years old) Conchobar went to a feast prepared by Culann. He asked the little boy to accompany him, but Cú Chulainn was playing and said he would follow. When Conchobar came to the house, Culann wanted to know if anyone was still to come, and the king, forgetting about the boy, said no. So Culann let out his savage watch-dog to guard the place. The little boy came along at last, playing with his toys to shorten the way:

The hound attacks him ... and he did not interrupt his play though the hound was making for him ... Now when the hound came at him, he throws away his ball and his club, and tackles the hound with his hands; he puts one hand to the hound's throat and puts the

---

[1] *Lebor na hUidre*, ed. R. I. Best and O. Bergin (Dublin 1929), 153; transl. L. W. Faraday, *The Cattle-Raid of Cualnge* (London 1904), 17–18.

other to the back of its head. He strikes it against a standing stone beside him so that every limb of it sprang apart.[1]

The story goes on with Culann's regret for the loss of his valuable hound and Cú Chulainn's judgment: a pup of the hound's breeding to be reared, and until it is mature the boy himself will guard Culann's herds. This is how he got his name, 'the hound of Culann'.

These two short incidents well illustrate some of the conventions of the Irish story-teller. The audience must have liked the spirited dialogue, the ironic understatement, the careless courage and gaiety of the little boy, the savage details,[2] the sheer impossibility of his feats. And if the tables could be turned on an opponent in a single twist, as in the Tale of Mac Dathó's Pig,[3] so much the better. The confrontation here between Cét and Conall must have been greeted with a roar of applause.

The values of this society, which emerge in the literature, were the heroic ones of honour, courage and generosity. When, in the twelfth century Colloquy of the Ancients, Patrick asks Caílte, 'Was he a good lord with whom you were; Finn mac Cumaill that is to say?' Caílte replies:

> 'Were but the brown leaf
> Which the wood sheds from it, gold,
> Were but the white billow silver,
> Finn would have given it all away.'

And when Patrick goes on, 'Who or what was it that maintained you so in your life?' Caílte answers:

---

[1] *Lebor na hUidre*, 157-8; Faraday, *op. cit.*, 24-5.

[2] I am not sure how far this implies a violent background to life. If a historian in 1,500 years time has to base his conclusions on contemporary novels he might get some very distorted ideas about, say, the sexual habits of the majority of present-day citizens.

[3] *Scéla Mucce Meic Dathó*, ed. R. Thurneysen (Dublin 1935). This story is evidence for the archaism of the Irish tradition, since the contest for the champion's portion, which forms its subject, took place also among the Gaulish Celts. See J. J. Tierney, 'The Celtic ethnography of Posidonius', *PRIA*, LX (1960), C 202.

'Truth that was in our hearts, and strength in our arms, and fulfilment in our tongues.'[1]

These are some of the most admired heroic qualities. The ideal
hero gives a fair judgment, as the boy Cú Chulainn does when he
has killed the hound of Culann. The ideal hero sticks to his
bargain, as Cú Chulainn does in Bricriu's Feast. A hideous giant
comes to the hall of Emain and boasts that the world over he
cannot find anyone brave enough to accept his challenge; it is to
cut off a warrior's head tonight and let the warrior cut off his the
next night. After some discussion he agrees to reverse the order,
and one of the Ulster heroes, Munremar, strikes off his head. But
the giant picks it up and walks out of the hall. When he returns
the next night Munremar refuses his part of the bargain. It is not
until the fourth night of his return that Cú Chulainn is in the hall
and beheads him, but Cú Chulainn meets the giant on his return:
'Death awaits me, and I would rather have death with honour.'
The giant's descending axe makes a noise like a wood tossed in a
storm, but he brings it down on the blunt side and proclaims Cú
Chulainn worthy of the champion's portion of Ulster.[2]

The stories tell us what the Irish audience appreciated and found
amusing. They also provide examples of Irish institutions.
Hospitality is constantly mentioned. The Ulstermen, 'if they have
no dry cows will kill their milch cow for companies and satirists
and guests for the sake of their honour.'[3] This is an expression of the
ultimate act of generosity in a pastoral society, though I doubt if
one should take too literally such statements of economic suicide.
The nearest we come in historic fact to the Dagda's never-empty
cauldron is the *briugu* (brewy), equal in honour-price to the petty
king. 'He repels no condition of person. He refuses no company.'
One class of *briugu* has 'an ever-stocked cauldron'.[4]

The first satire in Ireland was said to have been caused by a

[1] S. H. O'Grady, *Silva Gadelica* (London 1892), I, 96; II, 104.

[2] G. Henderson, *Bricriu's Feast*, 116–28.

[3] C. O'Rahilly, *Táin Bó Cualnge* (Book of Leinster version) (Dublin 1967),
41, 80.

[4] *ALI*, V, 76–8. Mac Neill, *PRIA*, XXXVI (1923), c 276.

failure in hospitality. It is told in The Second Battle of Moytura that a poet came to the house of Bres. 'He entered a cabin narrow, black, dark, wherein there was neither fire nor furniture nor bed. Three small cakes and they dry were brought to him on a little dish. On the morrow he rose and he was not thankful.' Then he uttered the first satire to be made in Ireland, and ill-luck was on Bres from that time. Satire brought bad luck in the stories and in the historic period it was a social weapon, for the satirised man could not ignore it.[1] The Irish aristocracy lived very much in the public eye, and their reputations were an important possession. It was only when Medb sent her satirists to Fer Diad that he would consent to fight with Cú Chulainn, 'for the sake of his honour ... for he deemed it better to fall by shafts of valour and prowess and bravery than by shafts of satire and reviling and reproach.' The dramatic quality of this encounter was enhanced by the fact that both Fer Diad and Cú Chulainn had the same foster mothers, for the ties were close between foster brothers, or between foster parents and children.

The heroes in the stories are sometimes to be seen seeking 'protection' (*faesam, commairge*).[2] Of course it was of no use to seek protection from an inferior: this is why Cú Chulainn insisted that the youths on the green at Emain should come under his protection.[3] To contravene protection was a life and death matter. Three of the heroes of Ulster guaranteed their protection to the sons of Uisliu before they would return with Deirdriu to the court of Conchobar; but when the sons of Uisliu were treacherously killed and the three heroes' protection and honour violated, they were so enraged that they attacked Emain and afterwards left Ulster for the court of Ailill and Medb of Connacht. We have already seen the annalists' horror when the king of Cianachta was

---

[1] A man could lose his honourprice by not giving a pledge after he had been satirised (*CG*, lines 304–5). This ranked with false witness, default of suretyship, etc.

[2] See Binchy, *CG*, 106–7; *Contrib. to a Dict. of the Irish Language*, relevant fascs.

[3] *Supra*, 183.

killed in 851, 'in spite of the guarantees (*di foesmaib*) of the nobles
of Ireland and the coarb of Patrick'.[1] An individual was normally
under the protection of his family, and children could be adopted
into the *fine* by special contract. The extent of 'protection' which
a man might confer varied with his rank.[2]

In this heroic society of violence and honour it is surprising to
find the theme of love, though it is the griefs of love which are
emphasised, not its joys, as in later European literature. They are
present here in Deirdriu's lament for Noisiu.[3] They are in Créde's
love song for Dínertach, beginning: 'These are the arrows that
murder sleep.'[4] But probably the most moving of all is the lament
of Líadan the nun for the poet Cuirithir, whom she refused:

> Joyless is the thing I have done. I have angered the one I loved.
> It would be madness not to do what pleased him were it not for
>   fear of the King of Heaven.
> Do not hide it! He was my heart's love, though I had loved every
>   one else beside.
> A blast of flame has pierced my heart. Most certainly, it will not
>   endure without him.[5]

In another poem the Old Woman of Beare, in old age, looks back
on the time when she was loved by kings.[6] Whereas heroic ideals
are universal in the Latin west, in the extant literature love poems
are highly unusual before the twelfth century. The fact of their
survival emphasises the independence of the Irish tradition.[7]

The love poems bring us near to the tragic theme which, in
spite of the rumbustious comedy of some Irish literature, is never

---

[1] *Supra*, 132.

[2] For these and other references see under *faesam, Dictionary*.

[3] *Longes mac nUislenn*, ed. and transl. V. Hull (New York 1949).

[4] K. Meyer, *Ancient Irish Poetry* (London 1911), 63–4; or D. Greene and F.
O'Connor, *A Golden Treasury of Irish Poetry 600–1200* (London, 1967), 78–80.
(These editors think the lament should be put into the mouth of Guaire's wife.)

[5] The first and last two stanzas, transl. Greene and O'Connor, *op. cit.*, 74.

[6] *Ibid.*, 48–55.

[7] Anglo-Saxon literature very occasionally depicts the woman divided
from her lover, for example in the Exeter Book fragment now generally known
as Wulf and Eadwacer. For early nature poetry, see *infra*, 202–4.

far in the background. Death was always near; violent, painful and harrowing. If it came to the warrior in a contest of honour it was welcomed as glorious. But death might come with the elements of tragedy, by jealousy, misunderstanding or blind fate. The story of how Rónán killed his son is such a situation and it ends in a holocaust, Rónán's young wife having induced him, through a lie, to slay his son.[1] Moreover the Irish hero was surrounded by magical taboos, and he might be placed in situations where it was impossible not to contravene them. In The Destruction of Da Derga's Banqueting House the dramatic quality of the story gathers pace as Conaire one by one contravenes his taboos, moving inevitably towards disaster.[2] Even in the historic period a king might still have had his traditional taboos (*gessa*) and the things it was lucky for him to do (*buada*). When the tract on the taboos of the kings was transcribed in later medieval manuscripts it must have been a record of antiquarian lore; but the language of the prose may be Old Irish and the tract shows some Christian influence. The *buada* of the King of Munster are:

> to despoil Cruachain (the capital of Connacht) at the call of the cuckoo; to burn the Laigin to the north of Gabair; to chant the passion in Lent in Cashel; to travel over Sliab Cua with a company of fifty after pacifying the south of Ireland; to go with a dark grey army on Tuesday across Mag nAlbe.[3]

If the kings follow these taboos and prescriptions they will live to old age without misfortune or disturbance, plague or pestilence. In actual fact a run of bad luck, disease, failure in battle, was likely to lead to a king's overthrow.[4]

A consciousness of the supernatural must have pervaded early

---

[1] This story is partly translated by D. Greene in *Irish Sagas*, ed. M. Dillon (Dublin 1959). The lament of Ronan is translated in *A Golden Treasury*, 96–7. It is edited by D. Greene, *Fingal Rónáin and other stories* (Dublin 1955).

[2] *Supra*, 173, note 2.

[3] For this tract see M. Dillon, *PRIA*, LIV (1951), C 1–36.

[4] See the career of Aed Alláin, introductory chapter by Hughes in J. Otway-Ruthven, *A History of Mediaeval Ireland* (London 1968), 13–14.

Irish society. The story-tellers move from reality to magic as if they do not recognise any boundary. There are visitors from the *síd*, a man may enter a fairy dwelling, or have a fairy lover.[1] The poet was also a 'seer', so that vision and prophecy were his proper medium. In the historical sagas and saints' Lives the writer seems sometimes unable to distinguish fact and fiction, in the religious literature he is close to the powers of the spiritual unseen. This is the tradition in which he lived. The Irish audience did not ask, as we do, 'Is this story true?' meaning 'Is it literal fact?' They wanted to be amused. They wanted their heroes to behave well. And sometimes they wanted to share an experience of beauty, which might mean entering a world of enchantment.

The quality of some of this literature is a historic fact. The Irish aristocracy were used to good stories and they had a professional learned class whose business it was to provide them. It is also a fact that the learning of the *filid* belongs to a tradition different from that of the Latin learning introduced with Christianity, even though the monks transcribed their stories and panegyrics and may have recited them to each other (for the devout and ascetic monks of Iona in the seventh century did not hold themselves aloof from the songs of the poets).[2] The *Táin* itself is consistently pagan. One early ninth-century panegyric in praise of Aed, lord of a kingdom with its northern border on the Liffey, shows us how deeply rooted in the past was the panegyric poetry.[3] Aed is extolled for his noble lineage, for his hospitality, for his reputation as a fighter. There is no trace of Christian influence anywhere in this poem; in fact, the bard wishes 'every good to him of gods or ungods', exactly the old blessing of the pagan sagas.[4]

The secular literature is the necessary background to Irish social history. It shows that although Irish society shared many ideals in

---

[1] See G. Murphy, 'Notes on Aisling Poetry', *Éigse*, I (1939), 40–50.

[2] In Adamnán's seventh-century Life of Columba, I, 42, the monks ask the saint: 'When the poet Crónan was leaving us, why did you not *according to the custom* ask for a song of his own composition, sung to a tune?'

[3] *Thesaurus Palaeohibernicus*, ed. W. Stokes and J. Strachan (Cambridge, 1903), II, 295.

[4] Reading *cach maith do dé no anddae*; cf. LL *Táin*, 57, 197.

common with other heroic cultures it had definite points of difference. Its professional learned class was more highly evolved than that of Anglo-Saxon England. The stories have striking archaisms, which take us back to descriptions of the pre-Roman Gauls. The institutions of fosterage and surety and of satire as a legal weapon are peculiar. Ireland was cultivating love poems and love stories[1] within her heroic literature long before the twelfth-century renaissance.

Always the historian must bear in mind the interpenetration of myth and reality. As Mlle Sjoestedt remarks, the Romans thought of their myths historically but the Irish thought of their history and geography mythologically. When records belong to a Latin tradition, as the annals do, this is not apparent, but as soon as we come to narrative sources such as later saints' Lives and historical sagas, we must expect to find conventions similar to those observed in the secular tales.

The genealogies and placelore were 'history' to the Irish poet. He venerated the past and strove to perpetuate it, though he was not above improving on it when the occasion demanded. The tales were primarily good stories. As one item in a fifteenth-century manuscript says, they are not the truth but something like it.[2] They should be read first and foremost as literature.

[1] And nature poetry: see *infra*, 202–4.
[2] Quoted by B. Ó Cuív, *PBA*, XLIX (1963), 238.

CHAPTER 6

Ecclesiastical Learning

I

I have already discussed, or will discuss, two of the major classes of literature which monastic men of learning were composing, those are the annals and the saints' Lives. Much of their other work is of less direct use as historical evidence, and one chapter on it is bound to be superficial.[1] But historians need to know something about the intellectual life of the period they are considering. So here I shall try to indicate what were the main intellectual interests of Irish scribes, giving references to some of the books they were composing, touching on the characteristics and quality of their learning.

These men had to learn Latin. Latin presented difficulties, as a language with a very different structure and word-order from their own. We have some text books from which Irish masters taught: the Würzburg glosses on the Pauline Epistles are generally dated about the mid-eighth century, the Milan glosses on the psalms about 800, and the MS of the St Gall Priscian 845.[2] Anyone who starts to learn Old-Irish today will probably use these books. They were annotated not only with glosses, but with a series of construe-marks to help the master guide his Irish-thinking pupils through the unfamiliar Latin. For example, Latin is based on the period, whereas a long Irish sentence is a chain of short ones, so that students badly needed guidance in linking the various elements in a Latin sequence. The Irish students found difficulty with the relative pronoun, for Irish has almost no relative pronouns and it marks relativity through altering the verbal forms;

[1] Kenney's 800 pages are devoted to this subject.
[2] These glosses are edited by W. Stokes and J. Strachan, *Thesaurus Palaeo-hibernicus*, 2 vols (Cambridge 1901-3); Supplement (Halle 1910). See also R. Thurneysen, *Old Irish Reader*, transl. D. A. Binchy and O. Bergin (Dublin 1949). For grammatical MSS circulating in Ireland see Kenney, *Sources*, 674 ff.

so construe marks often link the relative pronouns in Latin to their antecedents. Professor Maarte Draak has demonstrated Irish teaching methods in two fascinating articles;[1] a page of the St Gall Priscian interpreted by her shows an Irish master at work with his class, making sure not only that his pupils were able to translate a particular text, but also that they understood the structure of the language.

These manuscripts belong to the period of the Carolingian renaissance, but there are much earlier treatises on Latin grammar by Irishmen. These have been discussed in a recent edition of the *Ars Malsachani*.[2] Two ninth-century manuscripts of this text exist, and it was glossed about 700.[3] Malsachan was thus a seventh-century Irish grammarian. It is very probable that he made use of another treatise by an Irish scholar, the unedited *Anonymous ad Cuimnanum*. There is thus proof that Latin grammar was seriously studied in seventh-century Irish schools.

The Irish knew something of classical writers, but probably most of it was at second hand, through the Fathers and, most particularly, through Isidore of Seville. The works of Spanish authors reached Ireland remarkably quickly.[4] The only seventh-century manuscript of Isidore's *Etymologiae* which is known to exist was written in Irish minuscule,[5] and the Irish author of *De Duodecim Abusivis Saeculi*, probably writing between 630 and 650, knew the work. A treatise, *De Ordine Creaturarum*, which seems

---

[1] M. Draak, 'Construe Marks in Hiberno-Latin manuscripts', *Mededelingen der Koninklijke Nederlandse Akademie van Watenschappen afd. Letterkunde*, Nieuwe Reeks, XX (1957), 261–282; 'The higher teaching of Latin grammar in Ireland during the ninth century', *ibid.*, XXX (1967), 109–44.

[2] Bengt Lofstedt, *Der hibernolateinische Grammatiker Malsachanus* (Uppsala 1965). [3] *Ibid.*, 25.

[4] J. N. Hillgarth, 'Visigothic Spain and Early Christian Ireland', *PRIA*, LXII (1962), C 167–94; 'The East, Visigothic Spain and the Irish', *Studia Patristica*, IV (1961), 442–56; O. K. Werckmeister, 'From Visigothic to insular illumination', *PRIA*, LXIII (1963), 167–89. Cf. on computi, C. W. Jones, *Bedae Opera de Temporibus* (Cambridge, Mass. 1943), 97, 112–13.

[5] A. Dold and J. Duft, *Die älteste irische Handschriften-Reliquie der Stiftsbibliothek St. Gallen mit Texten aus Isidors Etymologien* (Beuron 1955); Lowe, *CLA*, VII (1956), no. 995.

to have been written by an Irish author known as pseudo-Augustine, was ascribed to Isidore. All this suggests the popularity of Isidore in Ireland.[1] His writings, with their compendia of classical knowledge and their mixture of erudition and fantasy, were just to the Irish taste. If they wanted information on men or monsters or almost any other subject, they could turn to his encyclopaedia. His 'three sacred languages' encouraged Irish scholars in their pursuit of Greek and Hebrew vocabulary, while his interest in words and etymological definitions gave authority to their own.

There seems to have been at least one classical author whom the Irish knew directly, Vergil. We have ninth- and tenth-century manuscripts which contain late seventh-century Irish glosses on the Bucolics and Georgics.[2] The commentary is ascribed to Adananus, who may be Adamnán of Iona.[3] Horace is another Latin writer whom the Irish probably read, for there are a number of allusions to him in Columbanus' works, and the Irish played a leading part in the transmission of his poems, which seem to have been 'practically unknown on the continent from the sixth to the eighth centuries'.[4] Other authors are used by Irish grammarians as illustrations for their teaching, but it is difficult to be sure that they knew them at first hand.

Adamnán of Iona probably had Greek glossaries in his library, for in his work on The Holy Places he tells us that the orthography of the name Thabor 'was found in Greek books'.[5] It was very probably from glossaries that Irish scholars took those obscure and esoteric words which they sometimes introduce into their vocabulary as marks of erudition.[6] The English Aldhelm protests against

---

[1] On Isidore, see R. McNally, *Theological Studies*, XX (1959), 432–42; Cf. Diaz y Diaz, *Sacris Erudiri*, V (1953), 147–66.

[2] Kenney, *Sources*, 286–7.   [3] For Adamnán, see *infra*, 222.

[4] L. Bieler, *Mélanges Columbaniens, Actes du Congrès International de Luxeuil* (Paris 1951), 99; 'The classics in early Ireland', *Classical Influences on European Culture*, ed. R. R. Bolgar (Cambridge 1971), 48.

[5] D. Meehan, *Adamnán's De Locis Sanctis*, SLH, 3 (Dublin 1958), 96.

[6] This style is called 'hisperic', Professor Bieler thinks that it originated in Britain, with the disintegration of the stylistic principles of antiquity. See *Revue du moyen âge latin*, VIII (1952), 220, note 17.

English students going to Ireland in pursuit of learning when they could have Latin and Greek teaching at home.[1] This sounds as if Greek was available in Ireland, but Aldhelm exaggerates and he is not a precise writer. There is no evidence that seventh-century Irish libraries possessed any Greek author in the original,[2] though Irish scholars knew the Greek alphabet and used Greek words, and may even have had some little-known works of Greek Fathers in translation.[3]

If the Irish were taking serious trouble to learn Latin well, you would expect them to write the language with ease. Patrick's Latinity was very unpolished.[4] Columbanus, about a century and a half later (he died in 615), belongs to a very different school. He had a great sense of style; what his editor, Dr G. S. M. Walker[5] calls 'a strenuous vitality' which can run to exuberant wordiness, but at its best is well-balanced, vigorous, precise. His poem to Fidolius contains a number of classical allusions. He writes it in light-hearted adonics, begging Fidolius to leave aside the more flowery songs of scholars and accept gladly his 'frivolities':

> Floridiora
> Doctiloquorum
> Carmina linquens,
> Frivola nostra
> Suscipe laetus.

---

[1] *MGH Auct. Antiq.*, XV, 488 ff.

[2] On this subject see B. Bischoff, 'Das griechische Element in der abendländischen Bildung des Mittelalaters', *Byzantinische Zeitschrift* XLIV (1951), 27–55, especially 39–48; or *Mittelalterliche Studien* (Stuttgart 1966–7), II, 246–75.

[3] The Irishman Virgil of Salzburg (died 784), now recognised as the Aethicus Ister who wrote a Cosmography, knew something about Greek thought. See H. Loewe, *Ein literarischer Widersacher des Bonifatius: Virgil von Salzburg und die Kosmographie des Aethicus Ister* (Akad. d. Wiss. und d. Lit., Mainz 1951, Wiesbaden 1952).

[4] C. Mohrmann, *The Latin of St Patrick* (Dublin 1961).

[5] *Sancti Columbani Opera SLH*, 2 (Dublin 1957). See the review by M. Esposito in *Classica et Medievalia*, XXI (1960), 184–202, and the convincing reply by Bieler, *ibid.*, XXII (1961), 139–50.

Then, at the end, he moves into sombre hexameters; he is now old,[1] 'overwhelmed by the bitter ills which I bear in my frail body and sad old age'.

> Haec tibi dictarum morbis oppressus acerbis,
> Corpore quos fragili patior tristique senecta.

Columbanus could change his style to suit his subject-matter. He was a man who knew what he wanted to say and who also had definite ideas about the best way to say it.

Columbanus spent much of his adult life on the continent, and it could be argued that he gained his fluent command of Latin there. But this is unlikely, for he was master of the schools at Bangor before he set out on pilgrimage, and his Latin style is not that of sixth-century Gaul.[2] The Antiphonary of Bangor at the end of the seventh century provides other evidence of Latin verse.[3] Here is the well-known hymn 'Draw nigh and take the body of the Lord', to be sung, as the text says, at the communion of the priests:

> Sancti, venite,
> Christi corpus sumite,
> sanctum bibentes,
> quo redempti, sanquinem.[4]

Another hymn, celebrating the monastic rule of Bangor, has an elaborate system of rhyme, with alternate two-syllabled rhymes. F. J. E. Raby ascribes to the Irish poets 'the credit of being the first important innovators in the use of rhyme'.[5] Other works were produced during the seventh and early eighth centuries, such as the *De Duodecim Abusivis Saeculi*, which show conscious awareness of

---

[1] 'our eighteenth olympiad', i.e., between 68 and 72.
[2] C. Mohrmann, 'The earliest continental Irish Latin', *Vigiliae Christianae*, XVI (1962), 216–33.
[3] Ed. F. E. Warren, 2 vols, *HBS*, 4 and 10 (London 1893, 1895).
[4] *Ibid.*, ff. 10v–11r.
[5] *A History of Christian-Latin Poetry* (Oxford 1953), 138.

linguistic effects.[1] The careful Latin teaching which is to be seen in the early ninth-century Latin text-book-readers may have been established by the late-sixth century and certainly was a feature of Irish ecclesiastical learning in the seventh and eighth.

Early Irish ecclesiastical learning was concentrated not on classical texts, but on the Bible. Secular men of learning had to master the genealogies and stories: Christian men of learning had to master a vast new set of texts, the scriptures. Consequently many of their pre-Carolingian works are Biblical commentaries.[2] The majority of these belong to the Alexandrine school of exegesis, which became accepted throughout the medieval west. They stress the moral and allegorical interpretation of the scriptures. Some belong to the much less popular tradition of the Antiochan school, with its emphasis on the literal meaning and historical context. A commentary on St Mark's Gospel, possibly written by the Cummean who urged his fellow clergy to adopt the Roman Easter c. 632,[3] will provide an illustration of the allegorical school:

> When Rebecca first saw Isaac, she sprang from the camel whereon she was, for humility of spirit. So, then, the Church has sprung from the camel of the pride and evil deeds whereon she had been when she beheld the bridegroom, i.e., Christ.[4]

On the other hand another commentator of about the same date prefers the historical method. He explains his purpose in the preface to his work *De Mirabilibus Sanctae Scripturae*:

[1] This work is edited by W. Hellmann (Leipzig 1909). There are also examples of bad writing, where the scribe does not seem to be in full command of the language. But the glosses are proof of serious effort, and men like Adamnán are the successful products of the system. For McNally's remarks on the style of the *Liber de Numeris*, *Der irische Liber der Numeris*, Inaugural-Dissertation (Munich 1957), 145–9.

[2] B. Bischoff, 'Wendepunkte in der Geschichte der lateinischen Exegese im Frühmittelalter', *Sacris Erudiri*, VI (1954), 189–281, or *Mittelalterliche Studien*, I, 205–73, provides the authoritative discussion, and lists the supposedly Irish exegetical works.

[3] The identification is Bischoff's, *Sacris Erudiri*, VI (1954), 200 f.

[4] Stokes and Strachan, *Thesaurus Paleohibernicus*, I, 488; *PL*, XXX, col. 592.

. . . to show, where any action seems to be outside the normal ordering, that there God does not make a new nature but governs the nature which he fashioned in the beginning. Moreover, in this work we have tried to explain the reason and order of actual events, excluding, at this stage, allegorical interpretations.[1]

Though the allegorical method was most sympathetic to the mystical ideas of many Irish writers, the literal method survived. About 800 a scribe named Diarmait, copying a commentary on the Psalms,[2] declares that he intends 'to come briefly to the meaning', which his glossator understood as the historical interpretation. He will leave 'opportunities for greater understanding to the readers themselves, if they wish to add things', and the glossator defines this as *sens* et *moralus*. 'We shall leave to them the exposition of the significance and the morality'.[3] Here a distinction is drawn between the literal meaning on the one hand, and the spiritual significance and moral application on the other. The fact that Irish monastic scholars possessed, and went on using, commentaries of the historical school gives their activity a singular interest.[4]

Early Irish commentaries are based on the Fathers, or rather on abstracts, summaries and isolated works, for their compilers seem rarely, if ever, to have grasped patristic thought in a comprehensive fashion,[5] and the patristic library available to any one commentator would have been scrappy and incomplete. Yet in spite of the defects in their sources, Irish exegetical tracts fulfilled a need in Europe and circulated there, often ascribed to well-known authors such as Augustine, Jerome or Cyprian.[6] Professor Bischoff's work has identified many unedited manuscripts and has

[1] *PL*, XXXV, col. 2151-2. Cf. Esposito, *PRIA*, XXXV (1920), 189-207.

[2] Now in the Ambrosian Library, Milan, C 301 inf. There is a facsimile reproduction with introduction by R. I. Best (Dublin 1936). See *supra*, 193.

[3] Stokes and Strachan, *Thesaurus Palaeohibernicus*, I, 13; Best, *op, cit.*, f. 14 d.

[4] Canterbury under Theodore and Hadrian used the Antichan authorities, but Bede belongs to the allegorical school, and he profoundly influenced subsequent Anglo-Saxon thinking. Cf. Bischoff, *op. cit.*, 189-95.

[5] R. E. McNally, *Annuale Mediaevale*, X (1969), 12-13.

[6] See P. Grasjean, *Sacris Erudiri*, VII (1955), 67-98.

shown these Irish commentaries in a European setting. Some were copied in south Germany during the late eighth and ninth centuries. They must have been taken there by Irish missionaries.

Irish scholars were interested not only in the canonical scriptures but in apocrypha. Early Ireland provided a home for some of the apocryphal literature which seemed destined to disappear on the continent.[1] Some incidents from the Gospel of Thomas occur in an Irish poem which Professor Carney dates to c. 700.[2] This starts with the story of the birds of clay, blessed by Jesus so that they flew away. His speech to the school-master Zacharias has that element of mystery which the Irish loved:

> Sage of the law of God, you think Joseph is my father. It is not he.
> I was before your begetting; it is I who am the sage; I know every thought that has been in your heart.
> You are certain in every science, you have read all; I have a lesson for you that no man knows.
> I have a wonderful matter to tell you without a trace of a lie; I have seen Abraham in the time when he existed.
> Thus did I see even you long ago through the mystery of the Holy Spirit; sage of the law, from all time before your begetting I was.[3]

There is rich material for a study of apocryphal tradition in Ireland, much of it not yet adequately examined. When the Irish were presented with anything unexplained or un-named they wanted to elaborate it, to find some mystical interpretation. They followed patristic tradition in naming the magi, Melchior, Caspar and Balthazar, and in explaining the significance of their gifts. One writer describes their appearance, age and dress, possibly follow-

---

[1] B. Bischoff, *Sacris Erudiri*, V (1954), 195.

[2] J. Carney, *The Poems of Blathmac . . . together with the Irish Gospel of Thomas*, etc., *ITS*, 47 (Dublin 1964), xv–xix, 90–105. See M. McNamara, 'Notes on the Irish Gospel of Thomas', *The Irish Theological Quarterly*, XXXVIII (1971), 42–66.

[3] Carney, *op. cit.*, 101–3. This passage is paralleled in non-Irish texts of the Gospel of Thomas.

ing a source which is no longer extant.[1] Another discusses the
significance of the colours of their robes; white for chastity, blue
for fasting, grey for ascetic martyrdom, red for martyrdom by
blood.[2] A collection compiled in the second half of the eighth
century, the *Liber de Numeris*, names the thieves crucified on the
right and left of Christ;[3] it discusses the attributes attached to the
names of the evangelists.[4] All this is typical of the Irish passion
for significant detail.[5] Mystical interpretations and apocryphal
elaborations cast a potent spell, and gave rein to fancy, as we may
see in the later text of the Evernew Tongue.[6]

Grammar and exegesis were, then, the major pre-occupations
of the early Irish schools. The Irish had a great respect for tradition, and their work in these fields was not original; yet, because
they glossed their manuscripts, some of it reaches us with personal
comment which is unusual in texts of this period. The Irish master
who glossed the Carlsruhe grammar of Priscian points out that
the author 'contradicts himself here', and notes his own query.[7]
The glossator of the St Gall Priscian criticised the misinterpreta-
tions of 'those blunderers', probably his fellow scholars: 'ut
erratici putant; Mael- et Cua-'.[8] A phrase in the text makes
another scribe think of a friend on pilgrimage: 'Sicut mac
Cialláin.'[9] Beside the phrase 'Judas Iscariot, who also betrayed

---

[1] *Pseudo-Bede*, PL, XCIV, col. 541 CD. See McNally, 'The three holy kings
in early Irish Latin writing'. *Kyriakon*, ed. P. Granfield and J. A. Jungmann,
667–90. For the Irish poem in a twelfth-century MS, Harl. 1802, which echoes
a similar imagery, see McNally, *op. cit.*, 687. This is a good example of Irish
archaism.

[2] 'Catéchèses celtiques', ed. A. Wilmart, *Studi e testi*, LIX (1933), 78; cited
Kyriakon, McNally, 686.

[3] McNally, *op. cit.*, 48–9. Fr. McNally is editing this text.

[4] *Ibid.*, 79–80.

[5] See the description of the high city of heaven from 'Catéchèses celtiques',
op. cit., 56 ff, translated with comment Hughes, *Studia Celtica*, V (1970), 50–1.

[6] Ed. W. Stokes, *Ériu*, II (1905), 96–162; III (1907), 34–5. Cf. *Celtica*, IX (1971).
For talking beasts and birds see McNally, *Annuale Mediaevale*, X (1969), 22.

[7] Stokes and Strachan, *Thesaurus Palaeohibernicus*, II, 227, f. 59 a 2.

[8] *Ibid.*, II, 84, f. 31 b 12.

[9] *Ibid.*, II, 235.

him', in the Armagh Gospels stands the word 'wretch'.[1] Irish scribes did not copy passively, and they sometimes jotted down the response their feelings prompted.

II

Their vivid response to the beauty of the natural world can be seen in the nature poetry. Much of what is known as Irish 'nature' poetry has been attributed to the hermits. Professor Jackson thinks that the special group of seasonal poetry might perhaps have had its remote origins in a pagan past,[2] but he follows Flower in attributing some of the other nature poems to the monks and hermits of the religious revival of the late eighth and ninth centuries.[3] Flower recognised this period as one when monks, retiring from the great monasteries to lead an ascetic life, saw nature with a new awareness.[4] Living much alone, surrounded by the sights and sounds of sea and forest, they turned with quickened imagination 'to adore the Lord, maker of wondrous works, great bright heaven with its angels, the white-waved sea on earth'. There is evidence that Irish religious felt a community with nature before the period of the ascetic revival, but Gerard Murphy, while emphasising monastic influence on the development of vernacular poetry in the seventh and eighth centuries, dates most of the nature poems which he edits in his *Early Irish Lyrics* to the ninth century, some to the tenth.[5] Thus, Flower, Murphy and Professor Jackson are in broad agreement.[6]

[1] *Book of Armagh*, 75 b (f. 38r). Many more glosses are noted by C. Plummer, 'On the colophons and marginalia of Irish scribes', *PBA*, XII (1926), 11–44.

[2] Jackson, *Studies in Early Celtic Nature Poetry*, 159. See also his *Celtic Miscellany*, Penguin 1971, revised edition.

[3] *Ibid.*, p. 96. 'One can scarcely avoid concluding that they, too, are the direct outcome of this anchoritic revival, and indeed that they are actually the work of monks and hermits'.

[4] R. Flower, 'The Two Eyes of Ireland', *The Church of Ireland AD 432–1932*, ed. W. Bell and N. D. Emerson (Dublin 1932), 66–79.

[5] *Early Irish Lyrics* (Oxford 1956).

[6] D. Greene and F. O'Connor, *A Golden Treasury of Irish Poetry* (London, Melbourne, Toronto 1967), 14–15, have given their opinion that 'nature poetry developed at some time in the tenth century as a result of hints in

These poems need a background. What sort of a background does the ascetic revival provide? There had been hermits in Ireland since the beginning of monasticism. The *céli dé*, or culdees, with whom the new asceticism is so closely associated, did not live in forest hermitages but in monastic communities. Groups of hermits were supported by the old churches, and seem to have lived near them, as many of the *dísert* names show.[1] It is clear from the annals that the word *anchorita* means not 'solitary', but 'ascetic'; for many of the scribes, busy heads of monastic schools, were also 'anchorites'. An active king even could be an 'anchorite'. Solitary life in remote places went on; it no doubt became more common during this period. Nevertheless the norm, even for the ascetics, was life in or near a community. Thus the ascetic reform, while it provides a suitable background, is not so peculiarly appropriate as the incidence of 'anchorites' in the annals might lead one to suppose. If it were possible to prove a direct connection between Irish and continental metres[2] this would provide a good dating criterion. But this is not easy. A twelfth-century French poem and an Irish poem could be independently derived from earlier Latin, so that a late parallel need not necessarily prove a late date for the Irish poem.

Many early Irish nature poems are distinguished by an extreme economy of words and clarity of vision. They convey an experience in which emotion and intellect are fused together by imagination. They have a complicated system of rhyme and alliteration. The vowels, generally speaking, must be identical, and the rhyming consonants of the same quality.[3] Alliteration is common. Because of their directness and brevity these poems convey an impression fresh and vivid, but it is based on a sophisticated virtuosity of technique:

contemporary Latin verse'. J. Carney, *Éigse*, XIII (1970), 292, wishes to date some of the poems considerably earlier.

[1] I owe this information to Mrs Flanagan. The neighbourhood of hermits and monastic cities is supported by the literary sources.

[2] This is what Greene and O'Connor suggest, *op. cit.*, 14–15.

[3] G. Murphy, *Early Irish Metrics* (Dublin 1961). More simply in the introduction to J. Carney, *Mediaeval Irish Lyrics* (Dublin 1967).

Int én bec
ro léic feit
do rind guip
   glanbuidi;
fo-ceird faíd
ós Loch Laíg
lon do chraíb
charnbuidi.[1]

Professor Greene and Frank O'Connor translate: 'The little bird has whistled from the tip of his bright yellow beak; the blackbird from a bough laden with yellow blossom has tossed a cry over Belfast Lough.'[2]

These are undoubtedly the poems of Irish monks, and the tone of many of them is extraordinarily buoyant and happy. The scribe is glad to get out in the spring 'I write well under the woodland trees.'[3] Marbán describes his hermit's hut, just the right size, with a fine view; near to nuts, berries and apple-trees. Stags leap out of the stream and the wild beasts come around the house, 'that is beautiful'. There are 'delightful feasts' of salmon, trout, eggs, honey, nuts and berries: (strawberries are 'good to taste in their plenty'). 'A pleasant constant thrush' sings above the house, with many other birds.[4] No wonder Marbán was content, and king Guaire envied him. I doubt if poems like this tell us much about Irish ascetics. Others are probably nearer the mark, although even the much more severe hermit's song which follows it in Murphy's collection expresses a wish, and does not describe the writer's present circumstances, while Manchán's poem (Murphy no. 12) describes the ideal ascetic community. They do tell us that, for these poets at least, religion was combined with an exquisite appreciation of and delight in life.

[1] Murphy, *Lyrics*, 6.   [2] *Op cit.*, 207.
[3] Murphy, *Lyrics*, 5. Greene and O'Connor, *op. cit.*, 84–5.
[4] Murphy, *ibid.*, 10–19.

III

The activity of the Irish not only as poets but as scholars is to be seen in the Martyrology of Oengus.[1] This text has both a date and provenance. It is a list of saints, foreign and Irish, in verse, arranged under the days of the year. The latest of all to be included is Máel-Rúain of Tallaght, who died in 792. The prologue mentions Máel-Rúain and, in the stanza immediately preceding, Donnchad and Bran of Leinster, whose tombs the author had visited. These kings died in 797 and 795. In the epilogue the author calls Máel-Rúain his tutor. This means that he must have written not very long after Máel-Rúain's death. The later Irish prefaces say that the author was Oengus, that he composed the martyrology in the time of Aed son of Niall (who died in 819) and showed it to Fothad when Aed went on a hosting to Dun Cuair. According to the annals that hosting was in 805. It seems almost certain that the Martyrology was written between 797 and 805. The author belonged to the circle of Máel-Rúain and may have completed it in Tallaght (near Dublin) as the prefaces say.

The Martyrology itself is full of clichés, but it has a fine prologue and epilogue written with complicated rhyme and alliteration. One of the most interesting passages contrasts the deserted pagan sites with the flourishing Christian cities. Here are some of the stanzas, in the translation by Professor Greene and Frank O'Connor:[2]

> The great settlement of Tara has died with the loss of its princes;
> great Armagh lives on with its choirs of scholars . . .
> The fortress of Cruachan has vanished with Ailill, victory's child;
> a fair dignity greater than kingdoms is in the city of Clonmacnoise...
> The proud settlement of Aillenn has died with its boasting hosts;
> great is victorious Brigit and lovely her thronged sanctuary.
> The fort of Emain Macha has melted away, all but its stones;
> thronged Glendalough is the sanctuary of the western world . . .

[1] Ed. W. Stokes, *HBS* (London 1905). See R. Thurneysen, *ZCP*, VI (1908), 6–8.

[2] Greene and O'Connor, *op. cit.*, 64–5. (I have made two small alterations.)

Old cities of the pagans to which length of occupation has been
refused are deserts without worship like Lugaid's place.

The little monastic sites settled by twos and threes are Romes[1] with
throngs, with hundreds, with thousands.

Paganism has been destroyed though it was splendid and far flung;
the kingdom of God the Father has filled heaven and earth and
sea . . .

The great hills of evil have been cut down with spear-points, while
the glens have been made into hills.

In Oengus' day the ruins of the pagan hill-top sanctuaries must still
have been in evidence:[2] he is rejoicing in the triumph of Christianity.

The turgid verse of the martyrology proper is in sharp contrast
with the beginning and end: 'Not a trace of imaginative power', 'a
calendar that can only be described as infernally dull', say his
editor and translators. But as a scholar Oengus is interesting. The
structure of the compilation is provided by foreign texts, in fact
Oengus names four of them.[3] As Stokes points out, he made
mistakes over the continental saints: for example he mistakes
Germanus of Paris (whom he probably knew nothing about) for
Germanus of Auxerre, turns a Roman virgin into a man, invents
saints out of a place-name.[4] These foreign saints form the core of
the compilation,[5] like the three who, on 17 May, unyoked their
chariots on the hill of heaven.[6] The most interesting aspect of the
martyrology, however, seems to me the very solid and detailed
tradition which, by 800, the Irish Church had built up about her
own past.

According to Adamnán, mass was being said in the lifetime of
Columcille to honour the feasts of particular saints. Columcille
celebrated the *natalis*[7] of St Brendan, and also of bishop Colmán.[8]

---

[1] See Hughes in *The English Church and the Papacy*, ed. C. H. Lawrence
(London 1965), 21–3, 27–8.

[2] *Supra*, 178, 32.   [3] Epilogue, 270.   [4] Stokes, xliv.

[5] A quick count for the first six months gives me 182 foreign saints, 156
Irish ones, but there may be slight errors in the numbers.

[6] As Stokes remarks, xlvii, this splendid imagery is not typical.

[7] *Adomnan's Life of Columba*, ed. A. O. and M. O. Anderson, III, 11. It means
his death, i.e., his birth into new life.   [8] *Ibid.*, III, 12.

Adamnán himself had been saddened by his separation by storms from Iona when the feast of Columcille was about to be held.[1] Armagh celebrated Patrick's feast with a special mass (*offertorium proprium*) and his own Irish hymn.[2] The day of a saint's death was continuously celebrated from his own epoch, and is thus one of the most reliable facts we can know about him.[3] An Irish martyrology composed c. 800 might be expected to include the great Irish monastic founders. Perhaps one might also expect the compiler to have access to lists of abbots of major houses, so that it is not surprising to find many who are mentioned in the annals, like Dunnchad of Iona (d. 717), Flann of Bangor (d. 728), Mac Óige of Lismore (d. 753). There are also famous scholars, like the seventh-century exegetist Laidcenn, who 'declared the mysteries of Christ'.[4] But dozens of saints occur here who are never mentioned in the annals,[5] some from houses which are rarely if ever mentioned. There are women saints about whom we otherwise hear little or nothing.[6]

Oengus must have had a considerable number of works of reference to build up such an Irish catalogue. Indeed, so complete a martyrology ('there is nothing that escapes us')[7] could not be a first attempt. He himself claims that he has searched multitudes of Ireland's host of books, the martyrologies of the Irish.[8] After its compilation, his text was corrected by a synod.[9] There must have been a mass of information available about the aristocracy of the Church, founders, abbots, scholars, virgins; not just localised information, but written information which was circulating. Oengus alludes to many stories and traditions; well known ones like 'the lasting liberation of the women of the Gaels' obtained by Adamnán,[10] and ones now unfamiliar, like the children playing

---

[1] *Ibid.*, II, 45.   [2] Book of Armagh, f. 16 a 1.

[3] The late Père Grosjean, Bollandiste, did not accept Mr Hennig's hypothesis that Ireland had no *sanctorale*.

[4] 12 Jan. On Laidcenn, see L. Gougaud, *Revue Celtique*, XXX (1909), 37–46.

[5] It is impossible to be certain that any one saint does not occur in *AU* without making a proper index, but the general impression is certainly true.

[6] *Infra*, 234.   [7] 22 June.   [8] Epilogue, 270.

[9] Epilogue, 268.   [10] 23 Sep. See *supra*, 81.

around Ultán, a saint of whom no Life exists.[1] The sort of 'Who's Who' of the Irish Church which Oengus compiled must have been a useful part of any monastic library—hence the synod's interest in it. The Irish enjoyed compiling lists and catalogues, and the Martyrology of Oengus presupposes that Irish Church historians had been busy before 800. It also proves the community of culture which existed within the Church.

If all this is true of the Martyrology of Oengus it is much more true of the Martyrology of Tallaght,[2] for where Oengus has two or three entries per day, Tallaght often has twenty or thirty. Whereas Oengus writes in Irish and in verse, the Martyrology of Tallaght is in prose, with its continental saints in Latin and its native saints in Irish and Latin. It is the immediate source of Oengus, and must thus have been earlier than Oengus. Gorman, writing his Martyrology in the twelfth century, complains that Oengus celebrated some saints on the wrong days. 'And this was surely, as we have ascertained, the reason why Oengus did so, because it was thus in the Martyrology of Tallaght, out of which he composed his martyrology.'[3] A comparison of Oengus and Tallaght shows that the twelfth-century scholar was quite right. This was accepted by the late Père Grosjean,[4] and has recently been further demonstrated by Mr Hennig.[5]

The continental entries of Tallaght are based on the Hieronymian martyrology.[6] In the continental, and occasionally in the Irish, entries there were difficulties in the exemplar. There are over eighty entries of the name *Zefanus*. Father Grosjean pointed out that all these 'Stephens' most probably arise from the sigla Z, which is found in the margin of the Book of Armagh, a manuscript of the early ninth century, with (in two cases) some elabora-

---

[1] 4 Sep.

[2] Ed. R. I. Best and H. J. Lawlor, *The Martyrology of Tallaght*, HBS, 68 (London 1931).

[3] W. Stokes, *HBS*, 9 (London 1895), 4. See *infra*, 283.

[4] 'Le Martyrologe de Tallaght', *Analecta Bollandiana*, LI (1933), 117–30.

[5] J. Hennig, *PRIA*, LXIX (1970), C 45–112.

[6] *Acta Sanctorum*, Nov. II. 2, ed. J. B. de Rossi and L. Duchesne (Brussels 1931), xii; Hennig, *Studia Patristica*, I (Berlin 1957), 104–11.

tion of the sign: '*Z incertus liber hic*'. The author of Tallaght was using written sources which were not always clear to him.

The Martyrology of Tallaght is a reference book: the Martyrology of Oengus was meant to be recited. The invocation of all these 'champions', these 'king folk' around 'the Lord of the seven heavens', was to bear the reciter into the heavenly kingdom. Both Oengus and Tallaght were obviously used, for the texts are heavily glossed.

Two Irish litanies, also meant for recitation, show a similar pleasure in cataloguing. One, the litany of the seven holy bishops,[1] was very probably compiled at Lethglenn. Its date has never been properly discussed, but I think it is at least as old as the late-eighth century, and may be earlier. It was to be said as a cure for disease. The other is a very interesting litany of pilgrim saints which seems to have been compiled c. 800.[2] In 1959 I argued that this was put together at Lismore, but Professor Bowen has recently shown good reason for thinking that its home was Wexford Harbour or its hinterland.[3] If this is so—and I find Professor Bowen's arguments convincing—it tells us more about the Church in south-east Ireland in the seventh and eighth centuries. It was very conscious of a spiritual dependence on Rome ('Roman pilgrims' and 'Romans' figure prominently in the litany): it was in touch with the Church abroad, for Gauls, Britons, Saxons and even Egyptians are mentioned here. The controlling idea behind this litany is that all are pilgrims. Some were ascetic pilgrims at home, like Brigit, who made 'a feast to Jesus in her heart', people who had no continuing city here. But some were pilgrims overseas, making voyages abroad. There are allusions here to stories which do not now exist, like Ibar's 'quest', or the 'twenty-four men of Munster who went with Ailbe to re-visit the Land of Promise, and are alive there until doom'.[4] This litany, like the

---

[1] C. Plummer, *Irish Litanies*, *HBS*, 62 (London 1925), 66–75.

[2] Hughes, 'On an Irish Litany of Pilgrim Saints compiled c. 800', *Analecta Bollandiana*, LXXVII (1959), 305–31.

[3] *Studia Celtica*, IV (1969), 68–71.

[4] There is an Island of the Family of Ailbe in the *Navigatio Brendani*.

martyrologies, shows that there was a mass of material available c. 800 to scholars compiling lists and catalogues about the Irish Church.

The language of the litanies, like the language of Oengus, is Irish. We have already seen that in the early ninth century the annals, a definitely foreign form of record, turn increasingly to Irish.[1] In the ninth century Latin was the language used by Irish scholars working in the Carolingian empire,[2] and Latin was still used at home; but, though Irish had been used by churchmen from an early period, now more and more texts were being written in Irish. Whereas seventh-century scholars had worked on the scriptures and written their exegesis, grammar, hagiology, annals, synchronisms and genealogy for a small monastic group, their interests in the Viking Age were extending beyond these limits and they were writing, increasingly in the vernacular, for a wider public.

IV

One of the most delightful of all Irish literary *genres* is that of the Voyages (*Immrama*). Monks had been voyaging in the later sixth century, for Adamnán tells us that Cormac sailed on three long journeys from Iona, seeking 'a desert in the ocean'.[3] On one occasion he made land in the Orkneys. He met *miràbilia* on his third voyage, in the shape of unknown creatures which almost pierced the leather covering of his boat with their stings.[4] Accord-

---

[1] *Supra*, 129.

[2] I have omitted these from this chapter, because they seem less good evidence for scholarship in Ireland than the material I have chosen to discuss. There is a long article by G. Murphy, *Studies*, XVII (1928), 39–50, 229–44; see more recently B. Bischoff, 'Il monachesimo irlandese nei suoi rapporti col continente', *Settimane di Studio del Centro Italiano di Studi sull' Alto Medioevo*, IV (Spoleto 1957) or *Mittelalterliche Studien*, I, 195–205. Professor Carney translates some of Sedulius Scottus' poems in *Mediaeval Irish Lyrics*. So does Helen Waddell, *Mediaeval Latin Lyrics* (London 1929).

[3] Adamnán's *Life of Columba*, I, 6.

[4] *Ibid.*, II, 42. He was sailing in a curragh, a boat with a wicker frame covered in hides.

ing to the Irish geographer Dicuil, writing in 825, Irish hermits
had been for nearly a century on islands to the north of Britain,
probably to be identified with the Faroes.[1] Stories of the voyage of
Brendan seem to have been known c. 800, for the Martyrology of
Tallaght seems to refer to him when it commemorates the
egressio familiae Brendini,[2] and the Litany of Pilgrim Saints alludes
three times to the voyage of Brendan,[3] each reference being to the
second voyage as it is recounted in the *Vita*, not the *Navigatio*.
   The voyage sections of the *Vita* are earlier than the *Navigatio*,
as Plummer showed.[4] There is disagreement on the date of the
Navigatio. Its editor thought that it was composed in the first half
of the tenth century.[5] But there are two tenth-century manuscripts of the text, each belonging to different families and showing considerable independent deficiencies. Taking this into
account, a ninth-century date seems more likely.[6] The *Navigatio*
has a fairly simple, well-constructed plot. It is a blend of classical
tradition, Christian legend, fairy lore and poetic invention,
combined into an exciting, indeed an entrancing, narrative.
Whether or not the *Navigatio Brendani* is earlier than other voyage
literature to which it is related is a matter of dispute but, even if
it does borrow, its author was still an artist of imaginative genius.
   He was undoubtedly a monk. As Professor Carney says, 'every
sentence, every character and every incident reflects Irish monastic society and ideals'.[7] Here are the monks on the *insula deliciosa*,
living in separate huts but saying divine office and eating together,
following a vegetarian diet.[8] On the island of Ailbe the monks,

[1] *Dicuil Liber de Mensura Orbis Terrae*, ed. B. Tierney, *SLH*, 6 (Dublin 1967),
76.

[2] 22 Mar.   [3] Hughes, *op. cit.*, 323.

[4] *ZCP*, V (1905), 124–41, especially 135–6.

[5] C. Selmer, *Navigatio Sancti Brendani Abbatis* (Indiana 1959).

[6] J. Carney, *Medium Aevum*, XXXII (1963), 40, suggests 'composition in
Ireland sometime about AD 800, possibly some decades later'.

[7] Other voyage tales are more secular in character, e.g., the Voyage of
Bran. These were written down in monastic *scriptoria*: how and by whom they
were composed is a more difficult question. The Voyage of Bran (generally
regarded as seventh century) must have drawn on pagan ideas.

[8] Selmer, *op. cit.*, 4–5.

who are vowed to silence, greet Brendan's voyagers with a liturgical procession. There is a description of the church and its services:

> When they had finished the evening office, St Brendan began to consider how that church was built. It was square—as long as it was broad—and it had seven lamps, three before the altar which was in the centre and two before the other two altars. The altars were made of square blocks of crystal and their vessels were similarly of crystal . . . and the twenty-four seats around the church. The place where the abbot sat was between two choirs. One side began from him and finished in him,[1] and the other side similarly. No one from either side would dare to presume to begin a verse without the aforesaid abbot.[2]

On the island of the three companies the boys are in white, the young men in blue (*iacinctinis vestibus*) and the seniors in purple dalmatics, singing in turn.[3] The hermit Paul is the eremitical ideal, living alone on his bare island crag, naked except for his hair, miraculously sustained by water from the spring.[4] Brendan and his monks are seeking 'the Land of Promise of the Saints', but they are allowed only forty days there before they must return to the ordinary world. The brief account of the islands which are a foretaste of hell[5] is also part of the ecclesiastical background of the story.

The voyage is full of marvels—the spring with water which puts men to sleep, the fresh food appearing daily, the sanctuary lamps lighted by a flaming arrow, the candles burning but never extinguished, the creatures on the ocean floor, the monsters, not to mention Jasconius on whose back, as on dry ground, they celebrate Easter Eve. There are sensuous delights—the fragrance of the isles of the blest, the singing birds, the taste of the marvellous fruits and foods, the shining light. These are part of the lure of the islands, but the attraction is, above all, a religious one, of the land 'where Christ is our light'.

---

[1] I think it means he began the chant, the choir on one side took it up, then he finished it.
[2] Selmer, *op. cit.*, 33–4.   [3] *Ibid.*, 50.
[4] *Ibid.*, 70–6.   [5] *Ibid.*, 61–70.

Just as the voyages appear in secular as well as ecclesiastical contexts, so do the visions. The earliest recorded ecclesiastical vision by an Irishman is Fursey's. Bede tells of Fursey's two visions, the first of the angelic hosts, the second of the fierce onslaughts of demons seeking to prevent his journey to heaven and of his vision of the blessed.[1] There is a seventh-century Life of Fursey,[2] and Bede must have been using a text very similar to this. But by far the most splendid of the visions is that of Adamnán, probably dating from the tenth century,[3] which shows first heaven, then hell with its rabble-host. This is how it begins:

> Noble and wonderful is the Lord of the Elements and great and marvellous are his power and his might. He is gentle and he is kindly, he is merciful and he is loving; for he calls to himself to Heaven the folk of charity and of mercy, of gentleness and forgivingness. But he abases and casts down to hell the impious, unprofitable flock of the sons of cursing. For he gives hidden things and divers rewards of heaven to the blessed and he bestows many diverse torments on the damned.[4]

Adamnán is first taken to the Land of the Saints where the blessed souls await the day of judgment. Through a golden portico they can see the family of heaven, but a veil of glass is between the saints and the Prince seated on his throne. 'None can tell his ardour and energy, his blazing and brilliance, his brightness and beauty, his splendour, and his bliss'. Around the Lord in the city of heaven are ranged saints and pilgrims, their faces all towards God, yet all face to face with each other. The soul has to climb up through the seven heavens, encountering tests and trials at each of the gates, until it is purged of sin. The righteous are

[1] *HE*, III, 19.   [2] Ed. B. Krusch, *MGH Script. Rer. Mer.*, IV, 34–40.
[3] Some scholars have put it in the eleventh. See Kenney, *Sources*, 445, n. 234, for various views.
[4] E. Windisch, *Fís Adamnáin, Irische Texte*, I (Leipzig 1880), 165–96, or R. I. Best and O. Bergin *Lebor na Huidre* (Dublin 1929), 67–76, for *LU* text only. Translated W. Stokes, *Adamnán's Vision* (Simla 1870, limited edition) or C. S. Boswell, *An Irish Precursor of Dante* (London 1908), and in part K. Jackson, *Celtic Miscellany* (revised edition Penguin), 290 ff.

welcomed with great pleasure. The unrighteous, having seen the joy of heaven, are cast out to be swallowed by twelve fiery dragons, one after the other, until the devil takes them into his mouth.

The main part of the original vision probably ended here; but there now follows an account of Adamnán's journey through the waste land of hell, where he meets erenaghs who have misappropriated Church property, masters of schools who have preached heresy, priests who have deceived the people. There are episodes which are mutually inconsistent.[1] The author (or compiler) combines motifs and images which derive from many different sources. The theory of the ascent of the seven heavens shows pythagorean, neo-platonic and gnostic elements, and the eschatology seems to derive ultimately from the eastern Church.[2] These images and ideas must all have been part of Irish tradition when the vision was composed. When and how they reached Ireland is an open question.

The voyages and visions, and much else in Irish scholastic tradition, are parodied in The Vision of Mac Conglinne.[3] This is a complicated text, confused in places: it has almost certainly gone through a number of recensions. Murphy thought that both the two versions were of the twelfth century,[4] but the version in TCD, H.3.18, seems the simpler and earlier,[5] so first of all I shall stick to this. The story opens with the statement that King Cathal of Munster had a demon of gluttony within him. It goes on to tell how the scholar Mac Conglinne, with one attendant, is doing the round of Ireland, seeking at all the great monasteries the hospitality which it was their legal duty and honour to provide. At last he comes to Cork. The abbot there merely provides him with a

[1] St J. Seymour, 'The eschatology of the early Irish church', *ZCP*, XIV (1923), 179–211.

[2] The fullest treatment of this is in a thesis by J. J. Colwell on the Vision of Adamnán, presented in 1952 for the degree of Ph.D. at Edinburgh. Cf. St J. Seymour, 'The seven heavens in Irish literature', *ZCP*, XIV (1923), 18–30.

[3] Ed. K. Meyer (London 1892).

[4] *Early Irish Literature*, introd. by J. Carney (London 1966), 138.

[5] Meyer, *op. cit.*, 114–29, 148–58.

fire and a bowl of oats. This is not good enough for Mac Conglinne, who utters a satire and is thereupon seized by the angry
abbot. But before he pays the penalty for his slander he is granted
a boon, a night in the abbot's bed; and on that night Mura (his
own patron) comes to him with a vision. This he repeats to King
Cathal, to cure him of his compulsive eating, and so secures his
own release.

In his vision, instead of an angel, a phantom guides Mac
Conglinne, one called 'Dirty-belch son of Fluxy'. They set off on
a voyage, but the curragh is made of beef and other foods, with
oars of flitches of bacon. In this splendid ship they sail over the
ocean's heaving waves, throwing up the sea's harvest, just like
other navigators. When they land, on a marvellous island made of
food, they ask for the hermit (an ascetic hermit is, of course, to be
expected on an island in voyage literature). They eventually
reach the church, in the glen between Butter-mount and Milk-
Lake, in the land of the Children of Early-Eating. The church is
described in detail;[1] its palisades of salt meat, a knocker of butter,
a bell with a tongue of salt, the rafters of flitches, the tiles of fat,
and so on. The hermit comes with great dignity from the house
in front of the church, his head crowned with lumps of butter and
seventeen bunches of leeks. In his two boots are stuffed the proper
contemplative reading, the *Táin* and the Destruction of Da
Derga's Hostel in the right boot and the Wooing of Étaín and the
Wooing of Emer in the left. The hermit utters a blessing on the
scholar: 'Be thou under the safeguard of good food.' Mac Conglinne explains that he wants to be cured of his greed, and the
hermit prescribes for him—a night of fasting, then a huge meal
served by a quick, white-toothed, white-handed, fine-breasted,
fair-thighed woman. The hermit says goodbye and puts a gospel
round the scholar's neck, a gospel made of bacon and sausage:
'Be thou under the protection of smooth juicy bacon. Be thou
under the protection of hard, yellow-backed cream.' So much for
vision and voyage, with their contemplative and ascetic ideals and
their sensuous (but not sensual) delights. Hearing this long story on

[1] Cf. *supra*, 212.

the theme of food, the demon of gluttony leaps from King Cathal's throat and Mac Conglinne, the scholar, is suitably rewarded.

This is just the bare bones of the story. In the longer version there are other parodies of the schools. It starts with the usual questions about *locus, persona, tempus* and *causa scribendi*. Mac Conglinne's nickname is 'never-refused', since he constantly bends his skill to satire and panegyric. He begins as an ecclesiastical scholar, but turns into a travelling poet. The princely guesthouse of the monks of Cork is described: a bath-tub full of yesterday's water with the cold stones in it, wind under the door and fleas in the blanket as thick as the dew on a May morning. Mac Conglinne recites the genealogy of the venerable abbot of Cork, but 'according to the pedigree of food'. So, instead of hearing the names of his illustrious ancestors, the abbot hears only insults: 'Son of Honey-bag, son of Juice, son of Lard', generation after generation back to Adam. There is a parody of the mystical significance of numbers when Mac Conglinne forces Cathal into giving away his apples one by one. Cathal's fury seizes him with a ridiculous copy of epic conventions: one eye jumps back into his head so that a crane could not have plucked it out, and the other starts out like an egg. All this is incidental decoration to the main story.

v

Parody like this indicates a secure tradition. Ecclesiastical learning had begun as grammar and the study of the scriptures. Ecclesiastical scholars had devoted themselves to hymns, hagiography, lists, calendars, martyrologies, annals. Because of these men's efforts early Ireland has a history, not just a lore. But from early times they were interested in legends, apocrypha, sagas, and there must have been many a cleric with the *Táin* and the Wooings in his memory, if not stuffed in his boots. Christian and secular men of learning were getting together as early as the seventh century, and by the twelfth they shared many of the same interests. Poetry, voyages, visions and hagiography all show how closely intermingled were the ecclesiastical and secular traditions.

CHAPTER 7

Hagiography

I

Hagiography is not history. The author is not concerned to establish a correct chronology. He is not interested in assembling and examining evidence and coming to a conclusion which takes all the evidence into account. He is rather writing the panegyric of a saint, stressing in particular his holy way of life and the supernatural phenomena which attended it. Sometimes the aim is didactic, sometimes more crudely financial. What he praises will depend on his audience and on the society for which he is writing. Hagiography will thus give reliable contemporary evidence about the aspirations and culture of a people.

This seems obvious enough. It is, however, sometimes assumed that the hagiographer is mainly interested in establishing his patron's claims to property. Although it is true that a considerable number of the Lives provide something like the title deeds of the monastery, and that after about 900 the emphasis on rights becomes common, to establish economic claims was not the primary motive of all hagiography. Some writers are much more spiritually aware than others of the moral qualities of the saint, so that it is imperceptive to lump all saints' Lives together as if they belong to a common pattern. Almost every Life is quite a complex production: in Cogitosus' Life of Brigit, though it is composed largely of miraculous elements often based on folk-tale themes, there is important historical information, while Adamnán's Life of Columcille, a major historical source, shows a sorcerer drawing milk from a bull[1] or the saint blessing a miraculous spike[2] and similar situations of folk-lore fantasy.

Some things are common to them all. Any saint's Life will tell something about the period in which it was written. The historian

[1] *Adomnan's Life of Columba*, II, 17.   [2] *Ibid.*, II, 37.

may sometimes be fairly sure when the Life was composed, and if so its criticism will be much easier. We can be fairly sure, for example, that the Life of Colmán of Lann was composed soon after 1122, when, as the text says, his relics were re-discovered and enshrined. The *Vita Tripartita* of St Patrick was probably compiled between 896 and 902; and here we can see how his legend had developed since the seventh century. Adamnán wrote his Life of Columcille almost certainly between 688 and 704. But most saints' Lives were re-written several times, and what we have is often the final and undated stage of re-writing. Such Lives may include revealing incidents which fit into circumstances which the compiler no longer understood. So a stratum of early material which will be very useful to the historian can be embedded in much later Lives. The Lives need detailed individual examination if this is to be extracted.

The vast majority of Irish saints' Lives have little genuine information about the saint. This is true even of the seventh-century Lives, except for that of Adamnán. There are often common hagiographical themes, borrowed from one Life into another, such as the multiplying of food and drink or the triple milking. There are hagiographical conventions: for example, the saint is severely ascetic; he is often in close harmony with the animal world; he can pronounce potent curses, so that people disregard him at their peril. The hagiographers are often influenced by the conventions of the secular story-tellers: exaggeration is used to excite laughter, and the saints may even borrow the pagan hero's attributes. Given such conventions, it is the incidental information in the Lives which is likely to be of most value to the historian, reports of political affiliations no longer· current, information about institutions, agriculture, social practices and the indirect evidence which reveals to us what it was the audience liked to hear.

There are several great collections of Irish saints' Lives. Two hundred pages of Kenney[1] are devoted to their discussion, and to

[1] *Sources* (New York 1929. Reprinted 1968). Vol. II on the secular sources was never written.

bibliographical and critical comment on the individual Lives. His work is indispensable to any serious study. The most valuable of all the collections is probably the *Codex Salmanticensis*, once at Salamanca, now at Brussels. This has been admirably re-edited since Kenney's day by Professor Heist.[1] It was transcribed in Ireland in the fourteenth century, and contains forty-eight Lives or fragments of Lives, all except one of Irish saints. Though the manuscript is late, the editing and revision seem to have been less thorough than those in other Latin collections.

The *Codex Kilkenniensis* survives in two manuscripts of about 1400, which are both independent copies of the same original. There are three manuscripts of *Codex Insulensis*, the earliest of which probably belongs to the first half of the thirteenth century. The second is a copy of the first and the third of the second, but all are defective, so that the edition needs to use them all. Most of the Lives from these two collections have been edited by Plummer.[2] Things likely to cause scandal have been toned down or left out, and the *Codex Insulensis* omits a lot of names of people and places.

The Book of Lismore, compiled in the second half of the fifteenth century, contains a number of saints' Lives in Irish, which have been edited and translated by Whitley Stokes.[3] Plummer's edition and translation of Irish saints' Lives[4] is taken from three seventeenth-century Franciscan manuscripts. Two of these were transcribed by Michael O'Clery, an extremely accurate copyist. The student of hagiography is comparatively well equipped with guide (Kenney) and editions. The real need is now for a modern text of Cogitosus' Life of Brigit,[5] a difficult undertaking, not least because of the multitude of manuscripts. Professor Bieler has this on his list of work to be done.[6]

---

[1] W. W. Heist, *Vitae Sanctorum Hiberniae*, Subsidia hagiographica 28 (Brussels 1965).

[2] *VSH*, 2 vols (Oxford 1910).

[3] *Lives of the Saints from the Book of Lismore* (Oxford 1890).

[4] *BNE*, 2 vols (Oxford 1922).

[5] It has to be consulted in Migne, *PL*, LXXII, cols. 775–90.

[6] I understand that Mr de Paor intends to provide a translation and study of Tirechán, which should also be very useful.

In this chapter I shall look first at three seventh-century Lives; then at some of the Lives which seem to have been written for an audience and in a milieu concerned to maintain the spiritual life; finally at some of those Lives which may accurately be described as the monastery's charter, Lives which are often determined to boost the saint's claims at any cost to his moral stature. I shall be selecting 'few things out of many' as the hagiographers frequently say they are doing.

II

Let us start with Adamnán, abbot of Iona, since, although he is not the earliest Irish hagiographer, he is probably the easiest for the historian to use.[1] Adamnán was an outstandingly able and versatile man. He was an ecclesiastical diplomat, actively concerned in the Easter controversy, engaged in Irish affairs, in touch with Northumbria. He was writing at a time when historical records—the annals—were taking shape at Iona, and he may have had a part in that enterprise.[2] He wrote a very good account of the holy places, both practical and well informed, a considerable feat both of scholarship and imagination (since, as far as we know, his information was all at second hand and he never visited them).[3] His Life of Columcille is divided into three books, dealing with the saint's miracles, his prophetic revelations, and his angelic visions. It is not what we should regard as history, yet it manages to include a great deal of historical information.

Adamnán's method of composition has been fully discussed.[4] Miss Brüning in 1917 set out the frequent borrowings of words and phrases, sometimes sentences, throughout his work.[5] The two

[1] *Adomnan's Life of Columba*, ed. A. O. and M. O. Anderson (London 1961). W. Reeves's edition (Dublin 1857) contains notes which are still helpful.

[2] *Supra*, 118.

[3] *Adamnán's De Locis Sanctis*, ed. D. Meehan, *Scriptores Latini Hiberniae*, III (Dublin 1958).

[4] G. Brüning, 'Adamnans Vita Columbae und ihre Ableitungen', *ZCP*, XI (1917), 213–304, and the introduction to the Andersons' edition, *op. cit.*

[5] These are set out in parallel columns, *ZCP*, XI (1917), 240–55.

prefaces and the final chapter are especially reminiscent of Evagrius' translation of Athanasius' Life of Anthony, of Sculpicius Severus' Life of Martin, of the *Gesta Silvestri* and of Jerome. There are other verbal reminiscences from these authors elsewhere in the Life, and from Gregory the Great, Vergil, Juvencus and the Scriptures. Yet on the one occasion where Adamnán paraphrases a whole incident from another source, he makes acknowledgment of it: one of his stories about Columcille reminds him of the Life of Germanus.[1] If he had deliberately lifted this story I doubt if he would have acknowledged it. He is prepared to borrow descriptive phrases, and his allusions show that he had a good verbal memory and probably a library to hand. They do not invalidate the truth of his own account. His purpose was didactic, and this must have influenced both his choice of material[2] and his manner of presentation. All the same, to claim that the Life is a purely artificial creation without regard to Columban tradition would be perverse.

Adamnán himself says that he used written sources about the saint: the scribe of the Schaffhausen MS, writing in or before 713, inserts a passage from the *acta* of Cummene, the seventh abbot of Iona who died in 669. But the main source must have been oral tradition. Adamnán says he obtained stories 'after diligent enquiry . . . from . . . certain informed and trustworthy old men'. He certainly claims that he used only sound tradition:

> Let no one suppose that I will write concerning this so memorable man either falsehood or things that might be doubtful or unsure, but let him understand that I shall relate what has come to my knowledge through the tradition passed on by our predecessors and by trustworthy men who knew the facts.[3]

When recounting the stories he often gives his source: that he had heard them, in his youth, from an old man who had been directly

[1] II, 34.
[2] He says that 'only a few out of very many things have been written down', Praef., I.
[3] Praef., II.

concerned;[1] that he had them through one intermediary, usually named;[2] that they came from abbot Failbe who, in his turn, had heard them from abbot Ségíne (624–52),[3] and so on. I think all this suggests that Adamnán was making a genuine attempt to report accurately.

We have then, in Adamnán's Life of Columcille, a very unusual thing; a Life written before 704, surviving in a manuscript written in or before 713, as well as in a ninth-century MS and in later transcripts. It was written by a learned man with conscientious scholarly standards. We should therefore be able to rely on its incidental information.

And amidst the prophesies, miracles and visions Adamnán does convey a surprising amount of information. He brings Columcille into contact with a number of important princes. We learn from him that Oswald of Northumbria 'had been in exile among the Irish' and that Columcille had appeared to him in a dream on the night before his battle with Cadwallon, prophesying his victory.[4] Columcille made prophecies about a number of kings. We hear from Adamnán of the Dál Riadic king Conall,[5] his cousin king Aedán[6] and of Aedán's sons, one of whom, Eochaid, succeeded;[7] of the Cenél Conaill king Aed and his son Domnall, both Uí Néill overlords; of Aed Sláine of Brega, also overlord of the Uí Néill; of Rhydderch son of Tuathal, king of Strathclyde. Whether these prophecies were made exactly as Adamnán and his predecessors believed does not matter to the historian, but his testimony is very valuable support and elaboration of the annals. It is the Life, not the annals, which tells us that the Dál Riadans fought in the battle of Mag Rath, a major landmark in the spread of Uí Néill power and the contraction of Ulster.[8] One cannot help wishing that Adamnán had been writing an 'Ecclesiastical History of the Scots' instead of a saint's Life, so that we might have explicit accounts where we now have tantalising allusions; for instance

---

[1] III, 23. Cf. I, 20. [2] I, 49. Cf. I, 2; III, 23.

[3] I, 1. Cf. I, 3. Cf. III, 19, from Commán who had the story from abbot Virgno. Cf. III, 23, etc.

[4] I, 1. [5] I, 7. [6] I, 8. [7] I, 9. [8] See *supra*, 102.

his references to the Synod of Druim Cett (575) do not tell us any of the things we want to know.[1]

The Life contains a lot of valuable information about Pictland. Bruide king of the Picts was a powerful overlord, for he had a sub-king of the Orkneys at his court.[2] In Columcille's day the Pictish areas which the saint visited were heathen.[3] *Magi* are frequently mentioned; Bruide had a *magus*, his fosterer Broichán, who was an enemy of Columcille. It is noteworthy that, though Columcille converted two Pictish households,[4] preaching through an interpreter, Adamnán never claims that king Bruide accepted Christianity. Other evidence suggests that the conversion of Pictland was a slow process.[5] But by Adamnán's day Columcille had monasteries within the boundaries of Pictland, for the Picts and the Irish in Scotland had twice in his own time (in 664–7 and in 683) been saved from plague by the virtues of the saint.[6] What Adamnán actually says is that Columcille preached to the pagan Picts and made some converts, though he does not mention the king among them; and that Christianity had spread in Pictland during the century between Columcille's time and his own. Bede makes a much greater claim for Columcille—that the saint had come to Britain 'to preach the word of God to the northern Picts', and that he had been successful in converting them,[7] and it is Bede's account which has been widely accepted. Adamnán's testimony here is preferable, and it fits in much better with the archaeological evidence.[8]

[1] This was where the position of Irish Dál Riata was discussed between Aed, Uí Néill overlord, and Aedán, king of Scottish Dál Riada, both of whom were claiming rights in Irish Dál Riata. See J. Bannerman in *Celtic Studies*, ed. J. Carney and D. Greene (London 1968), 1 ff.   [2] II, 42.

[3] II, 32, III, 14. (The Loch Ness Monster appears for the first time in II, 27.)
[4] II, 32, III, 14.

[5] Hughes, *Early Christianity in Pictland*, Jarrow Lecture 1971; cf. M. O. Anderson, 'Columba and other Irish Saints in Scotland', *Historical Studies*, V (1965), 26–36.

[6] II, 46.   [7] *HE*, III, 4.

[8] The whole question is discussed at length in my Jarrow Lecture, *op. cit.* (Please note that the *Amra* of Columcille, which I there—p. 14—date c. 800, ought to be dated c. 600.)

There are a great many allusions to life on Iona, some to its material as well as religious aspects.[1] We also hear a lot about books, and on two occasions there are references to an important scribal practice. A manuscript had to be checked through after it had been copied. 'I have need of one of the brothers to run through and emend with me the psalter I have written,' says Baíthéne.[2] And right at the end of the Life, after the 'Amen', the early eighth-century scribe Dorbene has written:

> I beseech all those that may wish to copy these books, nay more I adjure them through Christ, the judge of the ages, that after carefully copying they compare them with the exemplar from which they have written, and emend them with the utmost care; and also that they append this adjuration in this place.

This sentence is probably Adamnán's own colophon, transcribed by Dorbene.

Adamnán's Life of Columcille tells us many things which we would not otherwise know about Iona, Scotland and to a lesser extent Ireland in the century between the saint's death and his own lifetime. It supplements the annals and in one case modifies Bede. It also shows us a scholar writing confidently in Latin, a man with a good knowledge of the Fathers and some knowledge of the classics, basing his account on accepted literary models.

Cogitosus' Life of Brigit is a very different affair. Columcille did not die until 597 and there were probably written records at Iona from the very beginning. Brigit, by contrast, belongs to the early stages of Christianity in Ireland. Cogitosus claims that he had traditions[3] but, as we shall see, they were of a very different kind from Adamnán's. In spite of the conventions of hagiography,

[1] I, 38 (threshing grain), 37 (harvesting), 41 (a colony of seals), II, 23 (pig-slaughtering in autumn in a secular household on Islay), 29 (ironworkers among the monks of Iona).

[2] I, 23.

[3] 'Pauca de pluribus a maioribus et peritissimis tradita.' Writers of the Carolingian renaissance believed that Ultán and Ailerán had recounted the miracles of Brigit before Cogitosus (Esposito, *Hermathena*, XXIV [1935], 125–132). Cogitosus does not name these distinguished predecessors.

Adamnán's Columcille emerges as a person, not circumspect in youth, highly intelligent, determined and powerful, but also sympathetic and kindly: the Brigit of Cogitosus is a mythological figure.

This does not mean that Cogitosus's Life is valueless. Cogitosus may be the earliest formal Irish hagiography which we now possess.[1] He was a generation older than Muirchú (who seems to have written his Life of Patrick probably after c. 680 and certainly before 700,)[2] for Muirchú claims him as his 'father'. This would suggest that Cogitosus was writing about 650 or a little later. The beginning and the end of the Life deal with seventh-century affairs, things 'we have not only heard but seen with our own eyes', and they provide crucial contemporary evidence. The body of the Life is taken up with the miracles of Brigit, those 'few of the many things handed down by the great and most wise'.

Just as Adamnán belongs to the period of increasing detail in the reporting of the Iona Chronicle, so Cogitosus belongs to the period when the annal record for Kildare starts up. We have a record of the birth of Brigit in 457, which is an interpolated entry in *AU*. The annals give the deaths of Conlaed and Brigit; *AU* gives Brigit's death no less than three times. But the real history of Kildare starts with the entry in 639, of the death of bishop Aed Dub who was 'at first king of Leinster'.[3] There is a continuous series of entries from the year 686, opening with the death of a scribe. It looks therefore as if, during the seventh century, a scriptorium at Kildare had become active; as if the monastery had become involved in secular affairs and grown considerably in importance.

[1] It is possible that Cogitosus is not our earliest material about Brigit. There is an anonymous Latin Life which seems to use the same sources as Cogitosus (see Bieler, *Studia Patristica*, V [1962], 246–7) and the Latin portions of the eighth-century Old-Irish Life (ed M. O'Brien, *IHS*, I [1938–9], 121–34, 343–53) are very archaic.

[2] It is dedicated to Aed who died in 700, and who joined the *paruchia* of Patrick before Ségíne's death in 688.

[3] *Tig*. F. Ó. Briain, *Féil-sgríbhinn Eóin mhic Néill*, ed. J. Ryan, 460–1, writes on Leinster princes in the abbacy of Kildare.

This is also what Cogitosus implies in the opening and concluding sections of his Life. The original church had recently been rebuilt 'to hold the increased numbers of the faithful', and problems had arisen in its reconstruction.[1] He gives the only detailed description which we have of a seventh-century Irish church, a timber one hung with linen and decorated with paintings, which sounds considerably bigger than the early stone churches which we know.[2] The monastery housed a bishop with his school of clerics and an abbess with her virgins and widows, and presumably *manaig* (the monastic tenants), for Cogitosus speaks of the laity who attended the church. The settlement had its own water-mill,[3] which neighbours used.[4]

There is no mention of Patrick, and Cogitosus seems to be claiming for Kildare the sort of overlordship which Armagh achieved slightly later.[5] The bishop of Kildare is the 'chief bishop (*archiepiscopus*) of the Irish bishops', and the abbess is 'the abbess whom all the abbesses of the Irish venerate'. Kildare is 'a great metropolitan city', and Brigit's *paruchia* extends all over Ireland, 'from sea to sea'.[6] Even the lawyers of Armagh, when they drew up Patrick's claim to jurisdiction, did not dispute Brigit's supremacy in Leinster.[7] All this is contemporary, first-hand evidence.

The material about Brigit herself is in marked contrast. At the beginning comes a series of miracles of plenty, where Brigit gives her butter away and the deficiencies in her total are made up, where water is turned into beer, a stone into salt, and so on. There are also stories which show her in harmony with nature. She can hang her cloak on a sunbeam,[8] the wood supporting the altar at which she kneels when taking the veil burgeons into life.[9] There is a series of delightful tales about the animals and St Brigit. One,

[1] Migne, *PL*, LXXII, cols. 789 C–790 A.
[2] *Ibid.*, 788 D–789. *Infra*, 267.   [3] *Ibid.*, 787 C–788 B.
[4] *Ibid.*, 788 B C.   [5] See Hughes, *CEIS*, 84.
[6] Migne, *PL*, LXXII, cols 777–8 (Prologue).
[7] I take it that this is what the final sentence of the Book of the Angel means. Hughes, *CEIS*, 279.
[8] 779 D.   [9] 778 B–9 A.

which does not seem to belong to a well-recognised folk-pattern,[1]
goes like this:

An ignorant man saw a fox in the king's palace, the king's pet
fox, which had been taught all sorts of tricks. But the man did not
know this, and killed it. The king pronounced judgment on him:
an identical fox must be produced or the man should be killed and
his wife and children driven into slavery. The news was brought
to Brigit and she, grieving for the man, ordered her horses to be
yoked up and started to drive across the plain to the king's palace,
to plead for him. But a wild fox, commanded by God, came to her
as she travelled across the plain, jumped into the chariot and hid
under her robe. When she arrived, Brigit pleaded for the man, but
the king refused to free him unless he should be given another fox
of similar cunning. Whereupon Brigit produced the wild fox,
who proved able to perform all the tricks of the other. So the
victim was freed. However, when Brigit had gone home the fox
escaped back to the wild.[2]

The nature theme is prominent in the Lives of Brigit, and it has
often been remarked that she has many of the attributes of a pagan
goddess.[3] Among the pagan Irish 'a goddess used to be called
Brigit', says Cormac's Glossary, written c. 900, and we know of
three sister-goddesses of this name. So Brigit may well have
become confused with the goddess in people's minds. Her festival,
on 1 February, was *Imbolg*, the pagan festival of spring. Cogitosus
speaks in the conventional manner of the difficulties of his task,[4]
but he may genuinely have found some of his material hard to
translate into a Christian context.

Muirchú, composing a Life of Patrick, saw himself as following
in the footsteps of his 'father' Cogitosus, the only previous writer
of the *genre*. His Life is the first item in the Book of Armagh,
copied by Ferdomnach, who was transcribing the MS on 21

---

[1] Stith Thompson, *The Types of the Folktale* (Helsinki 1961).

[2] 782 D–783 A.

[3] Cf. *supra*, 32, P. Mac Cana, *Celtic Mythology* (London 1970), 34–5;
Macalister, *PRIA*, XXXIV (1919), 340–1.

[4] 'Quod opus impositum, et delicatae materiae arduum, parvitatis et ignor-
antiae meae et linguae minime convenit.'

September 807.[1] Muirchú had composed the Life more than a century earlier at the command of Aed of Sletty. Sletty joined the *paruchia* of Patrick when Ségíne was abbot of Armagh, between 662 and 688, and it seems likely that the Life was written as a result of that union.

Muirchú says that he is writing *incertis auctoribus*: nevertheless, he seems to have had some written sources. The first part of his Life is based on some text of Patrick's Confession, and on a narrative of his stay in Gaul.[2] With Patrick's return to Ireland the style becomes more rhetorical and the story more amusing.[3] Perhaps this change marks the end of the written sources and the beginning of oral legend. There is a long sequence about the contests between Patrick and king Lóegaire's druids, which ends in Lóegaire's conversion. There are stories about the north-east, where Patrick first set up an organised church, and the foundation of Armagh. (There was a north church standing here in Muirchú's day, a phrase which must imply a second church.[4]) The chapters mainly concerning his death and burial are added in the Book of Armagh as a *liber secundis*. Professor Bieler thinks that these all formed part of the same work by Muirchú.[5] This may be so, though they seem to me to show predominantly Ulster traditions rather different in emphasis from Book I.

When Patrick first set up his church in Ulster, that province must still have spread over much of northern Ireland, as it does in the *Táin*.[6] Armagh was certainly part of Ulster. Why else should an important church be established so close to the pagan sanctuary and royal capital of the Ulster kings? The expansion of the Uí

---

[1] See *Book of Armagh, Patrician Documents. Facsimiles in Collotype of Irish MSS* (Dublin 1937); *The Book of Armagh*, ed. J. Gwynn (Dublin, London, 1913), ff. 2–8v, 20; or W. Stokes, *Vita Tripartita* (London 1887), II, 269 ff; or transl. N. J. D. White, *St Patrick, his Writings and Life* (London 1920).

[2] It has been suggested that this part originally applied to Palladius.

[3] Professor Bieler says his style 'is not the solemn style of Adamnán: it might be called baroque. It certainly is the style of someone who had a definite idea of how one ought to write.' *Op. cit.*, 255.

[4] The Book of the Angel refers to a north and a south church. See *infra*, 267–8.   [5] *Four Latin Lives of St. Patrick* (Dublin 1971), viii.   [6] *Supra*, 178–9.

Néill began in the fifth century at Ulster's expense, and the contraction of Ulster took a long time. Its final stages were probably not achieved until the first half of the seventh century.[1] By Muirchú's time the Uí Néill were the dominant power in Ireland, and his Life presents Patrick not merely as founder of a Church in Ulster but as a missionary accepted by the Uí Néill. When Muirchú wrote, the grandsons of Aed Sláine of Brega were the ruling Uí Néill overlords and the whole scene for Patrick's trial of strength with the druids is set in Mag Breg, the central plain.

Patrick landed at the mouth of the Boyne, encamped at 'The Graves of the Men of Fiacc' near Slane, while Lóegaire was resident at Tara.[2] Tara is described as *caput Scotorum*, Lóegaire as *imperator barbarorum* and Niall, his father, as 'ancestor of the royal stock of almost the whole of the island'.[3] Mag Breg is the centre of the greatest kingdom of the Irish.[4] The contest in miracle-working ends in Lóegaire's conversion. Muirchú leaves no one in any doubt that the Uí Néill owed their Christianity to Patrick.

Yet the disturbances which lay behind the Uí Néill rise to power are evident in the additions. The Life says nothing about that all-important subject, Patrick's relics. The additions make it clear that Patrick died among the Ulaid. He intended to die in Armagh, but an angel made him return to Saul.[5] He was buried in Downpatrick. There was a dispute over the body between Airthir (in whose sub-kingdom Armagh lay) supported by the Uí Néill on the one side, and the Ulaid on the other. The Uí Néill were persuaded by a 'fortunate delusion' into thinking that they had got the body. Certainly the Book of the Angel, written probably early in the eighth century, says that Patrick's body lay at Armagh.[6]

[1] See F. Byrne, *Studia Hibernica*, IV (1964), 84.
[2] This is the area which is very well represented in early annals. See *supra*, 124–6.   [3] f. 2 a 2. Aed Sláine was Niall's great-great-grandson.
[4] 'In campo maximo, ubi erat regnum maximum nationum harum', f. 3 a 2.
[5] East of Downpatrick. Both Saul and Downpatrick are near the south-west end of Strangford Lough.
[6] But not the *Vita Tripartita*. Hughes, *CEIS*, 278.

One, at least, of Muirchú's aims was to attach Armagh to the Uí Néill, who were now clearly in the ascendant. The additions show that Patrick originally belonged to Ulster. His relics may have been taken eastwards as Ulster contracted; but the future of Armagh had to lie with the Uí Néill, as Muirchú's Life recognised. The Uí Néill overlords between 658 and 695 were all Brega kings, descendants of Aed Sláine, and it is interesting to find that the annals are concerned with that area, where Armagh later had her own steward.[1] The written sources for the Uí Néill annal entries may go back to this period in the later seventh century when Armagh was accumulating material to support her own claims and was anxious to link herself with Uí Néill power.

These three seventh-century Lives, of Brigit, Patrick and Columcille, are all very different, but they all add substantially to our historical information and understanding. The scribal activity which is evident here is, I believe, also reflected in the annals at the same period. Some Irish *scriptoria* certainly began before about 650, but the second half of the seventh century saw a great growth of activity in the production of historical, pseudo-historical and legal documents.[2]

III

We turn to a few examples of hagiography which seems to have been intended to build up the spiritual life. These were probably written for a religious audience, though, in each case, the author is unknown and the date must be a matter of conjecture. One of the least problematic is the Life of Samthann.[3] The annals say that she died in 739, and a Life was probably composed at the end of the eighth or the beginning of the ninth century. This is the basis

[1] See *supra*, 133-4.
[2] I have omitted Tírechán. He wrote, at about the same time as Muirchú, a document which aimed to establish Armagh's claims to property and jurisdiction. The sequence of places is determined by the circuit made by the abbot of Armagh, and the whole is cast into the form of a narrative of Patrick's journeys. It is thus evidence for Patrick's *paruchia* in the late-seventh century.
[3] Plummer, *VSH*, II, 253-61.

for our present Life. It mentions Niall, son of Fergal, king of Cenél Éogain, and Uí Néill overlord from 763–770, who ornamented the staff of Samthann with gold and silver. The Life echoes some aspects of the teaching of the culdee movement.[1]

Máel-Ruain of Tallaght, a leader of the *céli Dé*, had discouraged pilgrimage, for by the early Carolingian period it was clear that pilgrimage might become an abuse.[2] Samthann is shown as sharing his views. 'Since God is near to all who call on him there is no need for us to go oversea. It is possible to come to the kingdom of heaven from every land.'[3] Like the culdees, she recognised the importance of learning. When a master named Dairchellach wanted to quit study in order to give himself up entirely to prayer, she asked him how it would be possible to stabilise his mind if he neglected study? This does not imply any lack of interest in the spiritual life. Her answer to the monk who asked what was the proper position for praying, lying or sitting or standing, might be taken as a guide for the religious: 'One must pray in every position.'[4]

The Life of Íte[5] has much in common with this teaching. If her virgins will only persist without hindrance in prayer and meditation, God will always be present with them.[6] 'You are the temple of God, in body and in spirit,' said the angel to her.[7] According to her Life she would accept only a very small amount of land, because she did not wish to be weighed down by secular cares.[8] She taught that the three things most pleasing to God were a believing heart, a simple life, and generosity with charity.[9]

Her personal kindness emerges very strongly in the Life. She was a woman 'compelled by Christ',[10] and her love pursued the erring. One nun, who had committed fornication and left the monastery, had a son born to her in Connacht, where she fell into

---

[1] Some of the Tallaght documents also show that there was a connection between Samthann and the culdees.

[2] Hughes, 'The changing theory and practice of Irish pilgrimage', *JEH*, XI (1960), 143–51.

[3] *VSH*, II, 260.   [4] *Ibid.*, 259. *Omni statu est orandum.*

[5] *Ibid.*, 116–30.   [6] *Ibid.*, 119.   [7] *Ibid.*, 117.

[8] *Ibid.*, 119.   [9] *Ibid.*, 123–4.   [10] *Ibid.*, 117.

slavery. Knowing this, Íte sent a message to Brendan, who procured the woman's freedom, so that she and her child might return to live in Íte's community, where she was received with rejoicing.[1] It was Íte whom the Irish poet saw as the foster-mother of Christ.[2]

It is difficult to date her Life. The annals say she died in 570.[3] The Life claims to be written in the generation immediately following Íte's, for it speaks of a man 'whose son still lives' being brought to her. This is very hard to credit, even though a decided impression of her personality seems to have survived—a tolerant, humorous old woman,[4] who must have made an excellent abbess. Yet there are aspects of this Life which are not consistent with an early monastery. A skilled craftsman might join the settlement and marry there, presumably like the manach.[5] Íte herself performs severe fasts, sustained by an angel; but some of her virgins appear not to have been following a strict regime.[6] If this Life contains early elements, it would seem to have been substantially rewritten later. Its purpose remains didactic, and it seems to have been rewritten for a religious community.

Irish women's houses are of considerable interest, and their place within the monastic constitution has never been adequately studied. At least 119 Irish women saints or groups of women are mentioned in the Martyrology of Tallaght (and all November and part of December is missing). Yet we have Lives of only four women saints, Brigit of Kildare, Samthann of Clonbroney, Íte of Killeedy in Co. Limerick and Monenna of Killeevy in Co. Armagh.[7] There is another woman's house mentioned on a number of occasions in the annals, Cloonburren in Co. Roscommon. This enormous discrepancy between the minute number of

[1] VSH, II, 129.

[2] G. Murphy, Early Irish Lyrics (Oxford 1957), 26–9. Professor Murphy dates the poem c. 900.

[3] AU and Tig. AU gives another date as well, 577.

[4] VSH, II, 127–8.   [5] Ibid., 121–2.   [6] Ibid., 121, 125.

[7] Monenna's Lives would certainly repay study. It should be possible to reconstruct a seventh-century text. There is also a list of abbesses drawn up in the early ninth century. See Esposito, PRIA, XII (1910), C 202–51.

women's houses and the very large number of pious women must be due to the Irish law of inheritance. For a woman could not acquire more than a life interest in the land she inherited: on her death it passed back to her kin. Only if she acquired land for services rendered or by gift could she transmit it to her heirs. I think that many monasteries were set up on family lands; there is some good evidence for this, and it explains many of the peculiar features of Irish monasticism.[1] The pious women who appear in the martyrologies probably supported a few like-minded friends during their lives, but their households must have broken up with their deaths. Only in the few cases where a substantial grant of land was obtained by some gift could a perpetual monastic community have been founded. With the exception of Kildare, the women's communities seem to have been less ambitious, less competitive than many men's houses, and this may account for the accent of genuine piety in the Lives of Samthann and Íte.

The Irish Life of Columcille[2] was composed for preaching on the saint's festival, 9 June. Its main purpose was to instruct the faithful, and it was probably intended for a monastic audience. Columcille represented the Irish idea of the perfect pilgrim, and the Life begins with a homily on pilgrimage, taking as its text the 'friendly counsel' which God gave to Abraham: 'Leave thy country and thy land and thy neighbour in the flesh and thine own fatherland for my sake, and get thee into the country that I shall show thee.' The author goes on to distinguish between the three different ways in which men may be called to pilgrimage, and the three different kinds of pilgrimage.

He must have known Adamnán's Life, for he makes use of many of his stories. But he usually tells them more briefly and simply than Adamnán, and some incidents gain an added poignancy. At the end of his life Columcille says to his monks that at Easter 'I should have liked to go to heaven, but I did not wish you

---

[1] Hughes, *CEIS*, 76 f.
[2] Ed. and transl. Stokes, *Lismore*, lines 655–1119. The language of this Life is mainly Middle Irish, mixed with some Modern Irish. A few Old Irish forms remain, and there may have been an Old Irish nucleus.

to have grief or sorrow after your toil, so I have stayed with you from Easter to Whitsun'. When the horse comes and weeps against him and his attendant would have driven it away the saint stops him: 'Let him be, until he suffices himself with tears and sorrow in lamenting me.' It is all in Adamnán, but muffled in words.

Some things are added, for the legend of Columcille had by now developed much further. In Adamnán the first death on the island came about naturally after some time:[1] in the Irish Life it is deliberately requested by Columcille to consecrate the ground, and takes place immediately on landing.[2] The writer must by now bring Columcille into contact with Ireland's major saints: he has to be prophesied by Patrick, go to school with Finnian of Clonard, and he and Ciarán of Clonmacnoise are the gold and silver moons which shine over northern Ireland and Scotland and over central Ireland. The books written by Columcille which are occasionally mentioned in Adamnán have now become 300 books, and the churches founded by him have become 300 churches.

The common exemplar of the Irish MSS is an eleventh-century abridgement of a ninth- or tenth-century Life.[3] Although the date of the exemplar is an open question, it seems to me that the ninth century is the more likely. It was undoubtedly written in one of Columcille's monasteries in Ireland, but it does not show any clear provenance. It does, however, describe the foundation of Kells, and Columcille's prophesy that it 'would be the loftiest cloister he should have on earth'. After a series of Viking attacks on Iona, Kells was granted to Columcille, and the church was built in 807. This may well have led the community of Columcille in Ireland to feel the need for a new Life. Whatever its precise date, whether it belongs to the period of severe Viking pressure in the ninth century or the worst period of secularisation in the tenth, it warns us against assuming that the Viking Age put an end to genuine religion in Ireland.

---

[1] III, 6.   [2] Stokes, *Lismore*, lines 1011–17.
[3] Kenney, *Sources*, p. 434.

IV

The Irish Life of St Finnian of Clonard[1] probably goes back to an original of the tenth century.[2] Its aim is different from that of the old Irish Life of Columcille, and it was intended for a different kind of audience. It was predominantly for laymen, to interest, impress and encourage their generosity. It stresses the virtues of Finnian's cemetery to save a man from hell and of his well to heal sickness, the powers of his community's prayers to banish disease, his own right to judge at Doomsday by the side of Patrick and Jesus Christ (note the order). Unpleasant fates overtake those who oppose the saint,[3] while those who do him any kindness are rewarded in this life.[4] There are stories to explain and illustrate local place-names which the audience would understand and appreciate. This Life takes care to state the saint's claims to property; even when the writer knows little or nothing about the foundation of a church and has to fill in with a borrowed miracle theme he names the locality of the church and, if possible, the lay donor.

The main historical interest of the Life is that it reflects political conditions which were long out of date when the compiler wrote. Clonard is on the borders of the Northern and Southern Half of Ireland. Long before the tenth century it was reckoned as a famous monastery of the Northern Half, and Finnian's heirs seem to have been building up a *paruchia* in Connacht in the eighth century.[5] During the reign of Niall Caille, king of Cenél Éogain and Uí

[1] Stokes, *Lismore*, lines 2504-786.

[2] Hughes, 'The historical value of the Lives of St Finnian of Clonard', *EHR*, LXIX (1954), 353-72; 'The cult of St Finnian of Clonard from the eighth to the eleventh century', *IHS*, IX (1954), 13-27. When I wrote these I said ninth or tenth century. I now think that the parallels with the Vita Tripartita of Patrick, written c. 900, must be reminiscences, and am therefore in favour of the later date. Otherwise I am relieved to find that I still agree with myself.

[3] Stokes, *Lismore*, 2587-97.

[4] *Ibid.*, 2700-3, the calf killed for his entertainment found alive under its mother; 2672-7, barren fields made fruitful in return for a praise-poem.

[5] *IHS*, IX (1954), 22.

Néill overlord, his protégé Éogan abbot of Armagh (died 834) also ruled Clonard. In 851 and 859 abbot Suairlech of Clonard led the clergy of the southern Uí Néill at royal meetings summoned by Máel-Sechnaill, king of Meath and Uí Néill overlord. In the tenth century Clonard and Clonmacnoise, another great monastery of the Northern Half, shared the same abbots, Colmán (died 926) and Celechair (died 954).[1] During the ninth and tenth centuries Clonard was the leading monastery of Meath and, with Armagh and Clonmacnoise, one of the three greatest monasteries of the Northern Half.

Yet the Life shows that Finnian had originally a Leinster *paruchia*. The compiler, who was using both written and oral traditions,[2] speaks at some length about the Leinster foundations. Finnian was born and brought up 'here in Leinster' and his Leinster foundations are all connected with kings of Leinster peoples. Aghowle, in Co. Wicklow, where there are the ruins of a twelfth-century church with an early cross slab, and the neighbouring Condal, still connected by local legend with the saint, seem to have been important churches. But Clonard was 'the place of his resurrection', i.e., the place where he died, and this church, which housed his relics, became the head of his *paruchia*.

In the 740s Clonard had been linked with a Leinster monastery, Kildare, with whom it shared an abbot (died 748). The first sign of royal Uí Néill interest in Clonard comes at 775, when there was 'a conflict between Donnchad (king of Meath) and the *familia* of Clonard'. We do not know what this 'conflict' was about, but thereafter Clonard is seen as a northern, not as a Leinster, monastery. It looks as if Finnian founded a Leinster *paruchia* but that, with the expanding power of the Uí Néill, Clonard came within a northern sphere of influence.

---

[1] And later Flaithbertach (died 1015), though this entry is in a hand of the additions in *AU*.

[2] Stokes, *Lismore*, 2643.

V

It is probably the Tripartite Life of Patrick[1] which determines the character of many of the later Lives. It shows us a saint protecting his own, extracting privileges, quick to revenge injuries, a devastating curser. It does not present a morally elevating picture of Patrick. The saint sulking on the mountain top 'in evil mind' and brow-beating the angel to wring greater benefits from God is poor spiritual teaching.[2] As Sechnall rightly remarks of his colleague, there is very little charity.[3] We see Patrick driving his chariot three times over his sister Lupait for her unchastity, but it is she who prays that he will not take heaven from her lover and his offspring.[4] The conventional version of the curse goes like this: 'There shall be neither king nor material of a king (*rígdomna*)[5] from the family of Trían; he himself shall perish early and shall go down into bitter hell.'[6] More unusually, an opposer is told: 'It shall be lawful for men of Munster to peel you always, every seventh year, like an onion.'[7] Angels serve Patrick, even performing menial jobs like cleaning the hearth for him.[8] The writer is presenting the dignity and power of Patrick, and if he belittles Christian teaching it does not seem to matter.

Claims to property and jurisdiction are given prominence. Churches are carefully named and the sites recorded, occasionally with measurements. The names of the first incumbents are usually given and sometimes those of the grantors. The writer knows the more recent history of these places, for of one he says 'Columcille hath it now through cunning', of others 'the community of Clonmacnoise afterwards obtained it', 'the community of Columcille and Ardstraw have come down upon it'. Sometimes

---

[1] Ed. and transl. W. Stokes (Rolls Series, London 1887). It is discussed by K. Mulchrone, ZCP, XVI (1926), 1–94, ed. *Bethu Phatrdic* (Dublin, 1939).

[2] Historians may be interested to note that one of the privileges Patrick obtains is that no Saxons are to dwell in Ireland. *Ibid.*, 116.

[3] *Vita Tripartita*, 244.   [4] *Ibid.*, 234.

[5] i.e., those who are eligible for kingship.   [6] *Vita Tripartita*, 218–20.

[7] *Ibid.*, 208.   [8] *Ibid.*, 14.

he reports later traditions connected with a church; Cinaed son of Írgalach (king of Meath 724–8) violated a man who was under the safeguard of Patrick's flagstone at Donaghpatrick, so that three drops of blood trickled from the stone, drops which had to be heavily compensated. One suspects that the claims to jurisdiction could not all have been consistently put into effect. 'No one is king of Cashel until Patrick's successor installs him and confers ecclesiastical rank on him' must be wish rather than fact.[1] This passage goes on with a reference to the bishop-kings of Cashel: 'Twenty-seven kings of the race of Ailill and Oengus ruled in Cashel under a crozier until the time of Cenn Gégáin.' Cenn Gégáin was king of Cashel from 896 to 902, and his reign provides an approximate date for the Life. The references to relics scattered throughout show a similar interest in power and income. According to this account, sleep came over the inhabitants of Rome when Patrick visited the city, so that he was able to bring away all he wanted of her relics. There were 365 Roman relics at Armagh,[2] beside all Patrick's own valuables which he left in his churches.

Yet embedded in the Life is evidence of a spiritual experience at odds with the grasping opportunism. Some poets' rendering of an early catechism was incorporated. Here are parts of it:

> Question: Who is God,
> and where is God,
> of whom is God,
> and where is his dwelling?
>
> Is he ever-living,
> is he beautiful,
> was his son
> fostered by many?
>
> Answer: He has a dwelling
> in heaven and earth and sea
> and in all things that are in them.
> He inspires all things,

---

[1] *Vita Tripartita*, 196.   [2] *Ibid.*, 238.

he quickens all things,
he is over all things,
he supports all things.[1]

The eighth-century Breastplate of Patrick, which seems to have
been attributed to the saint at an early date,[2] looks as if it was
interpolated into the *Vita Tripartita*.[3] Here, in the midst of the
black arts of paganism, the poet buckles on 'a mighty strength,
invocation of the Trinity, belief in the threeness, confession of the
unity (on my way) to meet the Creator'.

The *Vita Tripartita* was almost certainly intended for preaching
to the public on the three days of Patrick's festival.[4] It was not to
teach Christian behaviour but to build up revenue, to assert rights,
to frighten the non-co-operative. Much of it is entertaining stuff,
told with considerable zest. It seems to have set a fashion in saints'
Lives, for many of those compiled later show similar characteristics. They stress the saints' property rights and the power of his
relics (another aspect of the same thing): they have considerable
entertainment value. As saints' Lives became more popular,
characteristics of the secular saga become more noticeable.

The Irish Life of St Senán of Inis Cathaig is a good example of
these qualities.[5] The influence of the *Vita Tripartita* is apparent in
the opening phrases,[6] and Patrick is called 'chief prophet and high
bishop (or archbishop) of the island of Ireland'. It is Patrick who
foretells Senán's birth, who blesses the Corcu Bascinn[7] with
'excellence of shipping', who prophesies blessings on those who
pay tithes, first-fruits and alms to Senán and heavy vengeance
with ruin on men and cattle if they do not. Senán's own struggle

---

[1] J. Carney, *Mediaeval Irish Lyrics* (Dublin 1967), 3–7. I thank Professor Carney and the Dolmen Press for permission to cite this translation.

[2] *Book of Armagh*, f. 16 probably contains a reference to it.

[3] *Vita Tripartita*, 48–52. The date is discussed by Professor Binchy, *Ériu*, XX
(1966), 232–7. I quote his translation of the opening lines.

[4] See the conclusion of the narrative in each book, 60, 170, 256.

[5] Stokes, *Lismore*, lines 1775–2503.

[6] *Vita Tripartita*, 172–4, the opening of the third book.

[7] See sketch map, *supra*, 111.

to secure freedom from royal taxation[1] shows him determined to secure the material advantages of his monastery, using curses and blessings to gain his purpose.

Like many of the saga-writers, this hagiographer did not bother about chronology. The saint is made to visit Martin at Tours, though Martin died c. 400, before Senán's birth could have been foretold by Patrick. He succeeds Maedoc as abbot of Ferns (Maedoc died in 626) and Martin gives him communion at his death. Such inconsistencies are common to many saints' Lives.

Kenney regards the Life as dependent on an exemplar written at Inis Cathaig 'when that was still a flourishing monastery, that is, not later than the tenth century'.[2] But Mac Airt's edition of the Annals of Inisfallen had not appeared when Kenney wrote, and these annals show Inis Cathaig becoming prominent from the very end of the tenth century. Inis Cathaig seems, in fact, to have been flourishing during the eleventh and twelfth centuries, after the O'Briens restored order to the lower Shannon area. Moreover, the description of the sea monster whom Senán turned out of the island is in the kind of rhetorical, alliterative style popular in the twelfth century.

O'tchuala an peisd iat, rocraith [a cend], 7 adracht a guairi fuirre 7 a gairbh-driuch, 7 ros-feg co hainserg ainniardhai. Nir'bhó ciuin, cairdemail, cennais in fegad dorat forro, ar ba hingnad le nech aile da hindsaigid ina hindsi [gusin dallá sin]. Doching dono a n-andochum cotren 7 cotairptech, cu rocrithnuigh in talam foa cosaibh. Ba heitigh, anaithnid, angbhuidh, adhuathmhar an míl doeirig ann . . . Airrter eich lé: rosc loindrech lasamail 'na cinn os sí feigh feochuir fichda fergach fæbhrach fordherc fuilidhe firamhnus forluaimhnech.[3]

[1] 'He would not be under tribute or service (*fo chís na fa f hoghnam*) to an earthly king.'

[2] Kenney, *Sources*, 365.

[3] Stokes, *Lismore*, lines 2212–19. 'When the monster heard them, it shook its head, and its hair stood up upon it, and its rough bristles; and it looked at them hatingly and wrathfully. Not gentle, friendly, mild was the look that it bestowed upon them, for it marvelled that anyone else should come to visit it in its island. So it went to them strongly and swiftly, insomuch that the earth

I am inclined to think that this Life is considerably later than the tenth century. Both its style here and the history of Inis Cathaig would suggest this.[1]

The opening chapters of the Life of Declán,[2] which we probably have in a twelfth-century form, were taken over bodily from the secular sagas.[3] It begins with a story of triple incest, and goes on with the expulsion of the Déisi and their settlement in Munster. But it is probably the Life of Findchú[4] which comes closest to the conventions of the secular tales. Findchú is very much a warrior-hero. Even his name reminds us of that other hound, Cú Chulainn, and his career must have heroic models. Like Cú Chulainn, he was famous for his boyhood deeds,[5] deeds of spirit, anger and valour, with a judgment at the end. When he fought, the heat of his battle fury manifested itself in abnormal phenomena. His teeth flashed sparks of fire,[6] in his encounter with the Vikings at Ventry his 'wrath and indignation arose like flakes of red flame, or like the rush of a wave to the land', and 'the howling and rending of a hound possessed him in his valour on that day'.[7] Findchú's reputation as the warrior-saviour is emphasised: 'Let us send to the slaughterous warrior to the south of us,' says the king of Munster, 'even to Findchú of Brigown; for he promised me that, whenever stress of war should be on me, he would come with me to battle to help me, having with him the Cennchathach, even his own crozier.'[8] Before this battle Senán went three times right-handwise round his own host, crozier in hand.[9] On another

trembled under its feet. Hideous, uncouth, ruthless, awful, was the beast that arose there. A horse's mane had it; an eye gleaming flaming in its head, and it keen, savage, froward, angry, edged, crimson, bloody, cruel, bounding.'

[1] In *CEIS*, 225, I accepted Kenney's tenth-century date. I should like to revise my opinion now.

[2] P. Power, *Lives of Declan and Mochuda* (London 1914) for Irish version; Plummer, *VSH*, II, 32–59 for Latin version.

[3] As Kenney points out, *Sources*, 313.

[4] Stokes, *Lismore*, lines 2788–3302.

[5] Performed before he was nine. *Ibid.*, lines 2846–77.

[6] *Ibid.*, lines 2772–3. [7] *Ibid.*, lines 3180–6. [8] *Ibid.*, lines 3082–4.

[9] To bring good luck. Going round left-handwise (widdershins) brings ill luck in the sagas.

occasion he made a cairn of the enemy's heads.[1] The dues which he obtained from three princes have a ring of the Book of Rights —fifty bugle horns from the Uí Caissín, fifty foreign steeds from the Uí Tordelbaig, fifty silver pails from the Dál Cais.[2]

The usual allusions to material rights come into this Life,[3] though not as frequently as in some others. But of course Findchú's relics are powerful. Findchú marches into battle with the Cennchathach (his crozier; the names means 'head battler') in his hand, and when the king wants to borrow it he will not give it up, 'so that on himself might be the glory of routing the foe'. As entertainment, the Life of Findchú strikes me as one of the most successful of Irish saints' Lives, probably because the hagiographer has borrowed with so little reserve from the conventions of secular story-telling.[4]

These twelfth-century Lives often provide useful information about twelfth-century monasteries. At Lismore there is practically nothing left to recall the pre-Norman monastery, but the Life of Mochuda[5] speaks of many chapels and monasteries, a convent for women, one part of the main monastic enclosure forbidden to women, an anchoritic settlement in the glen below the great monastery. Lismore is also said to be a place of pilgrimage for the Britons and English.[6] The Life of Colmán of Lann (in Westmeath),[7] very probably written soon after 1122, shows indisputably that the erenagh was a married man,[8] and that there was

---

[1] Stokes, *Lismore*, lines 2978–80.

[2] *Ibid.*, lines 3127–9. Cf. *infra*, 285–7.   [3] *Ibid.*, lines 3269–72.

[4] The chronology is wildly inconsistent, even more so than in most Lives. He is born in the reign of Diarmait son of Aed Sláine (died 665), baptised by Ailbe of Emly (died *AI*, 528) and his parents settle on land provided by Óengus mac Natfraich king of Munster (died 492). He is educated by Comgall of Bangor (died 602) and later joins in battles against the Vikings.

[5] See Kenney, *Sources*, 452.

[6] I think this Life may contain much earlier traditions. To what period does the anti-British feeling go back? 'My city shall never be without men of the British race who will be butts and laughing stocks and serve no useful purpose.'

[7] Ed. and transl. K. Meyer, *Betha Colmáin maic Lúacháin*, Todd Lecture Series, 17 (Dublin 1911).

[8] *Ibid.*, cc. 28, 98.

hereditary succession to his office.[1] The monks of Lann must sometimes have attended the great fair of Telltown, for, when they are disappointed at being unable to go, the angels come and run races for them.[2] Tech Conan, 'the abbot's house of Colmán mac Lúacháin', had a famous goldsmith in residence. He made a gold and silver bridle which he took to sell to the king of Offaly: its price was twelve cows.[3] These are the sort of bits of information which such Lives contain.

The Life of Colmán, like so many others of this period, has a clear statement of financial rights, plus a claim to be exempt from royal taxes. This Life shows us very plainly that hagiography composed during the 'reform' period for popular consumption often exhibits remarkably little influence of any moral and didactic purpose. There is an amusing story here about king Cinaed of Offaly, who falls in love with the wife of the king of Tara and has an assignation with her. The wronged husband surrounds them with his troop. But Cinaed puts himself under the safeguard of Colmán, and he and the queen are turned into stag and fawn, so that they are able to make their escape. 'And God's name and Colmán's were magnified by that miracle'.[4]

VI

Much of these late Lives is pure folk-lore, so that we seem nearer the pagan past than in some of the Lives written centuries earlier. Plummer thought that the attributes of pagan divinities had been transferred to the saints, a view which Kenney rejected.[5] But Dr Máire Mac Neill's work on the *Festival of Lughnasa* suggests that Patrick displaced a former actor in the mythological legends, and that that actor was Lug.[6] The excavations at Knockaulin and Emain Macha emphasise the proximity of major pagan sanctuaries to two great monastic foundations.[7] Much of the hagiography probably represents continuity between Christian Ireland and the pagan past.

[1] *Ibid.*, c. 37.　　[2] *Ibid.*, c. 84.　　[3] *Ibid.*, cc. 40–1.　　[4] *Ibid.*, c. 86.
[5] *Sources*, 302.　　[6] *Festival of Lughnasa* (Oxford 1962), 409.
[7] *Supra*, 32, 74.

As Kenney says, the saints' Lives are 'one of the most extensive classes of material relating to the history of early Ireland'. Whether sermons or sagas, whether for a monastic audience or for popular preaching, whether written to explain a political situation or to prove a monastery's economic claims, their incidental information, properly criticised, will yield much that is of value. The picture of the saint is infinitely varied; either the monastic founder and missionary like Adamnán's Columcille, the spiritual teacher, or the saints who, as Gerald of Wales wrote, were more prone to anger and revenge and more vindictive than saints of any other country.[1] In one and the same Life you can meet a saint humble and charitable, or arrogantly cursing.

Where we have several Lives of a saint like Patrick, you can also see the same saint changing his features as time goes on. Patrick's Confession shows a man toiling, insulted, persecuted, someone with a blot on his copybook who has repented and worked for God, and who feels hurt and indignant that his efforts should be so badly misinterpreted by his fellow-Christians. It is a completely convincing, contemporary document.[2] Muirchú presents a heroic figure, protecting his followers, worsting his opponents, an infallible wonder-worker: St Patrick has become the hero of a saga. He remains so in the *Vita Tripartita*, but by now he is wringing privileges from God, concerned above all with his rights and status. Patrick's gifts to the pagan Irish described in his Confession have here become nine companions' load of gold and silver, which God promises to give to the Irish for believing.[3] This Life demonstrates clearly that precision does not imply truth in hagiography. For instance, Muirchú says that many of the heathens perished in Patrick's encounter with Lóegaire: the author of the *Vita Tripartita* knows the number, twelve thousand.[4]

[1] *Topographia Hibernie*, ed. J. J. O'Meara, *PRIA*, LII (1949), C 156.

[2] In the Book of Armagh version of the Confession some, but not all, the passages in which Patrick confesses his weaknesses have been omitted. See Bieler, *Libri Epistolarum Sancti Patricii Episcopi* (Dublin 1952), I, 18.

[3] Confession, cc. 51, 52, Patrick is defending himself against charges of corruption, saying that he took nothing from his converts: on the contrary, he made gifts to them. Cf. *Vita Tripartita*, I, 30.   [4] *Vita Tripartita*, I, 58.

The Lives inevitably reflect the age in which they were produced. In the seventh century the great monasteries were beginning to build up their history, making entries which then or later became annals, writing down traditions of their founders. Some Lives seem to reflect the spiritual teaching of the reform movement of the later eighth and ninth centuries. The *Vita Tripartita* and the Lives which follow it frequently show the secularisation which the Church underwent in the tenth century, and the character of many of the twelfth-century Lives makes one wonder just how deeply the twelfth-century reform really penetrated.[1]

---

[1] Against these we have, of course, to set the Life of Malachy by St Bernard (which I have not discussed because it is not by an Irishman), as well as other texts like *The Writings of Bishop Patrick, 1074–84*, ed. A. Gwynn, *SLH*, I (Dublin 1955). All the same, the hagiography is evidence, which has to be remembered when we use words like 'reform'.

CHAPTER 8

Art and Architecture

I

There have been, during the present generation, some fine studies of Irish art which provide detailed discussion of groups of objects and a coherent history of the development of styles.[1] Books and articles have been lavishly illustrated, so that it is easy for anyone to see something of the history of Irish art. There may be justification for thinking that modern work has made this chapter unnecessary. But art and architecture, like literature, are one of the ancillary sources of Irish history, so I shall try to indicate how they illustrate and add to the information supplied by the written evidence.

First of all, the objects themselves provide some direct evidence which the historical texts rarely, if ever, give. One wants to know how these things were made; also by whom, if possible where, and with what purpose (indeed the usual questions with which an early Irish historian begins his work).[2] The first question is less easy to answer than might be expected, for art historians seem generally much less interested in the technology of production than in the origins and borrowing of motifs. However, there is an admirable paper by Professor O'Kelly on the making of the Moylough belt-shrine,[3] an object which shows several of the techniques used by early Irish metalworkers, and there is some discussion by Mlle Henry and Mr and Mrs de Paor about

[1] F. Henry, *Irish Art in the Early Christian period to AD 800* (London 1965); *Irish Art during the Viking invasions, 800–1020 AD* (London 1967); *Irish Art in the Romanesque period, 1020–1170 AD* (London 1970). These are quoted as Henry I, II and III. L. and M. de Paor, *Early Christian Ireland* (London 1958). For other papers see bibliography.

[2] *Supra*, 216.

[3] 'The belt-shrine from Moylough, Sligo', *JRSAI*, XCV (1965), 149–88.

how the *objets d'art* were composed. Mr Powell, who bound the Book of Kells and the Book of Durrow, has written about their make-up,[1] and H. G. Leask has discussed Irish building techniques.[2] Many of the raw materials of production could have come from Ireland, for silver and gold are found there, and stones for jewellery can be picked up on the beaches. But amber and tin were imported, possibly gold and silver also. A cattle-rearing country, Ireland had plenty of calf-skins for vellum, and there was wood or stone in abundance for building.

Irish craftsmen used their talents on a variety of objects. The most familiar are those which have survived best; the stone-crosses and metalwork—brooches, pins, ecclesiastical equipment such as bells and book covers, hanging bowls, altar vessels and reliquaries. The Irish believed in the virtue of the relics of their own saints.[3] They saved from disease, brought success in battle and confirmed oaths and treaties, so they have legal and sociological implications. Reliquaries become common from c. 700, demonstrating the growing prestige and wealth of the Church. The art of the scribes has also survived, and, like the metalwork, has two periods of brilliance—the later seventh to the early ninth century and the later eleventh and twelfth centuries. There is some surviving ornamental leather-work,[4] and the literature mentions painting on wood. We know almost nothing about textiles, and the Irish did not follow the Carolingian fashion for ivories.

It must be clearly understood that in the earlier period of Irish art, the dating of the objects is highly controversial, since it rests only on stylistic grounds. Art historians are not even always agreed on whether objects belong to successive phases or to the same period.[5] In the later period the inscriptions on the metal-

---

[1] *Scriptorium*, X (1956), 3–26.

[2] *Irish Churches and Monastic Buildings*, I (Dundalk 1955).

[3] We hear of the relics of Peter and Paul, and the Cross of Cong was made from a fragment of the true cross. Nevertheless the vast majority of Irish reliquaries are for native saints.

[4] J. W. Waterer, 'Irish book-satchels or budgets', *Mediaeval Archaeology*, XII (1968), 70–82.   [5] See *infra*, 266.

work become more specific and so provide dating criteria.

The ornamental metalwork of the late-seventh and eighth centuries is basically constructed of bronze or silver, the former frequently tinned, the latter frequently gilt, embellished with panels of diverse ornament. Probably the most exquisitely detailed piece of all those now existing is the Tara brooch,[1] the ring 8·5 cms (3¼in.) in diameter. The back of this (which could not have been seen when it was being worn) has openwork silver panels overlying copper, set into the base of cast silver which was ornamented and gilded. There are studs of blue and red glass set in silver frames. The front of the brooch is cast with sunken panels, which contain filigree designs on various planes. The filigree is composed of twisted, beaded or plain gold wires, soldered or surface-melted[2] on to a base of gold foil. These filigree panels are held in place by stitching, a technique by which claws are cut in the frame and fold over to clasp the filigree panel. In addition to the filigree panels there are embellishments of circular and rectangular studs of amber and domed hemispheres of glass in various shades of blue, occasionally combined with red, set in silver-gilt depressions. To the hinge which connects the chain and brooch there are added two tiny human faces, cast in purple glass and placed chin to chin, a frequent arrangement in Irish art. The virtuosity of technique and versatility of design in this piece are hard to equal.

The Moylough belt-shrine shows the complicated processes and exquisite finesse of the jeweller. The leather belt is enclosed in tinned bronze strips, where molten tin has been run on the bronze.[3] The belt is in four segments, and roughly in the centre of each is a medallion made of cast bronze with little recesses filled with glass and enamel. Two of the medallions contain central round panels of silver bearing a triple triskele design.[4] The silver, which is 0·1 mm thick, was struck from an intaglio

---

[1] For illustrations, see Henry I, plates 38, 40, 41, 42. I am indebted to Dr Raftery for showing this to me and explaining its technique.

[2] For these processes see H. Maryon, *PRIA*, XLIV (1938), C 190–4.

[3] O'Kelly, *op. cit.*, 152.   [4] O'Kelly, plate 11, or Henry, I plate 35.

die,[1] which could have been cut in hard metal or stone or bone. This means that some of the bone 'trial-pieces' which are often turned up in Irish excavations might have had such a purpose. The glass studs in the buckle were made by laying a silver grid in a clay mould, putting glass on the back and applying heat through a blow-pipe until the glass softened and sank into the cells.[2] Finally a layer of glass was fused on to the back of the stud to give it the necessary height. Millefiori glass was frequently used to decorate panels in Irish jewellery. The usual method of manufacture was to group bars of differently coloured glass in a bundle, so as to give a pattern when seen end-on.[3] This was heated to fuse the glass, which was drawn out to give varying thicknesses. Sections could then be cut transversely from the patterned rod.

The expert jeweller had to be in command of a considerable number of difficult techniques, and, although some fall out of popularity in the later period, his work must always have required great skill and long training, as well as talent. The later seventh- and eighth-century objects show a most elaborate expertise. All the monasteries could not possibly have possessed artists of the calibre of the man who made the Ardagh chalice, though some great houses and some royal courts had resident metalworkers. A number of objects were recovered from the royal site at Lagore, where there was millefiori and glass-working. Enamel, glass and millefiori were prepared at Garranes. In ecclesiastical contexts, Mr de Paor's excavation at Inis Celtra has revealed part of a bronze-working furnace to the west of St Brigit's church, and crucibles and moulds were found in the excavation south of the cathedral in Armagh. The *Vita Tripartita* names Patrick's metalworkers: whether Patrick had them may be disputed on this evidence, but the hagiographer c. 900 thought

[1] i.e., a recessed carving, in which no part projects beyond the original face of the material. You can experiment by taking a piece of kitchen foil, supporting it on wax, putting the die face-down and pressing it. See O'Kelly, *op. cit.*, 184.

[2] O'Kelly, *op. cit.*, 175.

[3] For this and other methods see O'Kelly, *op. cit.*, 185–7.

it quite natural that he should have. It seems likely that ornaments were made at one place and taken to another. In the Life of Colmán of Lann we hear of the goldsmith from the abbot's house selling one of his productions to the king of Offaly. But the jeweller's equipment was easily portable—small crucibles, implements, and an anvil about the size of a shoemaker's last—so it is possible that the jeweller may have travelled. There is difference of opinion on this question.

In the later period the inscriptions on the shrines often enable us to see where and by whom the work was done. Patrick's bell was enshrined under the auspices of the abbot of Armagh by Cú-dulig Ua Inmainen and his sons. The Cathach of Columcille was sent to Kells where its shrine was made by Sitric Mac Mic Aeda, a craftsman who appears in one of the Kells charters.[1] Mlle Henry is inclined to attribute several objects associated with Clonmacnoise and North Munster to a workshop at Clonmacnoise.[2] If her interpretation of one of the inscriptions on the Cross of Cong is correct, the craftsman who made the shrine was abbot of Clooncraff, though the man who supervised the work for king Toirdelbach was bishop and abbot of Roscommon and Clonmacnoise.[3] Kells, Clonmacnoise and possibly Armagh and Lismore (for the Lismore Crozier was made for an abbot of Lismore who died in 1113) all seem to have had recognised workshops at this period.

We know some of these patrons from the inscriptions of late-eleventh- and twelfth-century reliquaries. Cathbarr king of Cenél Conaill is mentioned on the bookshrine holding the Cathach, made between 1062 and 1098. The cross of Cong was made for Toirdelbach Ua Conchobair king of Connacht.[4] Domnall Ua Lochlainn had Patrick's bell enshrined[5] and three princes of Desmond are associated with the shrine of St Lachtin's

---

[1] Henry, III, 89. According to *Tig.* certain Cenél Conaill relics (this one is not mentioned) were brought to Kells in 1090 with 120 ounces of silver, presumably for their enshrining.

[2] *Ibid.*, 100 ff.   [3] *Ibid.*, 107–8.   [4] *Ibid.*, plates 42, 43.

[5] *Ibid.*, plates 22, 23, 24, 27.

arm.[1] Eleventh- and twelfth-century kings wanted to establish their connection with these relics and enlist their support.

The manuscripts provide direct evidence about the *scriptoria*. Presumably the vellum was prepared in the monastery; and when we think of a *scriptorium* at work we should probably imagine men and boys pumicing vellum and repairing holes, seeing how to cut a skin the most economical way, as well as scribes writing and painting. Even in a beautiful illuminated gospel-book like Durrow the preparation of the vellum, its colour and thickness, varies.[2] One of the features of many Irish manuscripts is the irregularity of the gatherings.[3] Whereas the Book of Lindisfarne has regular gatherings of eight (that is eight leaves made up of four pairs of conjoint bifolia folded in half) the Book of Durrow, though the gatherings are often in tens, has single leaves inserted in more than half of them,[4] and the gatherings of the Book of Kells vary from four or five to twelve.[5] The Book of Armagh, the Book of Dimma, the Book of Mulling and the Stowe Missal all have irregular gatherings: the Cathach and the Schaffhausen Adamnán have regular gatherings of tens and twelves respectively, so this is not an absolute standard of assessing origin. Nevertheless, this sort of evidence of irregularity often goes with an Irish background.

By the end of the sixth century, *scriptoria* were sufficiently well established in Ireland for the scribes to have developed a fine tradition of caligraphy. The graceful majuscule of the psalter known as the Cathach ('Battler') of St Columba is one of the best illustrations. All the continental scripts grew out of the degenerate cursive hand of late antiquity. Irish caligraphy is different from them all, and seems to be an independent creation deliberately evolved in the Irish *scriptoria*.[6]

A book, especially an elaborate luxury book like the Book of

[1] Henry, III, plates 38, 39, 40.
[2] R. Powell, *Codex Durmachensis* (Olten 1960), 80.
[3] This is one of Lowe's criteria for Irish provenance, *CLA*, II, xii.
[4] R. Powell, *Scriptorium*, X (1956), 13, 17–21.   [5] *Ibid.*, 3, 5–12.
[6] See L. Bieler, *Ireland*, 16–18 for examples. Cf. Bieler, *Scriptorium*, III (1949), 273.

Kells[1] (perhaps two hundred years later than the Cathach), tells us something about the manner of its production. There seem to have been four major painters at work here, besides a number of other less skilled illuminators.[2] Someone must have planned the book, assigned the carpet page, chi-rho and initial pages to one artist, the portraits to another, and so on. Sometimes the plans went awry, as they did in the execution of the canon-tables. We have to imagine an experienced, wealthy and sophisticated *scriptorium*, in touch not only with Northumbria and with Pictland, but also familiar with Carolingian developments.[3] The poetry shows us scribes writing under the green wood; but only a big monastery would be likely to house several painters of Kells quality, and they would have needed all the resources of a well-established *scriptorium*.

The early crosses are simple designs incised on stone slabs, but subsequently the high crosses become free-standing, bearing ornament in relief. They have a carved base and, before the romanesque period, are often topped with a house or shrine-shaped cap. They fall into fairly well-defined groups, with rather different characteristics. Clear and sharply-cut designs distinguish the Ahenny group, generally recognised as of the eighth century; the Kells crosses which Mlle Henry dates to the later eighth and ninth centuries have very sensitive and well-modelled figures; the granite crosses to the west of the Wicklow Mountains and in the Barrow valley are rather roughly cut, and the crosses of Monasterboice and Clonmacnoise (tenth century in Mlle. Henry's dating) are carved in bold, rounded relief. The unfinished east cross at Kells shows that the stone was first cut out—it may have been obtained like that. Raised panels were then prepared, from which the scenes could be carved in relief. It looks as if the crosses at Ahenny, Kilkieran and Tibberaghny are by the same sculptor, and two crosses from Lorrha and another at Inis Celtra are very similar.[4] Did this sculptor travel? Miss Roe suggests

---

[1] *Codex Cenannensis* (Berne 1950–1).   [2] Henry, II, 73 ff.
[3] For the controversy over the origins of this book see *infra*, 262–3.
[4] Henry, *Irish High Crosses* (Dublin 1964), 21–2.

that the crosses were executed by travelling craftsmen: a master mason and his assistants moved about carrying out commissions.[1] Much later, perhaps in the twelfth century, Inis Celtra may have been producing sculpture for the Lower Shannon area.[2] There must also have been 'pattern books', probably kept by the masons,[3] since many of the scenes are similar. Indeed, the designs on metalwork, manuscripts and stone crosses all have striking similarities. Had the executors learned their basic designs in Irish schools before they specialised in their various arts? Were these the monastic schools? We have somehow to account for the community of design between illuminators, metalworkers and masons. We must add to these the men who painted scenes on wood, which have now disappeared but which are mentioned in the literary sources.

The stone crosses are in contrast to the very primitive design of the stone churches. The building of monasteries and forts was certainly by men of the locality. Early churches, except perhaps in very stony districts, were of wood, and have not survived. Cogitosus' description of the seventh-century church at Kildare[4] is our best source of information for these. The early stone churches and cells are corbelled, each course overhanging the course below so that the building gradually narrows and can be finished by a flat slab. When the building is circular the stones are wedged by their own pressure against each other, but in a rectangular building there is a tendency for the roof to collapse inside. This could be averted by building a round arch with a croft above, which served to prop the roof slopes. The earliest example is at Kells, if Columcille's House there is the church which the annals say was completed in 814. In the early churches no mortar is used on the outside, but the stonework is often finely finished and the stones are fitted together with great care. A great many men must have been capable of simple building. Tenants had to help their

[1] *Seanchas Ardmhacha*, II (1956), 80.

[2] Dr Liam de Paor's excavation here is in progress. *Bulletin of the Group for the Study of Irish Historic Settlement*, I (1970), 28.

[3] Miss Roe's suggestion, *op. cit.*   [4] *Supra*, 228.

lord build his cashel, and no doubt they put up their own houses and farm buildings. Every sizeable monastery must have had competent buildings, either in wood or stone. The simplicity of the architecture is remarkable, for the Irish knew the ground plans of continental churches. Adamnán, sitting in his small dark building on Iona, had probably drawn out some of the plans and had certainly described a number of eastern *basilicae*.[1] Yet Irish architecture is comparatively little influenced by foreign models.[2]

II

Whereas studies in technology are still few and far between, there has been a great deal of discussion about designs. These indicate the foreign contacts of the Irish and illustrate their history. The Church was almost certainly the primary channel for borrowings. In the Cathach of Columba, a psalter traditionally associated with the saint, which probably dates from the end of the sixth century, we can see an Irish *scriptorium* at an early stage:[3] the scribe wrote a clear and elegant hand, drew comparatively simple and very graceful initials decorated with the La Tène designs which are found on contemporary cross slabs. In the seventh century the repertoire of Irish artists widened, partly by contacts with the continent and with Pictland, but much more dominantly through the influence of Anglo-Saxon metalworkers' designs. The very close connection between Ireland (and this includes Scottish Dál Riada) and Northumbria is illustrated by the controversies besetting the origins of certain manuscripts. The Book of Durrow[4] was illuminated in a *scriptorium* intimate with earlier Irish style, with Anglo-Saxon jewellery and with Pictish symbol stones. It has a Vulgate text, though not the Italo-Northumbrian Vulgate of the Codex Amiatinus (which was definitely written at Monkwearmouth/Jarrow); the gospel symbols belong to the Old-Latin version and much of the prefatory material belongs

[1] D. Meehan, *Adamnán's De Locis Sanctis, SLH*, 3 (Dublin 1958).

[2] *Infra*, 261–2, for twelfth-century styles.

[3] Henry, I, plates 9 and 12.   [4] *Codex Durmachensis* (Olten 1960).

to the Old-Latin tradition. We might justifiably look for a *scriptorium* which could produce this book in Dál Riada or Northumbria or Ireland.

Continental influence on Irish art was present from at least the seventh century. It may be seen in designs on the early slabs and crosses, which Miss Roe has traced back to late-antique objects.[1] Mlle. Henry has argued that Carolingian ivories were the origins of many of the scenes depicted on the scripture-crosses.[2] The upper binding strip and collar-knop of the Kells crozier have an acanthus like foliage based on Carolingian models, and the Clonmacnoise plaque has similar ornament.[3]

Irish art up to about 900 reveals a country in intimate contact with the British Isles and the continent, teaching and learning, open minded, eager to adapt foreign themes, though with a pronounced tradition of her own, so that foreign influences were transmuted into Irish forms. The sculptors may have been aware of foreign models for a little longer. Then, about the middle of the tenth century, the English and continental influence which had played so dominant a part in the development of Irish art seems for a time to decline. It is now the Vikings who affect Irish art and architecture, at first indirectly, later directly.

Irish round towers seem to be an indirect by-product of the Viking raids. They may have been built first in the ninth century, and are mentioned in the annals from 948 on. They were excellent defensive structures and served a variety of purposes, as keep, treasury, look-out and bell-tower. It seems that in the Viking age the earlier wooden monastic structures gave way to building in stone, a change probably encouraged by Viking devastations.

The interpenetration of Irish and Scandinavian styles is an interesting comment on the relations between the two peoples. During the ninth century the Irish borrowed very little from Scandinavian art. The Hiberno-Viking brooches and the thistle brooches, both usually of silver with decoration of Scandinavian

---

[1] H. M. Roe, 'The Irish high-cross: morphology and iconography', *JRSAI*, XCV (1965), 213–26.   [2] Henry, II, 197 ff.
[3] M. Mac Dermott, 'The Kells Crozier', *Archaeologia*, XCVI (1955), 97.

type, look very different from earlier Irish metalwork and were made in the Viking colonies. It was not until the end of the tenth century that Scandinavian themes began to be adopted by Irish metalworkers.[1] From the mid-eleventh century Irish metalwork shows strong traces of a mixed Scandinavian-Irish style.

Bone trial pieces from eleventh- and twelfth-century Viking Dublin have close affinities with the side panels of the Cathach shrine and with the shrine of St Senán's bell. There was now close contact between Irish and Hiberno-Norse craftsmen. The manuscript illumination tells the same story. A group of late-eleventh- and early-twelfth-century manuscripts have foliage-and-animal decoration which has affinities with Scandinavian art.[2] The two manuscripts of the Liber Hymnorum[3] and the second part of Rawl. B 502[4] belong to this group, and the style seems to have connections with Leinster.[5] The beast-and-snakes decoration of some early-twelfth-century manuscripts has much in common with the Scandinavian Urnes style.[6] The painter of the Corpus Missal[7] took these Scandinavian elements and transmuted them into Irish art.

The Norsemen in the tenth century were already becoming Christian: in the eleventh century Dublin gained its own bishop. Irish illumination and metalwork agree with the literary evidence in showing that, by the mid-eleventh century at the latest, a genuine integration of the Viking colonies had taken place. By this time they were Hiberno-Norse.

Irish manuscripts show surprisingly little influence from English or French Romanesque art. Romanesque influence is more or less confined to the stone-work, and even here it is adopted in a very idiosyncratic style.

At a period when splendid new churches were being built in

[1] M. Mac Dermott, 'The croziers of S. Dympna and S. Mel and tenth-century Irish metalwork', *PRIA*, LVIII (1957), 193–5.

[2] F. Henry and G. Marsh-Micheli, 'A century of Irish illumination, 1070–1170', *PRIA*, LXII (1962), 126–36.

[3] *Infra*, 283.   [4] *Infra*, 274.

[5] Henry and Marsh-Micheli, *op. cit.*, 136. See plates 8, 9, 10, 12–16.

[6] *Ibid.*, 136–42.   [7] *Ibid.*, plates 17–21.

France and England, Irish churches remained small, without transepts, the nave undivided by arcading resting on pillars or columns. The Irish adopted the round-headed arch and delighted in lavish Romanesque decoration of arches and doorways. New churches were built, and Cormac's Chapel[1] (consecrated in 1134) combines a number of continental elements into a general appearance rather unlike most Irish romanesque churches, whose decoration is made up of borrowed elements mixed with traditional Irish motifs.[2] The fine high crosses of this period are an original Irish interpretation of Romanesque and Scandinavian themes.[3] As we shall see, though the Irish borrowed stories and literary motifs, the twelfth-century renaissance in Irish scholarship took a very different form from that of the continent.[4] The stone-workers proved ready to adopt new ideas, but even here romanesque borrowings were highly selective and very much controlled by past tradition.

The sketch of foreign influence on Irish art which I have just given is in broad outline true, but it is very oversimplified. Problems arise concerning the provenance of manuscripts and metalwork. In his Bede Lecture for 1971 Professor Julian Brown has argued that the lay-out, script, scribal ornament and minor initials of the Book of Kells are closely similar to the Durham Gospels (A. II, 17).[5] Since he believes, with Mr Bruce Mitford, that the Durham Gospels and the Book of Echternach are by the same scribe, this is a claim that Kells was written by a scribe trained under the influence of Lindisfarne.[6] If this claim is moderately expressed, it would be possible to reconcile it with Irish,

[1] Henry, III, plates 96, 98–106. See L. de Paor in *North Munster Studies*, 133–45.

[2] Henry, III, plates 73–9, 80–4, 91–3.

[3] *Ibid.*, plates 47–63. L. de Paor, 'The limestone crosses of Clare and Arran', *JGAHS*, XXVI (1955–6), 53–71. [4] *Infra*, 280–1, 301.

[5] The paper is to be published in the first volume of a new periodical entitled *Anglo-Saxon England*.

[6] The presence of Northumbrian features has long been recognised. An extreme form of the case was put by F. Masai, in *Essai sur les origines de la miniature dîte irlandaise* (Brussels 1947), where he claims Kells as Northumbrian.

Pictish and Carolingian features in the book. A scribe trained at Lindisfarne might easily have come to Iona, or to a monastery in Ireland. There were, in fact, English communities resident in Ireland.[1] What style was adopted by the English monks of Mayo, or by the monks of 'the distinguished fold' built by Egbert in Ireland for men 'of his own race', or by the inhabitants of those 'houses of Saxons' mentioned in the martyrologies? If Professor Brown's claim is taken as a statement that the Book of Kells is Northumbrian,[2] it will meet some well-founded opposition. Nor, I think, could any Pictish monastery c. 750 (a date which Professor Brown regards as palaeographically possible, but subject to archaeological confirmation) have produced several illuminators of such high calibre. Indeed, four or more first-class manuscript artists in one *scriptorium* seems to be very unusual, and the hypothesis that the Book of Kells was begun at Iona and finished elsewhere meets this particular difficulty best. The controversy about Kells, now just reviving, illustrates the complexities of the subject. We need more work on the text. The stone crosses, which remained in the vicinity where they were carved, should be brought more prominently into the argument.[3] If Kells were to be accepted as wholly English in origin, art historians would be in doubt about where the Tara Brooch and the Ardagh Chalice were produced (as some already are).[4] All this emphasises the fact that Ireland, Scotland north of the Antonine Wall and Northumbria belong to one culture area. Iona must have been historically extremely important in facilitating communications.

[1] I have assembled the literary evidence for contacts between Ireland and England during the pre-Viking period in *England before the Conquest*, ed. P. Clemoes and K. Hughes (Cambridge 1971), 49–68.

[2] Professor Brown does not think it was written at Lindisfarne.

[3] J. Henderson, *The Picts* (London 1967), 123–5.

[4] Irish art historians are at a disadvantage in that the circumstances of the finds of some of their greatest treasures of metalwork cannot now be established.

III

So far I have mentioned some conclusions of interest to the historian which can be directly deduced from the evidence of objects and buildings—facts about technology and craftsmanship, patronage, centres of production and foreign influences. Most of these facts are much more clearly conveyed by the objects than they are in any written sources. There are also a number of inferences which are suggested by the material, some of which illustrate or modify the documentary evidence.

The archaeology seems to suggest a fairly peaceful society, and this is at variance with the literary sources. A great stone fort like Cahercommaun, with its triple ring of defences, was a peaceful cattle-ranching community. In fact we know from the laws that the ramparts round the king's fort, erected by his base clients, were an indication of his status. 'It is then that he is a king, when ramparts of base-clientship surround him.'[1] There is no fine Irish armour from this period. The pre-Christian era has furnished the Lisnacroghera scabbards and the horse trappings from Attymon.[2] Archaeology certainly does not suggest a society of endemic war.

This is completely at variance with the literary sources. 'Since I took spear in hand', says Conall, the Ulster hero, 'I have never been without slaying a Connachtman every day and plundering by fire every night, and I have never slept without a Connacht-man's head beneath my knee.' This may be rhetorical exaggeration, but the annals, laconic statements of fact, report constant battles, some of them apparently quite major affairs where over-kings with their sub-kings were killed. For instance, in 743, at the battle of Sered-magh, Aed Alláin, king of Cenél Éogain and Uí Néill overlord, fought Domnall of the Clann Colmáin, king of Meath. Aed was killed with three Airgialla sub-kings, and as a result of the battle Domnall became the first Clann Colmáin overlord of the Uí Néill. Battles like this must have been considerable ones, with numbers killed on both sides.

[1] *CG*, lines 569–70. The tract goes on to describe the size of such ramparts.
[2] Henry, I, plates 4 and 6.

Can we reconcile the archaeological and literary evidence? The annals show that once the initial Uí Néill expansion had taken place (perhaps in the fifth and sixth centuries) territory was not annexed, forts were not captured. Battles were hardly ever at or beside a royal fortress, so the archaeologist would not expect to recover much evidence of them. The most common type of war according to the literary sources was the raiding of the borders, often done by an over-king. He thus asserted his superiority and captured supplies. Speed and surprise were the two main ingredients of success, and to sit down outside a fortress in order to besiege it was not part of the attacker's plan. The discrepancy between annals and archaeology is thus not a real one. The battles would not provide the kind of evidence which archaeologists would normally expect to find.

The sharp decline in metalwork and manuscript illumination at the beginning of the Viking Age bears out the annalists' claims that the country had to meet attacks of unprecedented ferocity.[1] Here the scripture crosses present a dating problem. Whereas the crosses of the Ahenny group (generally recognised as of the eighth century) have shafts bearing panels of spirals, interlace and other motifs, the shafts of the scripture crosses are carved with scenes from the scriptures and from Christian tradition, with ornament mainly on the side panels and on the ring of the cross.[2] To what period do these scripture crosses belong? The inscriptions on the crosses of Monasterboice and Clonmacnoise do not provide decisive dating criteria, but if Mlle Henry is right in seeing the scripture crosses as, in part, directly influenced by Carolingian ivories, then they must belong to the ninth century and later.

This view has much to recommend it. The effect of the Viking raids on stonework need not have been the same as their effect on metalwork and on book production: indeed, monasteries may have deliberately put their artistic effort and patronage into a medium which was less vulnerable to Viking attacks. Moreover,

[1] *Supra*, 157–8.
[2] See Henry II, plates 65, 71, 76, 77, 78, 80, 83, 85, 86, 90, 93, etc.

the crosses fit in very suitably with the period of the culdee reform. Some have a fairly coherent and didactic message,[1] prefiguring Christ in scenes like the murder of Abel and the sacrifice of Isaac, prophesying the salvation of God in Noah's deliverance from the flood or Daniel's from the lions, depicting scenes associated with the great festivals of Christmas, Epiphany and Easter.[2] The tenth-century crosses (accepting Mlle Henry's dating) introduce new motifs and invent new themes. As the culdee movement loses its force the logic and coherence depart from the iconography.[3] Then, in the second half of the tenth century, these splendid scripture crosses come to quite an abrupt halt. The crosses of the romanesque period are different in conception.

Another opinion on the dating of the scripture crosses is, however, possible. Miss Roe tells me that, in her view, a substantial amount of the subject matter on the scripture crosses finds its closest parallel in late-antique motifs, as illustrated on Gaulish sarcophagi and consular ivories. This would not necessitate so late a date as Mlle Henry proposes for some of the crosses, and would allow them to be considered as contemporaneous with other great works of Irish art in the eighth and early ninth centuries.[4] There is thus not complete agreement on the condition of Irish art in the Viking Age.

The crosses of the twelfth century show us in visual form one of the changes which came about in the twelfth-century church. The scripture crosses bear the crucifixion and judgment at the crossings on either side of the monument. Twelfth-century legislation was dividing Ireland into dioceses of Roman type, with bishops as administrative heads of the church. It is therefore interesting to find bishops given a prominent place on the

---

[1] Henry II, 143–4. R. Flower, 'Irish high crosses', *Jrnl. of the Warburg and Courtauld Institutes*, XVII (1954), 87–97.

[2] Henry, II, 145.   [3] *Ibid.*, 156 f.

[4] Mlle. Henry accepts late antique analogies for some of the scenes. Of course the designs of Carolingian ivories were themselves often based on late antique models. I am grateful to Miss Roe for allowing me to quote her opinion.

crosses. Sometimes they carry a new-style crozier with a curling head. The 'Doorty' cross at Kilfenora shows the bishop, with conical tiara and curling crozier in the crossing of the east face, and beneath his feet two smaller clerics carrying croziers of the earlier type, one tau-headed, the other headed like a walking-stick. The people who commissioned these crosses obviously intended bishops to catch the public eye.

The lay-out of an Irish monastery reflects the peculiar Irish ecclesiastical constitution. In a Benedictine house the monks not only worshipped together; they ate and slept in common. The cloister which adjoins a typical Benedictine church provides their living quarters and bears the marks of its origin, for it is well suited to a Mediterranean climate where the inhabitants need shade.[1] An Irish monastery had within an enclosure one or more small churches, a graveyard, standing crosses, probably a separate building for a *scriptorium* and a separate abbot's house; but the monks lived in small huts, either separately or in tiny groups. This physical lay-out did not lend itself to standardisation, and some monks might lead a much more ascetic life than their brethren. When the twelfth-century Irish adopted the Cistercian rule, they had to build an entirely different sort of monastery.

Some of the early churches within the monastic enclosures are very tiny. For example, Temple Kieran at Clonmacnoise is twelve by eight feet internally.[2] Such a church could not have been used for congregational worship, and may have been used to house the founder's tomb. In any case the term 'congregational worship' is very misleading. At the beginning the communities of religious must have been quite small, and ten or a dozen men might have assembled in a tiny church for mass and for some of the offices. The seventh-century documents show that by this time church administrators were dividing people up into groups for worship. At Armagh there were at least two churches. The

---

[1] For an early Benedictine plan see H. Reinhardt, *Der St Galler Klösterplan*, 2 vols (St Gall 1952).

[2] When (*Vita Tripartita*, I, 236) Patrick measures out monasteries the church is much the smallest building described.

church in the north quarter was for virgins and penitents and those serving the church in legitimate matrimony, the south church was for bishops and priests and anchorites.[1] When Kildare built its new church in the seventh century 'in order to hold the increased numbers of the faithful',[2] the building was partitioned into three sections. At the end by the sanctuary and altar stood the bishop with his school of clerics. This was partitioned off from the rest of the church, which was also divided into two sections by a longitudinal wall. 'Priests and lay persons of the male sex' entered by an ornamental door on the right, 'matrons and virgins' by another door on the left. 'In this way', says Cogitosus, 'one basilica is sufficient for a huge crowd, separated by walls according to state, grade and sex, but united in the spirit'.[3]

Canons of a comparable date seem to recognise different areas within the monastic enclosure; one, the 'most holy', contained the relics of the saints, another into which only clerics might enter, a third for laymen and women.[4] The ascetics sometimes lived separately from the main community, like those at Loch Cré, though they were supported by 'the patron's fruits'. Even when some monasteries grew very large, like Clonard in the tenth century, I am not sure that this means a very substantial increase in the numbers of religious who regularly attended the offices. It must mean an increase of *manaig*, the lay tenants to whom the church owed baptism, confession, burial and the education of the eldest son and every tenth son thereafter,[5] and it means an increase of clerical students. But of the spiritual life of the laity who were not either princes or monastic tenants we know almost nothing. The canons show that the boundaries of the monastery were not closed to them[6] but the legislation is

---

[1] Book of the Angel, Hughes, *CEIS*, 277.

[2] Cogitosus, Migne, *PL*, LXXII, col. 789.

[3] *Ibid*. The whole passage is translated Bieler, *Ireland*, 28. I give Professor Bieler's translation Hughes, *CEIS*, 85.

[4] For references see Hughes, *CEIS*, 148.

[5] See the Rule of the Céli Dé, *Hermathena*, Second Supplemental Volume (Dublin 1927), 79 ff. Hughes, *CEIS*, 134–42.

[6] For reference see Hughes, *CEIS*, 167.

concerned mainly with reciprocal rights and obligations and is not interested in the layman who had no status or property.

The cemeteries and grave-slabs show us that burials were important. The saints' Lives emphasise the spiritual privileges which accrue to the person buried in the saint's cemetery. 'Even as the angel promised to Paul that no one who should go into the clay of Rome should after doom become an inhabitant of hell, even so the angel promised to Finnian that no one over whom the mould of Ard Relic should go would be an inhabitant of hell after the Judgment.' This is a typical claim. The higher the reputation of the saint, the more popular was his burial ground, so that kings came to be buried at Clonmacnoise,[1] Glendalough, Armagh and similar churches. The seventh-century canons, drawn up before the Church became very rich and powerful, show us the other side of the coin—the advantages which the Church gained from rights of burial. When a *manach* was buried the burial fee laid down in the canons consists of a cow, a horse, and the clothing and bed-trappings of the dead man. For someone of higher rank the fee was two horses with a chariot, his bed trappings and the cup from which he drank.[2] One secular law tract lays down a scale of bequests according to the status of the dead man, ranging between three young heifers from the *ócaire* at the bottom of the free grades to the value of seven slaves from the king.[3] Both secular and ecclesiastical law recognise that disputes might arise if a man were buried away from his own church, and they legislate for a division of the bequest.[4] The possession of a cemetery was thus of great economic importance to the church. The inscriptions on the surviving grave-slabs usually just give the man's name, or the formula 'Pray for' with the name.[5] Very occasionally there is a scrap of information, as contained in the inscription

---

[1] *Supra*, 105.   [2] Hughes, *CEIS*, 142, for references.

[3] *ALI*, III, 42. What the tract actually says is three *sets* to seven *cumals*. These are units of value, usually translated as I have given them. A *cumal* usually equals six *sets*.

[4] *ALI*, III, 64–6. Cf. *Collectio Canonum Hibernensis*, XVIII, 7a.

[5] P. Lionard, 'Early Irish grave-slabs', *PRIA*, LXI (1961), C 95–169.

'Or do Thuathal saer' at Clonmacnoise,[1] where *saer* could mean either carpenter or mason; and we can identify a few of the names with reasonable confidence. The multiplicity of fragments of grave-slabs provides indisputable illustration of the documentary sources.

IV

Irish art illustrates, explains and elaborates the literary sources. It provides part of the physical background of early Irish life with which the historian needs to be familiar. At certain periods the quality of Irish art is very high. Irish craftsmen had the same sort of confidence in their own traditions as Columbanus shows when addressing Pope Gregory,[2] where he writes as a scholar addressing his equal. The art is, of course, an aristocratic art, commissioned by kings, nobles and abbots, and the craftsmen were respected members of society. They used their patterns with great variety, as the Irish scholar loved to play with words. They understood how to juxtapose the matt surface of a stone like amber with the smoothness of millefiori and enamel and the gleam of metal. At its best the colour is flamboyant without being crude. Above all, they could produce the most complicated and exquisite detail without losing sight of the controlling design. The historian who ignores so beautiful an art loses both pleasure and enlightenment.

[1] *Ibid.*, plate XXXII.
[2] Hughes, 'The Celtic Church and the Papacy', in *The English Church and the Papacy in the Middle Ages*, ed. C. H. Lawrence (London 1965), 13–14.

CHAPTER 9

Eleventh- and Twelfth-Century Histories and Compilations

I

The eleventh and twelfth centuries were a period of historical activity in Ireland. Men of learning were writing history and compiling collections of texts. In particular there were three great manuscript compilations. One of these was *Lebor na hUidre* (or *LU*), 'the book of the dun', the medieval name of the MS, which was derived from the dun cow which followed Ciarán to school, and whose hide ended up at Clonmacnoise. This MS, now only a fragment of the original, about half what it once was, has been edited by a great palaeographer and a great linguist.[1] It was written by three scribes. One is named, Máel-Muire, a man who in the fourteenth century was identified with Máel-Muire grandson of Conn of the Poor of Clonmacnoise, possibly on the evidence of a *probatio pennae* which is now illegible. If this identification is correct, the scribe must almost certainly be the Máel-Muire who was killed at Clonmacnoise by marauders in 1106.[2] Best thought that all the three hands belonged to the same school and period, and that the whole MS was written at Clonmacnoise.

Dr Oskamp, however, has recently argued[3] that Máel-Muire and the scribe who had begun the MS (probably in the last quarter of the eleventh century) had access to texts connected with the libraries of Armagh, Durrow and Monasterboice; the final scribe, the 'interpolator', who seems to have worked at Clonmacnoise, used different MSS from the first two scribes. Dr

[1] R. I. Best and O. Bergin, *Lebor na hUidre* (Dublin 1929). Cf. Best, *Ériu*, VI (1912), 161–73.   [2] *AFM.*

[3] H. P. A. Oskamp, 'Notes on the history of *Lebor na hUidre*', *PRIA*, LXV (1967), C 117–37. See also R. Powell, 'Further notes on *Lebor na hUidre*', *Ériu*, XXI (1969), 99–102.

Oskamp concludes that it seems 'not unlikely' that the interpolator worked in a different *scriptorium* from the first two scribes. This need not, I think, necessarily imply that the first two scribes were not connected with Clonmacnoise, for the compilation was deliberately 'copied and searched out from various books'. Medieval tradition certainly associates the MS with Clonmacnoise.

The interpolator's hand appears in the opening item of another manuscript of the late eleventh or early twelfth century, Bodleian Rawl. 502. The item is a fragment of the Annals of Tigernach, and it seems likely that these twelve folios came from Clonmacnoise. But the Irish scholar Sir James Ware bound two manuscripts together to make Rawl. B 502, at some date after July 1642. The second part may have had a completely different origin: indeed, its contents concern mainly Leinster affairs.[1] It is beautifully written with very fine initials. Both parts are in facsimile, with an introduction and indices by Kuno Meyer.[2] Professor Ó Cuív has shown that a poem in the second part can be dated to c. 1120 by the terminal names in the pedigrees. The manuscript must therefore have been written after this date, probably soon after.[3]

The third manuscript, the Book of Leinster, is the latest and the longest, a volume of 187 existing leaves. The major part of it has been edited by Best, Bergin and O'Brien.[4] None of these scholars lived to complete the final section, though it may be seen in a careful nineteenth-century transcription reproduced in facsimile.[5] Many of the items in all these three manuscripts have been separately edited, often with translations.[6]

Best maintained that the Book of Leinster was all written by one scribe, Aed, abbot of Terryglass on the Shannon: 'Aed Hua

[1] A. Gwynn, *Celtica* V (1960), 11–12, quotes a suggestion by Professor Ó Cuív that this part of Rawl. B 502 may be the book which Ware in 1627 calls 'the Leinster Book'.

[2] Oxford 1909.   [3] *Ériu*, XVI (1952), 159.

[4] R. I. Best, O. Bergin and M. A. O'Brien, *The Book of Leinster*, 5 fascs. (Dublin 1954–67). This is a modern name. It was once called the Book of Noghoval.

[5] *The Book of Leinster*, with an introduction by R. Atkinson (Dublin 1880).

[6] The introduction to the separate volumes give references.

Crimthainn wrote this book and compiled it from many books.'
If so, its writing must have been spread over Aed's adult life, for
the entries demonstrate that it was begun about 1152 and was still
being written in 1201. The hand varies considerably: so, if we
follow Dr Best, we must imagine Aed writing under different
conditions, copying one text here and another there, where he
found them.

Recently Mr William O'Sullivan has argued that the Book of
Leinster was put together from the work of several scribes.[1]
There is a letter in the manuscript from Find, bishop of Kildare,
to Aed of Terryglass;

> Life and health from Find, bishop of Kildare, to Aed son of Crim-
> thann, the man of learning of the chief king of the Southern Half,
> the coarb of Colum son of Crimthann, the chief historian of Leinster
> in wisdom, knowledge, cultivation of books, learning and study.
> Write out for me the conclusion of this little story.

> > Be sure of this keen-witted Aed,
> > Rich in the holy wealth of song,
> > Be thou long time or short away,
> > I always for thy coming long.

> Let the poem book of Mac Lonáin be brought to me so that we may
> study the meanings of the poems that are in it, et vale in Christo.[2]

Aed certainly wrote a considerable part of the book. Mr
O'Sullivan thinks that another scribe collected surviving manuscripts made by and for Aed and either by or for Find and bound
them together with much of his own.

The Book of Leinster has an enormous number and variety of
texts. It now has 197 leaves, and may once have had about 225.
It begins with the Book of the Taking of Ireland[3] and includes
king lists and genealogies, place-lore, poems, sagas and anecdotes.

---

[1] 'Notes on the scripts and make-up of the Book of Leinster', *Celtica*, VII
(1966), 1–31.

[2] Translated R. Flower, *The Irish Tradition* (Oxford 1947), 67, or Mrs
O'Sullivan, *Celtica*, VII (1966), 7.   [3] *Infra*, 281–3.

Rawl. B 502, in addition to the Tigernach fragment of annals, gives us place-lore, lists of kings and saints, genealogies, stories and poems. In *LU* there are, amongst other material, a collection of sagas of the Ulster cycle,[1] two voyage tales and the Vision of Adamnán.[2]

All this was part of the twelfth-century Irish monastic scholar's view of history, for the recording of history was still the prerogative of the monastic scribe. History was tradition: it gained respect by its antiquity. Genealogies were pushed back into the mythical past, Irish history was seen as beginning with the flood. Ancient tales must be accurately recorded, though they might belong to a pagan context. Indeed, twelfth-century monastic scribes seem to have felt very little conflict between the Christian and the secular. When the scribe copied the *Táin* in the Book of Leinster, he ended by remarking, 'But I, who have written this history, or rather fable, give no belief to the various incidents related in it. For some things in it are the deceptions of demons, others poetic inventions; some are probable, others improbable; while still others are intended for the delight of fools.'[3] Irish men of learning were too sophisticated to assume that they had to believe in all they wrote down. They venerated anything ancient, and age gave sufficient respectability.[4]

These three great compilations were contemporaneous with the ecclesiastical reform which turned the Irish Church from a loose confederation of monastic *paruchiae* into a hierarchical diocesan and provincial structure. Within the administrative revolution which was to bring the Church up to date, the monastic scribes were consciously collecting the traditions of her past: as the Irish Church came into line with the rest of Europe, scholars were gathering the evidences for their unique heritage. The changes in the Church certainly did not have the immediate effect of stifling antiquarian activity; if anything they stimulated it.

[1] *Supra*, 174 ff.   [2] *Supra*, 213–14.   [3] f. 104 v.

[4] There is an excellent introduction to Irish learning during this period in *Seven Centuries of Irish Learning*, ed. B. Ó Cuív (Dublin 1961). See also R. Flower, *The Irish Tradition*.

Perhaps men like Aed felt that a long era was now passing away and must have its record.[1]

II

How far, if at all, was Irish literary activity in the twelfth century indebted to the continental renaissance? On the continent the Latin classics were being studied with revived enthusiasm from the eleventh century. The growing power of the papacy encouraged a new concern in canon law, which culminated in Gratian's *Decretum* of c. 1150. The study of Roman law revived in Italy in the late-eleventh century, and in the twelfth century the special needs of Henry II in England led to the independent development of English law. Englishmen like Adelard of Bath and a number of others went to Spain in search of Arabic science. The twelfth century saw tremendous activity in the writing of theology and history; philosophical studies were pursued, and new techniques of argument were evolved. And while all this was happening, the goliardic poets introduced into medieval poetry new styles and new themes.

Irishmen must have been aware of this intellectual renaissance. There were Irish Benedictine monks in Germany who kept in touch with their friends at home.[2] We know most about the Irish community at Ratisbon, where a convent was handed over to a group of Irish pilgrims about 1070. There seem to have been fairly frequent journeys between Germany and Ireland, for there was a special fund for travelling expenses, and there are reports of missions to the king of Munster about 1130 and 1150, probably to recruit novices. Between 1026 and 1064 there were also a number of Irish royal pilgrimages to Rome, and at the end of the eleventh century an Irish community was established there; the death of 'Éogan, head of the monks of the Irish in Rome' is

---

[1] Cf. R. W. Southern, *Medieval Humanism and Other Studies* (Oxford 1970), 162.

[2] See Binchy, 'The Irish Benedictine congregation in medieval Germany', *Studies*, XVIII (1929), 194–210.

recorded by *AI* at 1095.[1] One direct link between Ireland and the papacy was opened with the appointment of Ua Dúnáin (died 1117) as first papal legate. The contacts between St Malachy (died 1148) and St Bernard of Clairvaux are very well known;[2] Mr Hancock's estimate that sixty-three houses of canons had been established in Ireland before 1170 is much less familiar.[3] Both Malachy and St Laurence O'Toole (archbishop of Dublin 1162–80) died on the continent, and their Lives were written there. Between 1140 and 1142 four Irish monks were at Cîteaux, and Cistercian manuscripts at Troyes in France illustrate the links between Clairvaux and her Irish daughter houses.[4] The lector of Armagh spent twenty-one years between 1133 and 1154 'learning among the Franks and Saxons'.[5] Professor Gwynn also thinks it likely that there were Irish scholars at Chartres in the twelfth century.[6] The close physical connection between Ireland and the continent is also demonstrated by the Vision of Tundal. Tnúdgal was a Munster soldier who had served in the army of Cormac Mac Carthy, king of south Munster. His vision was written down, probably in 1149 by the monk Marcus, a Munster man engaged in the ecclesiastical reform movement which was bringing the Irish Church into line with the continental pattern. It spread from Ratisbon all over Europe.

In addition, communications between Ireland and England were close, for Patrick, second bishop of Dublin from 1074 to 1084, was a Benedictine monk trained at Worcester;[7] his successor Donngus (1085–95) was trained at Christchurch, Canterbury;

[1] For the Irish names in Vat. MS Lat. 378 see A. Wilmart, 'La Trinité des Scots à Rome et les notes du Vat. Lat. 378', *Revue Bénédictine*, XLI (1929), 218–30. See also A. Gwynn, 'Ireland and the continent in the eleventh century', *IHS*, VIII (1953), 193–216.

[2] On Malachy see A. Gwynn, *IER*, LXXIV (1950), 17–29, 97–109. The Life of Malachy by St Bernard was translated by H. J. Lawlor (London 1920).

[3] J. A. Watt, *The Church and the two nations in mediaeval Ireland* (Cambridge 1970), 26.

[4] Gwynn, *IHS*, VIII (1953), 210. [5] *AU*, 1174.

[6] *IHS*, VIII (1953), 214.

[7] A. Gwynn, *The Writings of Bishop Patrick* (Dublin 1955), 6.

and Samuel, the fourth bishop (died 1121), was trained at St Alban's. Malchus, first bishop of Waterford (1096–?1135), had been a monk at Winchester, and Gilbert of Limerick (1107–40) had been a companion of Anselm. These were all bishops of Hiberno-Norse sees, but they were not cut off from their colleagues. During the second half of the eleventh and twelfth centuries Irishmen had thus plenty of opportunity to know what was happening in England and on the continent.

There is no doubt that the change in the constitution of the Irish Church was influenced by Irish contacts with the Church elsewhere: there is no doubt that continental developments affected Irish building and sculpture.[1] We should therefore expect that the twelfth-century renaissance, the most powerful intellectual movement that Europe had experienced since the ninth century, would penetrate to Ireland. Ireland was prepared to adopt and adapt stories, visions, literary motifs. Twelfth-century Irish scholars showed a lively interest in the classics and in history, but in a traditional Irish form. They had been adapting classical stories into Irish, probably since the ninth century.[2] They continued to interpret their texts for an Irish audience, supplementing, omitting, re-arranging, including typically Irish features and descriptions in Irish style. The classical stories are absorbed into the native idiom. A twelfth-century poem on the Christian kings of Ulster equals Conchobar to Priam, Fergus to Aeneas, Conall Cernach to Hector; for 'Asia and Ulster are equally famous in deed, in fame and in pride'.[3] The Irish were glad to enrich their own tradition with classical tales, but whereas in Europe there was an intellectual restlessness and a hunger after new knowledge, in Ireland the boundaries of imagination were well identified and there were few significant new departures in native learning.

Irishmen of the twelfth century were aware of the theological

---

[1] *Supra*, 261–2, 266–7.

[2] Professor Carney's view, quoted W. B. Stanford, in 'Towards a history of classical influences in Ireland', *PRIA*, LXX (1970), C 33, note 69.

[3] F. J. Byrne, 'Clann Ollaman Uaisle Emna', *Studia Hibernica*, IV (1964), 61–2, 76.

and philosophical ferment in the continental schools, but it had little effect on the structure of Irish learning.[1] Fairly recent studies have shown Irishmen interested in theology and philosophy. One Irish scribe, probably in the early twelfth century, transcribed John the Scot's *De divisione naturae*: his manuscript was a palimpsest which had contained some material similar to that in the Antiphonary of Bangor and the Stowe missal, and it seems likely that it was in Ireland when it was re-used.[2] In the twelfth century, and perhaps in the eleventh, there was discussion in Ireland over the doctrine of the real presence.[3] A manuscript of the four gospels written at Armagh in 1138 (BM. Harley, 1802) has a commentary which is copied from notes taken by an Irishman in one of the French schools at that date; an Irishman who had been listening to Peter Lombard, for the glosses seem to show a preliminary stage of the *Glossa Ordinaria*, not yet published in 1140.[4] That student may have been the man who later became lector of Armagh.[5] A manuscript of Peter Lombard's Sentences, now at Troyes (no. 900), was written in 1158 by an Irish scribe 'Michael Hiberniensis'.[6]

Such evidence shows that Irishmen were in touch with the continental renaissance; yet it remains true that no Irishman produced any work which contributed substantially to it, as Irishmen had done in the ninth century.

Ireland was nothing like so intellectually dependent upon France as was England in the twelfth century. There was intellectual revival in Ireland at this time, but learning continued in the old tradition. If the new learning had comparatively little direct effect

[1] Cf. C. W. Dunn, *Univ. of Toronto Quarterly*, XXIV (1954), 70–86.

[2] A. Gwynn, *IHS*, VIII (1953), 213–14. Lowe, *CLA*, II, no. 232.

[3] G. Murphy, *Mediaeval Studies presented to Aubrey Gwynn*, ed. J. A. Watt, J. B. Morall, F. X. Martin (Dublin 1961), 19–28.

[4] R. Glunz, *History of the Vulgate in England from Alcuin to Roger Bacon* (Cambridge 1933), 211, 339. Henry, *Irish Art*, III, 4, 65.

[5] *Supra*, 278.

[6] I owe this reference to Professor Ó Cuív. Professor Bieler was so kind as to examine the microfilm in NLI and reports: 'There is nothing "insular" about the codex.'

on Irish intellectual life,[1] the fact is sufficiently extraordinary to need explaining. Ireland lacked the centralised monarchy of England and France: the Angevins had a practical interest in law, whereas Irish law was in the hands of the glossators. On the continent there was a rapid growth in the floating population of students who were drawn to certain centres by the reputation of scholars. But now Irish *peregrini* were travelling to Rome, not generally wandering abroad in pursuit of learning, and the long stay abroad by the lector of Armagh was sufficiently unusual to be worth recording. The cathedral schools, established in busy towns in England and on the continent, were the centres of the new intellectual life. Their lack of a well-rooted tradition and freedom from a clearly defined routine of study made it easy for them to branch out in new directions.[2] Ireland had no cathedral schools, and her monastic schools were anchored so weightily in their past that a departure from tradition was extremely difficult. The combination of the administrative reform of the Irish Church and the Anglo-Norman settlement seems after a time to have discouraged the old literary activity of Irish churchmen. It looks as if students who might once have gone into monastic *scriptoria*, after the twelfth century found their way to the bardic schools. The monastic scribes' concern to learn from the poets and to record history as the whole of their past tradition, sacred and profane, hardly lasted into the thirteenth century.

III

The Book of the Taking of Ireland,[3] shows us how closely inter-

[1] I mean if we compare Ireland with France and England, and if we look at the body of traditional Irish learning contained in the three great codices mentioned at the beginning of this chapter.

[2] See R. W. Southern, *The Making of the Middle Ages*, 203.

[3] *Lebor Gabála Érenn*, ed. and transl. R. A. S. Macalister, 5 parts, ITS, 34, 35, 39, 41, 44 (Dublin 1938–56). Abbreviated *LG*. This is not a satisfactory edition to use. The LL text is edited by Best, Bergin and O'Brien, *Book of Leinster*, I, 1–56, with the kings following up to p. 99. The development of the text is an extremely complicated subject. See M. Dillon, 'Lebor Gabálá Érenn', *JRSAI*, LXXXVI (1956), 62–72.

locked were the monastic and secular traditions of learning in the period before the Anglo-Norman invasion. This is a history of the Gaedhill from the creation, with an appendix added on the kings of Ireland which brings the record up to 1166. One version of *LG* opens the Book of Leinster. Another, a simpler one, was known in the ninth century to the British historian Nennius:[1] 'Thus have the most learned of the Irish informed me,' he says, in giving his account of prehistoric Ireland.[2]

LG 'is a collection of pseudo-historical poems by various authors of different periods, arranged in a pattern of invasions'.[3] They are the means by which students could memorise their native history. As we have it, the compilation cannot be earlier than the later eleventh century. The history brings the final settlers, the sons of Míl, to Ireland from Spain. (We have already seen that intellectual links between Ireland and Spain were close in the seventh century.)[4] But there were seven invasions of Ireland before the sons of Míl arrived, for which the material is folklore and pagan myth. The story deals with euhemerised deities, eponymous heroes, genealogies and *dindshenchus* legends.

Yet *LG* is not, as you might expect, a product of the secular schools of the *filid*. Some versions were interpolated and elaborated in the medieval bardic schools, but the history was composed in a monastery. 'One thing is plain,' says Professor Dillon, 'namely that *LG* is a product of Latin learning.'[5] Some of the names are Latin or Latin derived. The whole structure of the story is based on Old Testament history, for Gaedel is a descendant of Japhet son of Noah. Like the children of Israel, the ancestors of the Irish set out from Egypt on their wanderings. They see Ireland from the top of Breogan's Tower in Spain,[6] as Moses saw the Promised Land from Mt Pisgah. Íth goes to spy out the land and finds it

[1] Both Nennius and the opening section of *AI* and *Tig.* have only three invasions.

[2] F. Lot, *Nennius et l'Historia Britonum*, 2 vols (Paris 1934), 158.

[3] Dillon, *op. cit.*, 66.

[4] *Supra*, 194–5. Macalister claimed to show that the Biblical quotations in *LG* are from an MS of Spanish origin, *LG*, I, 6–10.

[5] Dillon, *op. cit.*, 69.   [6] *LG*, V, 10–13.

full of fruit, honey, wheat and fish, with moderate heat and cold;[1] though he dies, like Moses, before the sons of Míl colonise it.

The story-teller is concerned to christianise the pagan elements. Fintan, son of Labraid, who was a year under the flood and survived until the coming of the saints, told the history to Patrick, Columcille, Comgall and Finnian, by whom, he says, it was written down. Since then it has been preserved by the saints and the sages, who 'have stitched together all knowledge into it'.[2]

'Stitching together' is a good description of the historian's technique. He had a mass of tradition and folklore which he had to fit into a Christian world-history and to synchronise into its time sequence. Some monastic historians must have been skilled in Irish *senchus*, rather as the poets were. Indeed, a cleric of Armagh and a lector of Monasterboice were among the men who composed the poems in *LG*, and presumably pupils in the monastic schools were learning them. *LG* demonstrates how far the fusion of secular and monastic learning had gone.

The metrical *dindshenchus*, like *LG*, was a compilation of tradition which had been growing up over the centuries. The eleventh-century *Liber Hymnorum*,[3] in two fine early twelfth-century manuscripts, is another antiquarian collection, as the title indicates: a 'Book of hymns which the saints of Ireland composed'. The passions and homilies in the *Leabhar Breac*[4] seem to have been written in the second half of the eleventh century and based closely on continental texts circulating in Ireland. The Martyrology of Gorman was compiled between 1166 and 1174 at Knock, an Augustinian house near Louth.[5] This was based on the Martyrology of Oengus and was intended to make good what the author regarded as the defects of the earlier work, attempting to adjust the Irish calendar to European practices. These compilations and revisions are all typical of the period.

[1] *LG*, V, 17.

[2] *Ibid.*, 224–5. From the Roll of the Kings; this passage is not in *LL*.

[3] Ed. J. H. Bernard and R. Atkinson, *HBS*, 13, 14 (London 1897).

[4] R. Atkinson, *The Passions and Homilies from Leabhar Breac* (Dublin 1887). Kenney, *Sources*, 739.

[5] Ed. W. Stokes, *HBS*, 9 (London 1895). Kenney, *Sources*, 483–4.

IV

Now turn to the original historical works of the eleventh and twelfth centuries, and the impact of Brian Bóruma is immediately recognisable. Until his day the Uí Néill king had been the most important king in Ireland: Brian achieved an overlordship more comprehensive than that of any previous king. Although none of his successors equalled him, the ascendancy lay mainly with the Munster kings for nearly a hundred years, from 1022 until 1118. After Clontarf the Uí Néill king Máel-Sechnaill II resumed the high-kingship until his death in 1022. Then Donnchad son of Brian held the kingship, though he was a 'king with opposition'. In 1063 Toirdelbach (Turlough), nephew of Donnchad and Brian's grandson, took the kingship of Munster, and Donnchad left the next year for Rome. Toirdelbach subsequently secured recognition in Leinster, Dublin, Osraige, Meath, Connacht, Breifni and Ulster. His son and successor Muirchertach (Murtagh) had a fierce rival in king Domnall of Ailech. Nevertheless, Muirchertach's triumphal circuit of Ireland in 1101 must have seemed to his contemporaries the apogee of power; his hosting was into Connacht, Ailech and Ulster, perhaps returning to Kincora via Meath. In 1114 Muirchertach was very ill, so that he became a skeleton and parted with his kingship: a number of his sub-kings now came under the dominance of Ailech, and although Muirchertach recovered, he never resecured his hold over Connacht, now under the lordship of Toirdelbach Ua Conchobair (Turlough O'Connor). In 1118 Toirdelbach was strong enough (with the support of the kings of Meath and Breifni) to make a hosting into Munster and divide it into two kingdoms, giving the north (Thomond) to the O'Briens and the south (Desmond) to the Mac Carthys, taking pledges from both. This removed the most dangerous obstacle to a bid for a 'national monarchy' by the O'Connors. Before Muirchertach's death in 1119, Toirdelbach was already the chief king of Ireland, a position he maintained until a few years before his death in 1156.[1]

[1] On Brian Bóruma and Irish history in this period see J. Ryan, *NMAJ*, II

This is the political background into which the historical texts have to be fitted. Consider first the Book of Rights.[1] It is a statement of the stipend which the king of Ireland pays to each provincial king, of the stipend which each provincial king pays to his subordinate kings, and of the tribute he receives from each tribe. This is stated first in prose, then in verse. The compiler has added or inserted several texts which seemed to him related: the testament of Cathaír Mor, the blessing of Patrick, and a poem on Tara.

Mac Neill thought that the main statement on the tributes was drawn up c. 900, but this view has for some time been steadily eroded. Now Professor Dillon argues that the language of the main tract belongs to the late eleventh century, and that the compilation may have been made in the twelfth.[2]

The tract must belong on historical grounds to the period of Munster's greatness. It begins with the king of Cashel, who has much the longest section, and it is here that the stipends which the king of Ireland pays to provincial kings are set out. Then we go round the province of Ireland, on a circuit which would have been made by kings of Cashel: Connacht, Ailech (as Cenél Éogain is now called), Airgialla, Ulster, Tara and Leinster, with a poem on Dublin added. Dublin is here a tributary state of Leinster. The Osraige are one of the free tribes of Leinster.

I think that the Preface to this tract must have been written at the beginning of the twelfth century. In 1101 a great reforming synod was held at Cashel. Its convenors were king Muirchertach and Úa Dunáin, bishop of Meath. At this synod Muirchertach made Cashel over to the Church. This diplomatic act of generosity caught the public eye, and there seem to be two oblique references to it in *LC*. The Preface says that the angel Victor prophesied to Patrick, 'proclaiming that the dignity and

(1941), 141–52; III (1942), 1–52; III (1943), 189–202. His O'Donnell Lecture for 1966 has been printed separately, *Toirdelbach O Conchubair (1088–1156)*.

[1] *Lebor na Cert*, ed. and transl. M. Dillon (Dublin 1962). Abbreviated *LC*.

[2] 'On the date and authorship of the Book of Rights', *Celtica*, IV (1958), 239–49.

primacy of Ireland would be always in that place [i.e. Cashel]. Accordingly that is Patrick's sanctuary and the principal strong-hold of the king of Ireland.' Now this is the most barefaced effrontery. Armagh had been claiming the primacy of Ireland since at least as early as the late seventh or eighth century,[1] and was recognised everywhere as Patrick's chief church. Her claims to dignity and primacy are stated in the Book of the Angel. Surely some incentive is needed for the Munster poet to formu-late so outrageous a claim, and this would be provided by the splendid grant of Cashel to the Church in 1101. Was that gift motivated by a wish to secure the leadership in the reformed Church for Cashel?[2] There seems to be another reference to the gift of 1101 in the poem on Tara appended to the main tract. One of the 'unlucky things' of the king of Tara is to be maintained in Cashel.[3] This taboo would seem to post-date the grant to the Church. Muirchertach's great triumphal circuit of 1101 might well provide the kind of stimulus needed for the composition of this tract. At any rate its compilation would seem to fall be-tween 1101 and 1119, when Muirchertach died.

We have therefore a contemporary poem which sets out stipends and tributes, provincial kings and sub-kings. It ought to be an extremely valuable historical document. But it is full of inconsistencies and contradictions. The lists of kings receiving stipends do not agree with the lists of tribes subject to tribute. The work divides Ireland into seven provinces, a division peculiar to the Book of Rights and one which does not seem to agree with the reality.[4] As Professor Dillon says: 'It is as though these poems are merely praise poems, without any pretension to recite the facts'; they give an impression 'of something schematic and imaginary'.

[1] See Hughes, *CEIS*, 110 ff, 275 ff.

[2] The text itself (p. 16) seems to contradict the statement of the preface: 'These are the teachings of Benén son of Sescnén, Patrick's cantor, and he was of the Cianachta of Glenn Gemin of the line of Tadg son of Cian from great Munster: that the heir to Cashel is the common head of all, as is the heir of Patrick . . .' The heir of Patrick was abbot of Armagh.

[3] p. 140. Professor Dillon points this out in a footnote.

[4] *LC*, p. xix.

Nor does the tract provide the evidence for the economic historian which at first sight it might seem to do. All these slave women distributed by the provincial kings to their subordinates are probably largely fiction. For example the king of Tara gives his sub-kings fifty-seven slaves in the prose version, seventy-two in the verse. Some are 'foreign slaves without speech'. But all that this means is that the poet was familiar with the presence of slaves in Ireland, and we already knew that the Vikings were great slave-dealers. It is little use for archaeologists to look for all these hundreds of coats of mail distributed by the provincial kings. All we can conclude is that by giving a stipend[1] a provincial king secured the recognition of his overlordship. The greater the king the grander the stipend, so the poets exaggerated in their traditional style. Similarly with the tribute; though it is probably true that it was taken mainly in cattle, pigs, cloaks and mantles, with some sheep and horses.

The man who composed this tract was a poet, reciting in the traditional conventions. The section on Tara claims that the king's rights have been memorised by a Latin scholar, i.e., St Benén; but it goes on to say that they are not a subject for 'every prattling bard', only for the poet (*fili*).[2] Patrick's blessing has several stanzas on the historian's duties, insisting that he must know the rents and stipends to qualify for entertainment and reward. 'Then he is a rock of an *ollam* when he understands the stipends and rents without doubt, so that he will recount them in every high assembly.'[3] The public recitation explains the panegyric quality of the tract.

Historically it is of interest as an expression of Munster's ascendancy. Her political ascendancy was probably generally recognised. The poet was also flattering Muirchertach by claiming ecclesiastical primacy for Cashel.

---

[1] The word used for stipend in *LC* is *tuarastal*. The older texts use the terms *rath* or *cumtach*, which were very modest in amount. See Binchy, *Celtic and Anglo-Saxon Kingship*, 51, note 65.

[2] *LC*, 96–8.   [3] *Ibid.*, 122–3.

V

The War of the Gaedhill with the Gaill[1] has probably shaped the public impression of Irish history more than any other single work.[2] It is an account of the destruction and oppression which the Foreigners wreaked on Ireland, and the rescue of the Irish by the two sons of Cennétig, Mathgamain and Brian, princes of the Dál Cais in north Munster. The first thirty-four chapters are a chronological account related to annals. At chapter 35 the narrator says he will now turn to Munster, and reports the arrival of Norse fleets at Waterford and Dublin. (This was in 914.) After a very rhetorical passage describing Viking depredations, we have a list of Viking battles. Then (at chapter 40) the Norse arrive in Limerick, and soon after this the work becomes a saga of Mathgamain (active from the 960s) and, more particularly, Brian, until it ends with the battle of Clontarf in 1014.

This part is in the normal saga form of prose interspersed with verse. It has a lot of very wordy rhetoric, using strings of adjectives, sometimes alliterating, to describe Viking oppression or Dál Cais prowess. To cite much of this would be tiresome, although to cut it reduces the deluging effect:

> Though numerous were the oft-victorious clans of many familied Ireland . . . yet not one of them was able to give relief, alleviation or deliverance from that oppression and tyranny, from the numbers and multitudes, and the cruelty and the wrath of the brutal, ferocious, furious, untamed, implacable hordes by whom that oppression was inflicted, because of the excellence of their polished, ample, heavy, trusty, glittering corslets, and their hard, strong, valiant swords, and their well-rivetted long spears . . .[3]

What is the date of *CGG*? It is an example of a new prose style in Irish, also to be seen in the Book of Leinster version of the Táin, probably composed in the first quarter of the twelfth

[1] *Cogadh Gaedhel re Gallaibh* (abbreviated *CGG*), edited and transl. J. H. Todd, Rolls S. (London 1867).

[2] See recently F. Henry, *Irish Art during the Viking Invasions*, c, 1, which depends a good deal on *CGG*.   [3] *CGG*, 52–3.

century, and in the 'Capture of Troy' of about the same period. The earliest copy of *CGG*, though fragmentary, is in the Book of Leinster. It used to be assumed that the work was written soon after the battle of Clontarf. But it contains material which is decidedly reminiscent of the Book of Rights. It is very definitely an O'Brien document. It was no use for the author to pretend that Dál Cais had always supplied the kings of Cashel, but *CGG* claims that Dál Cais, even before the time of Mathgamain and Brian, had always been a free tribe, paying no rent to Cashel. 'To them belonged the lead in entering an enemy's country and the rere on returning' (i.e., the champion's place of honour). This is paralleled by the Book of Rights, for when that book enumerates the stipends paid by the king of Cashel to the kings of his tribes, it starts: 'First, a place at his side, and ten horses, ten suits, two bracelets and two sets of chess to the king of Dál Cais; *and to lead with him an expedition into another territory and to return at the rere.*'[1] The slaves who are constantly given away in the Book of Rights also receive heavy emphasis in *CGG*.[2]

Probably *CGG* was later than the Book of Rights. At any rate, it belongs to the same milieu, and it seems to date from the first half of the twelfth century.[3] The author of *CGG* states specifically that before Brian's day the kingship of Cashel, that is the overlordship of Munster, alternated between the Eoganachta (the peoples around Cashel) and the Dál Cais (Brian's kingdom in north Munster). Professor Ryan suggests that this claim post-dates 1118, when Munster was divided into a northern and southern half.[4] This seems very likely, though we have to note that the obituary notice of Cennétig, Brian's father, which *AI* gives at 951, names him as royal heir of Cashel (*rígdamna Cassil*).[5] It is,

---

[1] *LC*, 28-9.   [2] e.g., *CGG*, 116-17.

[3] The opinion of J. Ryan, 'The battle of Clontarf', *JRSAI*, LXVIII (1938), 1-50. A. J. Goedheer, *Irish and Norse Traditions about the Battle of Clontarf* (Haarlem 1938), 103, puts it in the 1160s.

[4] 'The historical content of the *Caithréim Ceallacháin Chaisil*', *JRSAI*, XI (1941), 95.

[5] Professor J. V. Kelleher discussed 'The rise of the Dál Cais' in *North Munster Studies*, ed. E. Rynne (Limerick 1967), 230-41. He thinks it likely that

however, quite probable that this is a retrospective addition.[1]
CGG shows many of the characteristics of a historical saga.
There is the usual exaggeration. It is said that Ireland endured total
oppression from the Vikings: there were Foreigners over every
kingdom and church, stewards in every townland, soldiers
in every house, so that an Irishman could not give away a clutch
of eggs or use his own cow's milk to feed a new born child.[2]
We have already seen that Viking pressure was not unremitting
and did not fall equally hard on all sections of the population.[3]
Professor Ryan, comparing the account given in the annals with
CGG, shows that the numbers engaged in the battle of Clontarf
are greatly exaggerated in the saga.[4] Exaggeration is so much a
feature of the style that reports which may be substantially accurate are inevitably cast in doubt; for example the plunder taken at
the sack of Limerick,[5] although after the battle of Tara in 980
the annals say that a measuring-rod was required everywhere.

The story-teller here is more interested in chronology than
were the composers of many historical sagas. It seems very likely
that he was following a set of annals, for there is more correspondence between his account and AI than one would otherwise
expect.[6] Nevertheless there are slips. Professor Ryan cites examples
of false chronology in his article on the battle of Clontarf, and
there are occasions where the story-teller telescopes events
which the annals put several years apart.[7]

the Eoganacht and Dál Cais made an agreement of alternate kingship in 964,
when the Eoganacht were hard pressed.
[1] An O'Brien Chronicle begins AI, 972. The entries immediately before 972
might have been touched up to fit the new interests. I think it is possible that
the entries relating to events before 972, though they are certainly drawn up
from earlier written sources, may have been added to the O'Brien Chronicle as
a prologue, at some time after 972. See *supra*, 146, 108–14.   [2] *CGG*, 48–9.
[3] *Supra*, 148–59.   [4] *JRSAI*, LXVIII (1938), 16 ff.   [5] *CGG*, 78–81.
[6] It is also worth noting that his usual term to describe the Vikings is
'Foreigners' (*Gaill*), the term normally used in the Annals, not the *Lochlannaig*
of the literary-romantic tradition. For terminology of different types of
sources see P. Mac Cana in *Proceedings of the International Congress of Celtic
Studies 1959* (Dublin 1962), 84.
[7] e.g. *CGG*, 106–7. The battle of Belach Lechta (978) is followed by the

The heroic conventions are observed. Brian is shown as the epitome of honour and generosity. When Brian, according to custom, demands hostages or battle from Máel-Sechnaill of Tara, Brian allows him a month's delay to obtain support from his allies if he wishes for war.[1] When Brian demands hostages or battle from the kings of Ailech and Ulster, he allows them a year in which to decide.[2] After battles Brian is always shown distributing the plunder fairly and generously,[3] and his gifts to his supporters are open-handed. As a fighter Brian is ranked with Lug and Finn,[4] and his son Murchad is the Hector of Ireland.[5] At Clontarf a bird of prey flutters screaming over the heads of the warriors, as the war-goddess Badb does in mythological battle; the madmen fly, as Suibne turned mad and flew from the battle of Mag Rath.[6] Murchad, like Cú Chulainn, is seized with a fierce heat, rushes forward and slays fifty with his right hand and fifty with his left.[7] Such details make it plain that this is saga rather than history.

The whole saga is in fact based on a completely false view of history, the one implied by the title, 'The War of the Irish with the Foreigners'. But the annals make it absolutely clear that, even in the first fifty years when the pressure was greatest, it was never a national war. The Irish were too divided for this. During the ninth and first half of the tenth centuries the annals show us the Uí Néill kings gradually strengthening their over-lordship. To do this they fought battles with the Vikings, but with a great many other peoples besides.[8] In the tenth century there were marriage alliances with the Norse, and the Foreigners sometimes fought alongside the Irish in the second half of the ninth and tenth centuries. By Brian's time Máel-Sechnaill of Tara had achieved a position of considerable power.

plundering of the Déisi (985) and the taking of hostages from the principal churches of Munster (987). Then in the saga we go back to the events of 983.

[1] CGG, 118–19.   [2] Ibid., 134–5.   [3] Ibid., 136–7, 118–19.
[4] Ibid., 202–3.   [5] Ibid., 186–7.   [6] Ibid., 174–5.   [7] Ibid., 188–93.
[8] Professor Kelleher's paper on 'The Rise of the Dál Cais', op. cit., argues that the Meath kings of Tara encouraged the Dál Cais in order to keep Munster divided.

Once Brian was king of Cashel he brought the other kingdoms into submission, taking hostages from Osraige and Leinster
(983), making raids on Connacht and Meath. In 997 Brian and
Máel-Sechnaill of Tara agreed to divide Ireland between them,
Brian taking the hostages of Leinster and of the Foreigners.
The following year Brian marched to Athlone, took the hostages
of Connacht and gave them to Máel-Sechnaill. Máel-Sechnaill
and the king of Connacht took defensive action against Brian
in 1001, but in 1002 acknowledged his overlordship. After this
there remained the Northern Uí Néill and Ulster, who also came
into submission. The annals show not a war of Irish versus
Foreigners, but an attempt to build up a high-kingship, in
which the Vikings are merely one factor.

Yet there are passages where the saga is consistent with the
account of the annals and at the same time emphasises factors
which the annals record very briefly. It brings out the extreme
particularism of the Irish kingdoms. The annals tell how the
Eoganacht King Máel-muad submitted to Mathgamain in 969
but reasserted himself in 974. The king of Uí Fhidgeinte (one of
the kingdoms of Munster situated near Dál Cais) seized Mathgamain in 976 and handed him over to Máel-muad, who had him
killed; in 977 Brian avenged this deed on the Uí Fhidgeinte, and
in 978 he defeated and killed Máel-muad. The saga elaborates all
this, describing the envy and alarm of the Uí Fhidgeinte and
Eoganachta at the growing power of the Dál Cais. When Máel-
Sechnaill seeks the help of Aed of Ailech against Brian, Aed
gives a significant answer: 'that he would not risk his life in battle
against the Dál Cais in defence of the sovereignty for any other
man'.[1] The whole episode may be imaginary, but the story-
teller had grasped one of the primary facts of Irish politics, the
difficulty of persuading kings to unite and to remain in union.

This is part of a very important sequence in the story—how
Máel-Sechnaill took Brian as his lord. In the annals we merely
read that Brian took the hostages of Connacht and of Máel-
Sechnaill, but the story-teller understood that Máel-Sechnaill's

[1] *CGG*, 126.

submission was a major event in Brian's career, so he gave it prominence. When Brian demands battle or hostages from Máel-Sechnaill, Máel-Sechnaill asks a month's delay to muster the Northern Half. He sends a poet to the kings of Ailech and Ulster, and another messenger to Connacht, inviting these provinces to join him against Brian. The long poem (given here) incites Aed to battle, reminding him of his glorious ancestors, and of the Uí Néill inheritance at Tara. But Aed was only prepared to defend Tara when his own branch of the Uí Néill was in the kingship. Máel-Sechnaill then offered to accept Aed as his overlord if he would support him, but though Aed was willing, his nobles asked themselves what benefit they would derive in leading a battle against the Dál Cais? The mission was a failure and Máel-Sechnaill submitted to Brian. This long sequence marks a genuine turning point in Brian's career, which the annals pass over in a few laconic words. The details may all be fanciful, but the story-teller was expressing in dramatic terms a fundamental historical truth.

What are we to make of the oft-quoted claim that Brian sent scholars overseas to buy books because the Vikings' holocaust had destroyed Irish libraries? It comes in a long panegyric on Brian, following his triumphal circuit of Ireland.[1] The poet praises him for his successful efforts to secure and maintain order,[2] for his destruction and enslavement of the Vikings,[3] for his building and repair of causeways, roads, fortresses and churches.[4] Asser, in his Life of King Alfred, had described how the king had sent overseas to obtain teachers and had forwarded a building campaign, after the destruction inflicted by the Vikings. This does not mean that the Irish saga is directly derived from Asser. On the contrary, building and scholarship were activities which civilised kings were expected to encourage, and Brian no doubt

---

[1] *CGG*, 136–41.

[2] See Goedheer, *op. cit.*, 31, for Bede's description of the peace and security of the reign of Edwin.   [3] *Supra*, 288 ff.

[4] It mentions Killaloe, Tomgraney and Inis Celtra on Loch Derg. For the eleventh-century history of the first two, see *infra*, 297–8

did so. The intellectual and artistic flowering came in Ireland, however, well after the reign of Brian; and although the O'Briens undoubtedly gave rise to new literature, there is little evidence for books imported from the continent on any large scale at the beginning of the eleventh century.

The battle of Clontarf rises as a great landmark in the public eye, for it was the last of the great Viking battles and Brian met his death there. Yet it did not substantially change anything. It was caused by Leinster's attempt to re-assert her independence. According to *CGG*, immediately after the battle the Eoganachta tried to resume the kingship of Munster, and, though one would not know it from *AI*, *AU* shows that the position of Donnchad was at first insecure. The struggle for overlordship continued among the Irish kings throughout the eleventh and twelfth centuries, though now a king of Connacht successfully claimed it for the first time in the historic period.[1] A high-king had to conduct constant hostings to maintain his grip on his sub-kingdoms, and at best his hold was insecure; illness, old-age, a false move could turn success into failure, so that his pre-eminence passed to another claimant. Churches seem to have been vigorously harried during this period, if we are to believe the annals, though now it was by Irish kings.[2] It is significant that the Anglo-Norman invasion was touched off by the discontent of the king of Leinster. The arrival of Strongbow (or perhaps more accurately that of Henry II), not the battle of Clontarf, was the end of an era.

VI

Historically the most important part of the tract now known as *CGG* is not the saga section which we have been discussing, but the first thirty-five chapters which are closely related to annals. They start with the events of 811 and go up to 922, concluding with a reference to the mighty deeds of Vikings who had brought fleets to Limerick harbour and Dublin, and a final sentence which

---

[1] Toirdelbach Ua Conchobair (Turlough O'Connor). *Supra*, 284.
[2] *Supra*, 157–9.

reads: 'But their plunders and their battles and their conflicts are not fully in recollection and are not ennumerated in books.' This implies that the compiler was using both written and oral sources.

There is no doubt that he was consulting books. There are many occasions where passages containing strings of names can be closely paralleled from the annals. But which annals? Mr Leech has suggested that there are some occasions where the wording of *CGG* seems to be nearer *AI* than to any other extant set of annals.[1] The most convincing example of a parallel with *AI* in the first thirty-five chapters seems to me the plundering of Clonfert by Tomrar the Jarl in 866, whom St Brendan killed in revenge three days afterwards.[2] This entry is in *AI* but not in *AU* or *CS*. But anyone who goes through the first thirty-five chapters of *CGG* noting parallels in the annals will find a very much greater total of correspondence with *AU* than with *AI*. Many of the events in *CGG* are recorded in *AU* but are omitted altogether in *AI*. This is presumably because the compiler was using some version of the Chronicle of Ireland,[3] the source which lies behind all the annals and which *AU* preserves much more fully than does *AI*.

But the compiler of *CGG* was not making a straightforward transcription of that chronicle. For instance, after citing events of the year 866 he says that Ireland had some rest from the Foreigners for forty years before the fleets put in at Waterford.[4] After listing several battles he goes back to the events of 888. Then (c. 28) he again jumps forward to the story after the landing at Waterford, and the events of 914–16. Then we go back again (c. 29) to 867–8 before we get firmly launched once more in the narrative of 916 and the following years. Has a scribe copied interpolations slightly out of place?

Although *CGG* gives us a lot of original material, some of it fits well enough with entries in the other annals. For instance,

[1] R. H. Leech, '*Cogadh Gaedhel re Gallaibh* and the Annals of Inisfallen', *NMAJ*, XI (1968), 13–21. His list of 'probable' parallels begins at 922.
[2] *CGG*, 24.   [3] *Supra*, 101 ff.   [4] *CGG*, 26.

fleets put in at Lough Neagh (*AU* 839) and Louth (*AU* 840), and Armagh was attacked. *CGG* then tells how the Viking Turgeis usurped the abbacy of Armagh and Forannán, Patrick's coarb, was driven out with Patrick's shrine and went to Munster, where he stayed for four years. There was a Viking fleet on Lough Ree in 845 (*AU*) and the houses of the Shannon were plundered. Men from the Limerick fleet carried off Forannán from Cluain Comairdi and broke Patrick's shrine. Turgeis was, however, killed by Máel-Sechnaill (*AU* 845) and Forannán returned to Armagh. *AI* says nothing about the expulsion of Forannán, but it does record that he and Diarmait brought the law of Patrick to Munster in 842. His capture is reported in *AI* and *AU* at 845 (though only *AI* says that the shrine was broken) and his return from Munster with the reliquaries of Patrick is given by *AU* at 846. Thus it appears from the annals that Forannán was in Munster for four years. Is the story of Turgeis at Armagh just a highly-coloured legend, or is there some truth here which has been suppressed by the Armagh-dominated Chronicle of Ireland?[1]

There is a lot of material in the annalistic section of *CGG* which is not in *AU*, *AI* or *CS*. Some of it is from oral sources, like the story of Selbach the anchorite, bound three times by the Vikings and loosed by an angel. But some of it seems to come from written sources, with details of battles which are synchronised with known events.

Whereas the normal Irish annals are largely about Irish affairs with some entries about Viking attacks, the *CGG* annals concentrate entirely on the Vikings and the opposition they met. They are definitely written from an Irish point of view, but the Vikings are not merely 'Foreigners'. Quite often the writer knows, or claims to know, the names of men who commanded the Viking fleets, the battles they fought and the fates they met with. It seems likely that some of this information comes from a time when there was exchange between Irish and Norse, so that traditions of the Norse heroic age could pass into Irish society. This could easily have happened when the O'Briens were in residence at

[1] *Supra*, 129 ff.

Limerick, from the early twelfth century. The form of the saga requires hostility towards the Norse, but *CGG* is much better informed about the Viking heroes than are the contemporary annals.

Can we say where the annals at the beginning of *CGG* were compiled? It must be somewhere in Munster. Lismore is mentioned several times, once with special comment, when St Mochuda avenges an attack on his monastery of Lismore.[1] The emphasis, however, is on the lower Shannon area,[2] that is the territory in or near Dál Cais. It looks as if these annals were compiled in O'Brien territory, from written sources and oral tradition, as a prelude to the saga of Brian Bóruma.

VII

The Book of Rights and The War of the Gaedhill with the Gaill were both O'Brien documents. So were the Annals of Inisfallen from 972 onwards. Professor Gwynn, in a beautifully written article, has shown the whereabouts of *AI* in the eleventh and twelfth centuries.[3] Mathgamain is first mentioned at 967. From 972 some of the entries become fuller, and Mathgamain and Brian are the central figures of the annals. Between 1003 and 1042 there is a sudden spurt of interest in Tomgraney, a church only mentioned previously three times in *AI*. Killaloe also enters the annals for the first time. Killaloe, on the southern shore of Lough Derg, is only a short distance from Brian's palace at Kincora, and Tomgraney is a little farther north, to the west of Lough Derg. During this period *AI* shows a considerable interest in the area that is now Co. Clare, and its sympathies are definitely with Donnchad son of Brian. Then from 1061 to 1092, when *AI* was transcribed, there is a spate of entries about Killaloe. The main character is Toirdelbach Ua Briain until his death in 1086. It is natural enough that Killaloe should be the home of an O'Brien

[1] *CGG*, 32.

[2] See chapters 9, 11, 13, 17, 18, 20, 21, 22, 24, 25, 26, 33, 34.

[3] A. Gwynn, 'Were the Annals of Inisfallen written at Killaloe?', *North Munster Antiquarian Journal*, VIII (1958), 20–33.

chronicle, situated as it was in the heart of Dál Cais territory and with its patron Flannán a collateral ancestor of Brian.

Between 1092 and 1130 (when there is a lacuna in the manuscript) the annals were kept up to date by nineteen different scribes. When Muirchertach fell ill in 1114 and his younger brother Diarmait seized power, the sympathy of the annalist was with Muirchertach. In 1116 Muirchertach went to Lismore and died three years later. Before his death the province of Munster had been divided between the Mac Carthys and the O'Briens, and for some years after 1116 we hear a good deal about Lismore and south Munster. Professor Gwynn suggests that the annals were brought south in Muirchertach's company. By the middle of the century they had migrated to Kerry and they remained at Inisfallen until the seventeenth century.

It seems exceedingly likely that the annals were transcribed in 1092 at Killaloe. If so, Killaloe had a good *scriptorium*, for the manuscript (which has been reproduced in facsimile)[1] is, as Professor Gwynn says, one of the finest surviving specimens of early medieval Irish caligraphy. It is by far the most valuable of the Munster historical documents of this period. Killaloe was concerned with history in the Latin tradition. Was she also concerned with history in the Irish tradition? When Domnall Ua hÉnna, bishop of Munster, corresponded with Lanfranc, he asked him about certain *quaestiones saecularium literarum*. Lanfranc replied that it was not proper for him to answer, and stuck to the theological queries.[2] The family of Énna had connections with Killaloe:[3] a son of Énna had died as its coarb in 1030 and a grandson of Énna died as a member of its community in 1095. We shall never know what were the 'questions of wordly learning' put by this other grandson of Énna, but his knowledge, like that of other Irish ecclesiastical scholars, must have embraced tradition both sacred and profane.

---

[1] *The Annals of Inisfallen*, with a descriptive introduction by R. I. Best and E. Mac Neill (Dublin, London 1933).

[2] J. Ussher, *Whole Works*, ed. C. R. Elrington (Dublin 1847–64), IV, 495–7.

[3] Gwynn, *op. cit.*, 30.

VIII

There is one other historical saga from Munster dating from this period, The Battle-Career of Cellachán of Cashel.[1] It is later than The War of the Gaedhill with the Gaill and is plainly modelled on it, composed in a similar style, though it is less wordy and it tells a better story. Cellachán was of the Eoganachta who, before the rise of the Dál Cais, had provided the kings of Cashel. He was reigning in 936[2] and died in 954. The theme is similar to that of *CGG*—the oppression suffered by Munster, an oppression described in both sagas in almost identical words,[3] and the rise of a saviour. The first event after Cellachán's election as king of Cashel is an attack on Viking Limerick, comparable to the battle of Sulcoit at the beginning of Mathgamain's victorious career. Both sagas stress the superiority of Viking armour. There is a great battle at Dublin, where Cellachán is captured, and an exciting battle in the harbour at Dundalk where Cellachán is tied to the mast of the Viking Sitric's ship. The Munster fleet arrives just in time to rescue him before the Foreigners carry him off. Cellachán behaves throughout in heroic style. A prisoner of the Vikings of Dublin, he tells the Munster men not to accept the Foreigners' terms but to make Cennétig their king. There is a moving passage where Cellachán, a prisoner, identifies the heads of his Munster friends as they are carried in by the Norse. The parentage of 'The Battle-Career of Cellachán' is clear enough, though it has lively, romantic incidents absent from *CGG*; for example, the story of how Cellachán, before his election, spends a year on intelligence work, travelling round incognito to get to know the countryside and its landowners; or of how the wife of the Viking prince of Dublin betrays his plans to Cellachán, since she fell in love with him the day she saw him at Waterford.

Although the Dál Cais are represented as allies—Cennétig is in fact recognised as the *tánaise ríg*[4]—the story must detract from

---

[1] *Caithréim Cellacháin Caisil*, ed. A. Bugge (Christiania 1905). For a critical study see J. Ryan, *JRSAI*, LXXI (1941), 89–100.

[2] *CS*, 935.   [3] *CGG*, 48–51; *CCC*, 1–2, 58.   [4] *CCC*, 16, 74.

the splendours of Brian, since it is claiming for his predecessor Cellachán an almost identical success. It therefore seems unlikely that this saga was produced during the period of O'Brien ascendancy. A date after 1118, when the Mac Carthys were ruling in Desmond and may have been trying to revive the glories of south Munster, seems probable.[1] As Professor Ryan shows, the main events of this saga seem to be almost entirely fiction. Nevertheless it has some historical interest for the twelfth century. The writer's aim was to produce a work of art, dramatic in quality, distinguished in diction. His very freedom from the restraints of fact emphasises the contrast between The Battle-Career of Cellachán and The War of the Gaedhill with the Gaill. Neither author is writing annals. Both are imposing a pattern on history which is not supported by other evidence. Yet The War of the Gaedhill with the Gaill draws on genuine historical material and follows the main events of Brian's career as they are outlined in the annals. The author of The Battle-Career of Cellachán was not basing his account on any such sources; he was trying to evoke an image of the king of Cashel's greatness which fits in well with Mac Carthy ambitions.

IX

The modern historian owes a great deal to the antiquarian activity of Irish monks in the eleventh and twelfth centuries. As one scribe wrote:

> I send my little dripping pen unceasingly over an assemblage of books of great beauty, to enrich the possessions of the men of art—whence my hand is weary with writing.[2]

[1] Professor Ryan wants to date it before 1118 on the grounds that the attitude to the Dál Cais is not sufficiently 'independent' for a later date. But the O'Briens and Mac Carthys were sometimes on the same side, as in 1127.

[2] G. Murphy, *Early Irish Lyrics*, 70–1. I have said nothing in this chapter of the poetry of the period, since my subject is history. See briefly D. Greene and F. O'Connor, *A Golden Treasury of Irish Poetry*, 15–17.

Works such as *Lebor Gabála* and the sagas of Brian and Cellachán are the Irish examples of early medieval 'histories', stories of the destiny of a people or the grandeur of a personality. There are no contemporary Irish equivalents to new historians like William of Malmesbury, men who, at their best, were attempting a narrative with general philosophical implications based on original research, on the comparison of title deeds and examination of archives. The main Irish historical sources for the eleventh and twelfth centuries are still the annals, though the other texts tell us about the minds and methods of the men who wrote them.

The most exciting period of early Irish history seems to me the seventh, eighth and ninth centuries. Ireland was then an integral part of Europe, learning from the classical heritage surviving in Europe and contributing to the civilisation of the Germanic barbarians. There are very good sources for Irish history at this time; a mass of legislation and annals, some saints' Lives, letters, poetry and early works of learning and piety, to say nothing of the sagas. In the tenth, eleventh and twelfth centuries the annals become fuller and are certainly contemporary: they have still much to divulge. The sources for the tenth century are literary as well as historical—visions, prophesies, poetry, in addition to annals and genealogies. Historians have neglected the tenth century even more than the earlier period, and our historical knowledge is here particularly obscure. The position improves with the eleventh, and even more with the twelfth century. The learning is still of traditional type; for the annals, the historical sagas, the *dindshenchus* legends, the *mirabilia* (Ireland's scientific lore), the nature poetry, all have their roots in the Irish past. It is no use looking for learned treatises about government, and the Book of Rights reads like a fairy tale beside Domesday Book. The twelfth century in Ireland is not the beginning of a new learning: it is the culmination of the old. Here again much work is still to be done. For the research student who will study the history of early Ireland there are still major voyages of discovery ahead; the maps have still to be drawn out and the routes charted.

BIBLIOGRAPHY

Chapter 1: Archaeology

Archaeological Survey of Northern Ireland: County Down (Belfast 1966).

BOWEN, H. J. *Ancient Fields* (London 1961).

Bulletin of the Group for the Study of Irish Historic Settlement, I (Dec. 1970).

CASE, H. J., DIMBLEBY, G. W., MITCHELL, G. F., MORRISON, M. E. S., and PROUDFOOT, V. B. 'Land use in Goodland townland, Co. Antrim', *JRSAI*, XCIX (1969), 39–54.

COLLINS, A. E. P. 'Excavations in Lough Faughan crannog, Co. Down', *UJA*, XVIII (1955), 45–80.

— 'Settlement in Ulster 0–1100 AD', *UJA*, XXXI (1968), 53–8.

DAVIES, O. 'The Black Pig's Dyke', *UJA*, XVIII (1955), 29–36.

DE PAOR, L. 'A Survey of Sceilg Mhichíl', *JRSAI*, LXXXV (1955), 174–87.

DE PAOR, M. and L. *Early Christian Ireland* (London 1958).

DOLLEY, R. H. M. *The Hiberno-Norse Coins in the British Museum* (London 1966).

DUIGNAN, M. 'Irish agriculture in early historic times', *JRSAI*, LXXIV (1944), 124–45.

FOWLER, P. J., and THOMAS, A. C. 'Arable Fields of the pre-Norman period at Gwithian', *Cornish Archaeology*, I (1962), 61–84.

HARTNETT, P. J., and EOGAN, G. 'Feltrim Hill, Co. Dublin', *JRSAI*, XCIV (1964), 19–34.

HENCKEN, H. O'N. 'Ballinderry Crannog No. 1', *PRIA*, XLIII (1936), 103–239.

— *Cahercommaun* (Dublin 1938).

— 'Ballinderry Crannog No. 2', *PRIA*, XLVII (1942), 1–76.

— 'Lagore Crannog', *PRIA*, LIII (1950), C 1–247.

HENRY, F. 'Remains of the early Christian period on Inishkea North, Co. Mayo', *JRSAI*, LXXV (1945), 128–55.

JOPE, E. M. 'Chariotry and paired draught in Ireland during the early Iron Age', *UJA*, XVIII (1955), 37–44.

LUCAS, A. T. 'The horizontal mill in Ireland', *JRSAI*, LXXXII (1953), 1–36.

MITCHELL, G. F. 'Evidence of early agriculture', *JRSAI*, LXXVI (1946), 16–18.

— 'Post-boreal pollen diagrams from Irish raised-bogs', *PRIA*, LVII (1956), B 185–251.

— 'Radiocarbon dates and pollen zones in Ireland', *JRSAI*, LXXXVIII (1958), 49–56.

— 'Littleton Bog, Tipperary: an Irish agricultural record', *JRSAI*, XCV (1965), 125–32.

NORMAN, E. R., and ST JOSEPH, J. K. S. *The Early development of Irish Society* (Cambridge 1969).

O'KELLY, M. J. 'St. Gobnet's house, Ballyvourney, Co. Cork', *JCHAS*, LVII (1952), 18–40.

— 'Excavation and experiments in Ancient Irish cooking places', *JRSAI*, LXXXIV (1954), 105–55.

— 'An island settlement at Beginish, Co. Kerry', *PRIA*, LVII (1956), C 159–94.

— 'Church Island near Valencia', *PRIA*, LIX (1958), C 57–136.

— 'Beal Boru, Co. Clare', *JCHAS*, LXVII (1962), 1–27.

— 'Two-ring forts at Garryduff, Co. Cork', *PRIA*, 63 (1962), C 17–125.

— 'Problems of Irish Ring-forts', *The Irish Sea Province in Archaeology and History*, ed. D. Moore (Cardiff 1970).

Ó RÍORDÁIN, S. P. 'Excavations at Cush, Co. Limerick', *PRIA*, XLV (1940), C 83–181.

— 'The excavation of a large earthen ring-fort at Garranes, Co. Cork', *PRIA*, XLVII (1942), C 77–150.

— *Antiquities of the Irish Countryside* (London 1942).

— 'Lough Gur excavations: Carraig Aille and the "Spectacles"', *PRIA*, LII (1949), C 39–111.

Ó RÍORDÁIN, S. P., and FOY, J. B. 'The excavation of Leacanabuaile', *JCHAS*, XLVI (1941), 85–99.

OTWAY-RUTHVEN, J. 'The organisation of Anglo-Irish agriculture in the Middle Ages', *JRSAI*, LXXI (1951), 1–13.

PROUDFOOT, V. B. 'Ancient Irish Field Systems', *Advancement of Science*, XIV, No. 56 (1958), 369–71.

— 'The economy of the Irish rath', *Medieval Archaeology*, V (1961), 94–122.

PROUDFOOT, V. B., and WILSON, B. C. S. 'Further excavations at Larrybane promontory fort, Co. Antrim', *UJA*, XXV (1962), 91–115.

SCOTT, J. H. 'Analysis of pre-Christian Irish skeletal material', *UJA*, XX (1957), 4–7.

STEPHENS, N., and GLASSCOCK, R. E. (eds.) *Irish Geographical Studies in honour of E. Estyn Evans* (Belfast 1970).

TOHALL, P. 'Team-work on a rotary quern', *JRSAI*, LXXI (1951), 70–1.

WATERMAN, D. M. 'The excavation of a house and souterrain at White Fort, Drumaroad, Co. Down', *UJA*, XIX (1956), 73–86.

— 'The excavation of a house and souterrain at Craig Hill, Co. Antrim', *UJA*, XIX (1956), 87–91.

Chapter 2: The Secular Laws

Ancient Laws of Ireland, 6 vols, Rolls Series (Dublin, London 1865–1901).

BEST, R. I., and THURNEYSEN, R. *Ancient Laws of Ireland*, Irish MSS. Comm. Facs. in Collotype of Irish MSS (Dublin 1931).

BINCHY, D. A. '*Bretha Crólige*', *Ériu*, XII (1934), 1–77.

— 'Sick Maintenance in Irish Law', *ibid.*, 78–134.

— *Críth Gablach*, Mediaeval and Modern Irish Series 11 (Dublin 1941).

— 'The Linguistic and Historical Value of the Irish Law Tracts', *PBA*, XXIX (1943), 195–228.

— '*Bretha Nemed*', *Ériu*, XVII (1955), 4–6.

— 'Irish Law tracts re-edited', *ibid.*, 52–85.

— 'The date and provenance of *Uraicecht Becc*', *ibid.*, XVIII (1958), 44–54.

— 'The fair of Tailtiu and the feast of Tara', *ibid.*, 113–38.

— '*Bretha Déin Chécht*', *ibid.*, XX (1966), 1–65.

— 'Ancient Irish Law', *The Irish Jurist*, I (1966), 84–92. (This paper contains a bibliography.)

— *Celtic and Anglo-Saxon Kingship*, O'Donnell Lectures for 1967–68 (Oxford 1970).

DILLON, M. (ed.), *Early Irish Society* (Dublin 1954).

— *The Celtic Realms* by M. Dillon and N. Chadwick (London 1967), chapter 5.

MAC NEILL, E. *Early Irish Laws and Institutions* (Dublin, 1935).

— *Phases of Irish History* (Dublin 1919).

— *Celtic Ireland* (Dublin, London 1921).

— 'Ancient Irish Law: the law of status or franchise', *PRIA*, XXXVI (1923), C 265–316.

MAC NIOCAILL, G. 'The "heir designate" in early medieval Ireland', *The Irish Jurist*, III (1968), 326–9.

— 'Admissible and inadmissible evidence in early Irish law', *The Irish Jurist*, IV (1969), 332–7.

PLUMMER, C. 'Notes on some passages in the Brehon Laws', *Ériu*, VIII (1916), 127–32; IX (1921–23), 31–43, 109–118; X (1926–28), 113–29.

THURNEYSEN, R. '*Cóic Conara Fugill*' (*Abh. d. Preuss. Akad. d. Wiss.*, *Phil.-hist. Kl.*, 7, 1925, Berlin 1926).

— 'Die Burgschaft im irischen Recht' (*ibid.*, Kl. 2, Berlin 1928).

— 'Irisches Recht' (*ibid.*, Kl. 2, Berlin 1931).

— 'Aus dem irischen Recht', ZCP, XIV (1923), 334–94; XV (1924–25), 238–76, 302–76; XVI (1926), 167–96; XVIII (1930), 353–408.

THURNEYSEN, R., POWER, N., DILLON, M., MULCHRONE, K., BINCHY, D. A., KNOCH, A., and RYAN, J. *Studies in Early Irish Law* (Dublin, London 1936).

Chapter 3: Ecclesiastical Legislation

BEST, R. I. 'The Canonical Hours', *Ériu*, III (1907), 116.

BIELER, L. *The Irish Penitentials* (Dublin 1963).

— 'Patrick's Synod: a revision', *Mélanges offerts a Mlle. Christine Mohrmann* (Utrecht Anvers 1963), 96–102.

— 'Interpretationes Patricianae', *Irish Ecclesiastical Record*, 5th ser., CVII (1967), 1–13.

BINCHY, D. 'Patrick and his biographers', *Studia Hibernica*, II (1962), 7–173.

— 'The Old-Irish Table of Penitential Commutations', *Ériu*, XIX (1962), 47–72.

— 'St Patrick's "First Synod" ', *Studia Hibernica*, VIII (1968), 49–59.

GWYNN, E. J. 'The Teaching of Máel-Ruain', *Hermathena*, XLIV (2nd supp. vol., 1927), 1–63.

— 'Rule of the Céli Dé', *ibid.*, 64–87.

— 'An Irish Penitential', *Ériu*, VII (1914), 121–93.

GWYNN, E. L., and PURTON, W. J. 'The Monastery of Tallaght', PRIA, XXIX (1911), C 115–79.

HADDAN, A. W. and STUBBS, W. *Councils and Ecclesiastical Documents relating to Great Britain and Ireland*, 3 vols (Oxford 1869–73).

HUGHES, K. 'The Changing theory and practice of Irish pilgrimage', *Journal of Ecclesiastical History*, XI (1960), 143–51.

— *The Church in Early Irish Society* (London 1966).

HULL, V. 'Cáin Domnaig', *Ériu*, XX (1966), 151–77.

MAC ECLAISE 'The Rule of St. Carthage', *Irish Ecclesiastical Record*, 4th ser. XXVII (1910), 495–517.

MAC NEILL, J. T. *The Celtic Penitentials and their influence on continental Christianity* (Paris 1923).

MAC NEILL, J. T., and GAMER, H. *Mediaeval Handbooks of Penance* (Columbia 1938, reprinted New York 1965).

MEYER, K. *Cáin Adamnáin* (Oxford 1905).

MURPHY, G. *Early Irish Lyrics* (Oxford 1956).

O'KEEFE, J. G. 'The Rule of Patrick', *Ériu*, I (1904), 216–24.

OAKLEY, T. P. 'Cultural affiliations of early Ireland in the penitentials', *Speculum*, VIII (1933), 489–500.

O'NEILL, J. 'The rule of Ailbe of Emly', *Ériu*, III (1907), 92–115.

REEVES, W. *Adamnán's Life of St. Columba* (Dublin 1857).

RYAN, J. *Irish monasticism, its origins and early development* (London 1931).

— 'The abbatial succession at Clonmacnoise', *Féilsgríbhinn Eóin Mhic Néill* (Dublin 1940), 490–507.

STOKES, W., and STRACHAN, J. *Thesaurus Palaeohibernicus*, 2 vols (Cambridge 1901–3).

STRACHAN, J. 'An Old-Irish Metrical Rule', *Ériu*, I (1904), 191–208.

— 'Cormac's Rule', *Ériu*, II (1905), 62–8.

WALKER, G. S. M. *Sancti Columbani Opera* (Dublin 1957).

WASSERSCHLEBEN, H. *Die irische Kanonensammlung* (Leipzig 1885).

Chapter 4: The Annals

BANNERMAN, J. 'Notes on the Scottish entries in the early Irish annals', *Scottish Gaelic Studies*, XI (1968), 149–70.

BEST, R. I. and MAC NEILL, E. *The Annals of Inisfallen reproduced in facsimile* (Dublin, London 1933).

BYRNE, F. J. 'Clann Ollaman Uaisle Emna', *Studia Hibernica*, IV (1964), 54–94.

— 'Seventh-century documents', *Irish Ecclesiastical Record*, CVIII (1967), 164–82.

— *The Rise of the Uí Néill and the High-Kingship of Ireland*, O'Donnell Lecture (Dublin 1969).

GLEESON, D., and MAC AIRT, S. 'The Annals of Roscrea', *PRIA*, LIX (1958), C 137–80.

GWYNN, A. 'Cathal Mac Maghnusa and the Annals of Ulster', *Clogher Record*, II (1957), 230–43, 370–84.

HENNESSY, W. M. (ed.), *Chronicon Scotorum*, Rolls S. (London 1866).

— *Annals of Ulster*, 4 vols (Dublin 1887–1901).

LUCAS, A. T. 'Irish-Norse relations: time for a reappraisal?', *Journal of the Cork Historical and Archaeological Society*, LXXI (1966), 62–75.

— 'The plundering and burning of churches in Ireland, 7th to 16th century', *North Munster Studies*, ed. E. Rynne (Limerick 1967), 172–229.

MAC AIRT, S. (ed.) *The Annals of Inisfallen* (Dublin 1951).

MACALISTER, R. A. S. 'The sources of the Preface to the "Tigernach" Annals', *IHS*, IV (1944), 38–57.

MAC NEILL, E. 'The Authorship and structure of the Annals of Tigernach', *Ériu*, VII (1914), 30–113.

MURPHY, D. (ed.), *Annals of Clonmacnoise* (Dublin 1896).

O'DONOVAN, J. (ed.) *Annals of Ireland by the Four Masters*, 7 vols (Dublin 1856).

— *Three Fragments* (Dublin 1860).

Ó hINNSE, S. (ed.), *Miscellaneous Irish Annals* (Dublin 1947).

Ó MAILLE, T. *The Language of the Annals of Ulster* (Manchester 1910).

O'RAHILLY, T. F. *Early Irish History and Mythology* (Dublin 1946).

Proceedings of the International Congress of Celtic Studies, 1959 (Dublin 1962).

SAWYER, P. H. *The Age of the Vikings* (London 1962).

STOKES, W. (ed.) 'The Annals of Tigernach', *Revue Celtique*, XVI (1895), 374–419; XVII (1896), 6–33, 116–263, 337–420; XVIII (1897), 9–59, 150–303, 374–91.

WALSH, P. 'The dating of the Irish Annals', *IHS*, II (1941), 355–75.

YOUNG, J. I. 'A note on the Norse occupation of Ireland', *History*, XXXV (1950), 11–33.

Chapter 5: Secular Literature

It is impossible to give an adequate bibliography of early Irish literature here. I have cited a number of the more important secondary works, texts and translations.

BINCHY, D. *Scéla Cano meic Gartndin* (Dublin 1963).

CARNEY, J. *Studies in Irish Literature and History* (Dublin 1955).

— *Early Irish Poetry* (Cork 1965).

DILLON, M. (ed.) *Irish Sagas* (Dublin 1959).

DILLON, M. (ed.) *The Cycles of the Kings* (London 1946).

— *Early Irish Literature* (Chicago 1948).

— 'Irish Literature'. Chapter 5 in *The Celtic Realms*, by M. Dillon and N. K. Chadwick (London 1967).

DOBBS, M. E. *Sidelights on the Táin* (Dundalk 1917).

FARADAY, L. W. *The Cattle-raid of Cualnge* (London 1904).

GREENE, D. *Fingal Rónáin and other stories* (Dublin 1955).

GREENE, D., and O'CONNOR, F. *A Golden Treasury of Irish Poetry, A.D. 600–1200* (London, Macmillan, 1967).

GWYNN, E. *The Metrical Dinnshenchas*, Todd Lecture Series 7–12 (Dublin 1900–35).

HENDERSON, G. (ed.) *Fled Bricriu ITS*, 2 (London 1899).

HULL, V. (ed.), *Longes Mac n-Uislenn* (New York 1949).

JACKSON, K. H. *A Celtic Miscellany* (London 1951).

— *The Oldest Irish tradition: a window on the Iron Age* (Cambridge 1964).

JOPE, E. M. 'Chariotry and paired draught in Ireland during the early Iron Age', *UJA*, XVIII (1955), 37–44.

KNOTT, E. *Togail Bruidne Da Derga* (Dublin 1936).

KNOTT, E., and MURPHY, G. *Early Irish Literature* (London 1966).

MAC NEILL, M. *The Festival of Lughnasa* (London 1962).

MEYER, K. *The Death Tales of the Ulster Heroes*, Todd Lecture Series 14 (Dublin 1906).

— *Ancient Irish Poetry* (London 1911).

MURPHY, G. 'Bards and *filidh*', *Éigse*, II (1940), 200–7.

O'GRADY, S. H. *Silva Gadelica*, 2 vols (London 1892).

O'RAHILLY, C. *Táin Bó Cualnge, ITS*, 49 (Dublin 1967).

O'RAHILLY, T. F. *Early Irish History and Mythology* (Dublin 1946).

ROSS, A. *Pagan Celtic Britain* (London 1967).

SJOESTEDT, M. *Gods and Heroes of the Celts*, transl. M. Dillon (London 1949).

STOKES, W. 'The second Battle of Moytura', *Revue Celtique*, XII (1891), 52–130.

— 'The Destruction of Da Derga's Hostel', *Revue Celtique*, XXII (1901), 9–61, 165–215, 282–329, 390–417.

— 'The adventure of the sons of Eochaid', *Revue Celtique*, XXIV (1903), 191–207.

— 'The battle of Allen', *Revue Celtique*, XXIV (1903), 41–67.

STRACHAN, J. *Stories from the Táin*, 3rd ed. revised by D. Bergin (Dublin 1944).

Bibliography

THURNEYSEN, R. *Die irische Helden- und Königsage* (Halle 1921).
— *Scéla Mucce Meic Dathó* (Dublin 1935).
TIERNEY, J. J. 'The Celtic Ethnography of Posidonius', *PRIA*, LX (1960), C 202.

Chapter 6: Ecclesiastical Learning

BERNARD, J. H., and ATKINSON, R. *The Irish Liber Hymnorum*, HBS, 13, 14 (London 1898).
BIELER, L. 'The Humanism of St. Columbanus', *Mélanges Colombaniens* (Paris 1951), 95–102.
— 'The island of scholars', *Revue du Moyen Âge Latin*, VIII (1952), 227–34.
— *Ireland, harbinger of the Middle Ages* (London, Oxford, New York 1963).
— 'The classics in early Ireland', in *Classical influences on European culture*, ed. R. R. Bolgar (Cambridge 1971).
BISCHOFF, B. 'Das griechische Element in der abendländischen Bildung des Mittelalters', *Byzantinische Zeitschrift*, LXIV (1951), 27–55; 'Wendepunkte in der Geschichte der lateinischen Exegese im Frühmittelalter', *Sacris Erudiri*, VI (1954), 189–281.
— *Mittelalterliche Studien. Ausgewählte Aufsätze zur Schriftkunde und Literaturgeschichte*, 2 vols (Stuttgart 1966–67).
BOSWELL, C. S. *An Irish Precursor of Dante* (London 1908).
BOWEN, E. G. *Saints, seaways and settlements in the Celtic lands* (Cardiff 1969).
— 'The Irish sea in the age of the saints', *Studia Celtica*, IV (1969), 56–71.
CARNEY, J. The Poems of Blathmac, *ITS*, 47 (Dublin 1964).
— *Mediaeval Irish Lyrics* (Dublin 1967).
DRAAK, M. 'Construe-marks in Hiberno-Latin manuscripts', *Mededelingen der Koninklijke Nederlandse Akademie van Watenshappen afd. Letterkunde*, Niewe Reeks, XX (1957), 261–82.
— 'The higher teaching of Latin grammar in Ireland during the ninth century', *ibid.*, XXX (1967), 109–44.
FLOWER, R. 'The Two Eyes of Ireland', *The Church of Ireland A.D. 432–1932*, ed. W. Bell and N. D. Emerson (Dublin 1932), 66–79.
— *The Irish Tradition* (Oxford 1947).
GREENE, D., and O'CONNOR, F. *A Golden Treasury of Irish Poetry* (London, Melbourne, Toronto 1967).

GROSJEAN, P. 'Le Martyrologe de Tallaght', *Analecta Bollandiana*, LI (1933), 117–30.

HENNIG, J. 'Studies in the Latin Texts of the Martyrology of Tallaght, of *Félire Oengusso* and of *Félire Húi Gormáin*', *PRIA*, LXIX (1970), C 45–112.

HILLGARTH, J. 'The East, Visigothic Spain and the Irish', *Studia Patristica*, IV (1961), 442–56.

— 'Visigothic Spain and Early Christian Ireland', *PRIA*, CXII (1962), C 167–94.

JACKSON, K. *Studies in Early Celtic Nature Poetry* (Cambridge 1935).

— *A Celtic Miscellany* (London 1951).

KENNEY, J. F. 'The Legend of St. Brendan', *Trans. of the Roy. Soc. of Canada*, 3rd ser., XIV (1921), 51–67.

— *Sources for the Early History of Ireland: Vol I, Ecclesiastical* (Columbia 1929, reprinted New York 1966).

LOFSTEDT, B. *Der Hibernolateinische Grammatiker Malsachanus* (Uppsala 1965).

MCNALLY, R. E. *Der irische Liber de Numeris: eine Quellenanalyse*, Inaugural-Dissertation (Munich 1957).

— 'The imagination and early Irish Biblical exegesis', *Annuale Mediaevale*, X (1969), 5–27.

MEEHAN, D. *Adamnán's De Locis Sanctis*, SLH, 3 (Dublin 1958).

MEYER, K. *The Vision of Mac Conglinne* (London 1892).

MOHRMANN, C. *The Latin of St. Patrick* (Dublin 1961).

— 'The earliest continental Irish Latin', *Vigiliae Christianae*, XVI (1962), 216–33.

MURPHY, G. *Early Irish Lyrics* (Oxford 1956).

PLUMMER, C. 'Some new light on the Brendan legend', *ZCP*, V (1905), 124–41.

— 'On the colophons and marginalia of Irish scribes', *PBA*, XII (1926), 11–44.

— *Irish Litanies*, HBS, 62 (London 1925).

RABY, F. J. E. *A history of Christian-Latin Poetry* (Oxford 1953).

SELMER, C. *Navigatio S. Brendani Abbatis* (Indiana 1959).

SEYMOUR, ST J. 'The eschatology of the Early Irish Church', *ZCP*, XIV (1923), 179–211.

STOKES, W. 'The Voyage of Snedgus and Mac Riagla', *Revue Celtique*, IX (1888), 14–25.

— 'The Voyage of the Húi Corra', *ibid.*, XIV (1893), 22–72.

— 'The Evernew Tongue', *Ériu*, II (1905), 96–162.

Bibliography

STOKES, W. *The Martyrology of Oengus*, HBS, 29 (London 1905).

— 'The adventure of St Columba's clerics', *Revue Celtique*, XXVI (1905), 130–70.

STOKES, W., and STRACHAN, J. *Thesaurus Palaeohibernicus*, 2 vols (Cambridge 1901–3).

VAN HAMEL, A. G. *Immrama* (Dublin 1941).

WALKER, G. S. M. *Sancti Columbani Opera*, SLH, 2 (Dublin 1957).

WILMART, A. 'Catéchèses Celtiques', *Studi e Testi*, LIX (1933), 29–112. Professor McNally is re-editing this text in *Corpus Christianorum*.

WINDISCH, E. 'Fís Adamnáin', *Irische Texte* (Leipzig 1909), I. 165–96.

Chapter 7: Hagiography

ANDERSON, A. O. and M. O. *Adomnan's Life of Columba* (London 1961).

ANDERSON, M. O. 'Columba and other Irish saints in Scotland', *Historical Studies*, V (1965), 26–36.

BANNERMAN, J. 'The Dál Riata and Northern Ireland in the Sixth and Seventh Centuries', *Celtic Studies: Essays in memory of Angus Matheson*, 1912–62, ed. J. Carney and D. Greene (London 1968).

BIELER, L. 'The Celtic hagiographer', *Studia Patristica*, V (1962), 243–65.

BRÜNING, G. 'Adamnans Vita Columbae und ihre Ableitungen', *ZCP*, XI (1917), 213–304.

BULLOUGH, D. A. 'Columba, Adamnán and the achievement of Iona', *Scottish Historical Review*, XLIII (1964); 111–30, XLIV (1965), 17–33.

ESPOSITO, M. 'Conchubrani Vita Sanctae Monennae', *PRIA*, XII (1910), C 202–51.

— 'On the earliest Latin Life of St Brigid of Kildare', *PRIA*, XXX (1912), C 307–26.

HEIST, W. W. *Vitae Sanctorum Hiberniae*, Subsidia hagiographica, 28 (Brussels 1965).

HUGHES, K. 'The historical value of the Lives of St Finnian of Clonard', *EHR*, LXIX (1954), 353–72.

— 'The cult of St Finnian of Clonard from the eighth to the eleventh century', *IHS*, IX (1954), 13–27.

— 'The changing theory and practice of Irish pilgrimage', *Journal of Ecclesiastical History*, XI (1960), 143–51.

— *The Church in Early Irish Society* (London 1966).

— *Early Christianity in Pictland*, Jarrow Lecture, 1971.

311

KENNEY, J. F. *Sources for the Early History of Ireland: Vol I, Ecclesiastical* (New York 1929. Reprinted 1968 with addenda by L. Bieler).

MACALISTER, R. A. S. *The Latin and Irish Lives of St Ciarán* (London 1921).

MEYER, K. *Betha Colmáin maic Lúacháin*, Todd Lecture Series 17 (Dublin 1911).

MULCHRONE, K. 'Die Abfassungszeit und Überlieferung der *Vita Tripartita*', *ZCP*, XVI (1926), 1–94.

O BRIAIN, F. 'The hagiography of Leinster', *Féil-sgríbhinn Eóin Mhic Néill*, ed. J. Ryan (Dublin 1940), 454–64.

O'GRADY, S. H. *Silva Gadelica*, 2 vols (London 1892).

PLUMMER, C. *Vitae Sanctorum Hiberniae*, 2 vols (Oxford 1910).

— *Bethada Náem nÉrenn*, 2 vols (Oxford 1922).

POWER, P. *Lives of Declán and Mochuda*, *ITS*, 16 (London 1914).

REEVES, W. *The Life of St Columba* (Dublin 1857).

STOKES, W. *Vita Tripartita*, 2 vols, Rolls S. (London 1887).

— *Lives of the Saints from the Book of Lismore* (Oxford 1890).

WHITE, N. J. D. *St Patrick, his Life, Times and Writings* (London 1920).

Chapter 8: Art and Architecture

DE PAOR, L. 'The limestone crosses of Clare and Aran', *Journal of the Galway Arch. and Hist. Soc.*, XXVI (1955–56), 53–71.

— 'Cormac's Chapel: the beginnings of Irish Romanesque', *North Munster Studies*, ed. E. Rynne (Limerick 1967), 133–45.

DE PAOR, L. and M. *Early Christian Ireland* (London, New York 1958).

DUFT, J. and MEYER, P. *The Irish Miniatures in the Cathedral Library of St. Gall* (Berne-Olten-Lausanne 1954).

Evangeliorum Quattuor Codex Cenannensis, 3 vols (Berne 1950–51).

Evengeliorum Quattuor Codex Durmachensis, 2 vols (Olten 1960).

FLOWER, R. 'Irish high crosses', *Jrnl. of the Warburg and Courtauld Institutes*, XVII (1954), 87–97.

HENRY, F. 'Les débuts de la miniature irlandaise', *Gazette des Beaux Arts*, XXXVII (1950), 5–34.

— 'Early monasteries, beehive-huts and dry-stone houses in the neighbourhood of Caherciveen and Waterville (Kerry)', *PRIA*, LVIII (1957), C 45–166.

— 'Remarks on the decoration of three Irish Psalters', *PRIA*, LXI (1960), C 23–40.

— 'The effects of the Viking invasions on Irish art', *Proc. of the International Congress of Celtic Studies*, 1959 (Dublin 1962), 61–72.

Bibliography

HENRY, F. *Irish High Crosses* (Dublin 1964).

— *Irish Art in the Early Christian Period to AD 800; Irish Art during the Viking Invasions, 800–1020 AD; Irish Art in the Romanesque Period, 1020–1170 AD* (London 1965–70).

HENRY, F., and MARSH-MICHELI, G. 'A century of Irish illumination, 1070–1170', *PRIA*, LXII (1962), 101–64.

KILLANIN and DUIGNAN, M. *The Shell Guide to Ireland*, 2nd ed. (London 1967).

LEASK, H. J. *Irish Churches and Monastic Buildings*, I (Dundalk, 1955).

LÍONARD, P. 'Early Irish Grave-Slabs', *PRIA*, LXI (1961), C 95–169.

LOWE, E. A. *Codices Latini Antiquiores*, 11 parts (Oxford, 1934–66).

MAC DERMOTT, M. 'The open-work crucifixion plaque from Clon-macnoise', *JRSAI*, LXXXIV (1954), 36–40.

— 'The Kells Crozier', *Archaeologia*, XCVI (1955), 59–114.

— 'The croziers of St Dympna and St Mel and tenth-century Irish metalwork', *PRIA*, LVIII (1957), 167–95.

MICHELI, G. L. *L'enluminure du haut moyen age et les influences irlandaises* (Brussels 1939).

O'KELLY, M. J. 'The Cork horns, the Petrie crown and the Bann disc: the technique of their ornamentation', *JCHAS*, LXVI (1961), 1–12.

— 'The belt-shrine from Moylough, Sligo', *JRSAI*, XCV (1965), 149–87.

POWELL, R. 'The Book of Kells. The Book of Durrow', *Scriptorium*, X (1956), 3–26.

RAFTERY, J. 'Ex Oriente', *JRSAI*, XCV (1965), 193–204.

ROE, H. M. 'The high crosses of Co. Louth', 'The high crosses of Co. Armagh', 'The high crosses of East Tyrone', *Seanchas Ardmhacha*, I, 1 (1954), 101–14; I, 2 (1955), 107–14; II, 1 (1956), 79–89.

— *The High Crosses of Western Ossory* (Naas 1958).

— *The High Crosses of Kells* (Longford 1959).

— 'The Irish High Cross: morphology and iconography', *JRSAI*, XCV (1965), 213–26.

WERCKMEISTER, O. K. 'Three problems of tradition in pre-Carolingian figure-style', *PRIA*, LXIII (1963), C 167–89.

Chapter 9: Eleventh- and Twelfth-Century Histories and Compilations

BERNARD, J. H., and ATKINSON, R. *The Irish Liber Hymnorum, HBS*, 13, 14 (London 1897).

BEST, R. I. 'Notes on the script of Lebor na hUidre', *Ériu*, VI (1912), 161–74.

BEST, R. I., and BERGIN, O. *Lebor na hUidre* (Dublin 1929).

BEST, R. I., BERGIN, O., and O'BRIEN, M.A. *The Book of Leinster* (Dublin, 1954–   ).

BUGGE, A. *Caithréim Cellacháin Caisil* (Christiania 1905).

CALDER, G. *The Irish Aeneid, ITS*, 6 (London 1907).

— *Togail na Tebe: The Thebaid of Statius* (Cambridge 1922).

DILLON, M. 'Lebor Gabála Érenn', *JRSAI*, LXXXVI (1956), 62–72.

— 'On the date and authorship of the Book of Rights', *Celtica*, IV (1958), 239–49.

— *Lebor na Cert, ITS*, 46 (Dublin 1962).

DUNN, C. W. 'Ireland and the twelfth century renaissance', *Univ. of Toronto Quarterly*, XXIV (1954), 70–86.

FLOWER, R. *The Irish Tradition* (Oxford 1947).

GWYNN, A. 'Ireland and the Continent in the eleventh century', *IHS*, VIII (1953), 192–216.

— *The Writings of Bishop Patrick, 1074–1084* (Dublin 1955).

— 'Were the Annals of Inisfallen written at Killaloe?' *NMAJ*, VIII (1958), 20–33.

— 'Some notes on the history of the Book of Leinster', *Celtica*, V (1960), 8–12.

GOEDHEER, A. J. *Irish and Norse traditions about the battle of Clontarf* (Haarlem 1938).

KELLEHER, J. 'The rise of the Dál Cais', *North Munster Studies*, ed. E. Rynne (Limerick 1967).

MACALISTER, R. A. S. *Lebor Gabála Érenn, ITS*, 34, 35, 39, 41, 44 (Dublin 1938–56).

Ó CUÍV, B. (ed.), *Seven centuries of Irish learning* (Dublin 1961).

— 'Literary creation and Irish historical tradition', *PBA*, XLIX (1963), 233–62.

OSKAMP, H. P. A. 'Notes on the history of Lebor na hUidre', *PRIA*, LXV (1967), C 117–37.

O'SULLIVAN, W. 'Notes on the scripts and make-up of the Book of Leinster', *Celtica*, VII (1966), 1–31.

RYAN, J. 'The battle of Clontarf', *JRSAI*, LXVIII (1938), 1–50.

RYAN, J. 'The historical content of the *Caithréim Ceallacháin Chaisil*', *JRSAI*, XI (1941), 89–100.

— *Toirdelbach O Conchubair, 1088–1156*, O'Donnell Lecture (Dublin 1966).

STANFORD, W. B. 'Towards a history of classical influences in Ireland', *PRIA*, LXX (1970), C 13–91.

STOKES, W. *Togail Troi: The destruction of Troy* (Calcutta 1882).

— *The Martyrology of Gorman, HBS*, 9 (London 1895).

TODD, J. H. *Cogadh Gaedhel re Gallaibh*, Rolls S. (London 1867).

WATT, J. A. *The Church and the Two Nations in Mediaeval Ireland* (Cambridge 1970).

Index

317

Printed in the United Kingdom
by Lightning Source UK Ltd.
131012UK00001B/334-342/P